Explorers in Eden

Explorers in Eden

PUEBLO INDIANS AND THE PROMISED LAND

JEROLD S. AUERBACH

UNIVERSITY OF NEW MEXICO PRESS ||| ALBUQUERQUE

©2006 by the University of New Mexico Press
All rights reserved. Published 2006
Printed in the United States of America
10   09   08   07   06   1   2   3   4   5

Library of Congress Cataloging-in-Publication Data

Auerbach, Jerold S.
  Explorers in eden : Pueblo Indians and the promised land /
Jerold S. Auerbach.
     p. cm.
  Includes bibliographical references and index.
  ISBN-13: 978-0-8263-3945-4 (cloth : alk. paper)
  ISBN-10: 0-8263-3945-x (cloth : alk. paper)
1. Pueblo Indians—History—Sources. 2. Pueblo Indians—Public opinion.
3. Pueblo Indians—Social life and customs. 4. Indians in literature.
5. Indians in art. 6. Indians in popular culture—Southwest, New.
7. Public opinion—Southwest, New. 8. Whites—Southwest, New—Relations
with Indians. 9. Southwest, New—Discovery and exploration.
10. Southwest, New—Description and travel. I. Title.
  E99.P9A84 2006
  978.9′04—dc22

                        2005035687

Design and composition by: Melissa Tandysh

To My Wellesley Students
Who Rekindled the Joy of Teaching
—You Know Who You Are

Contents

Introduction

American Holy Land

From their earliest encounters with Pueblo Indians in New Mexico Territory, Anglo-American visitors chose biblical images to express their sense of wonder and enchantment. Instantly and reflexively, they tapped into the deepest source of American self-understanding: here, surely, was the last lingering remnant of the newly promised land, the biblical homeland in America. During more than two centuries of settlement, the yearning for an Edenic garden of new possibilities had propelled Americans in their relentless migrations westward. Late in the nineteenth century, the pueblos of the Southwest inspired the last best hope of return to the wellspring of American distinctiveness as a chosen people.

Even before the first Puritans set sail from England, the Hebrew Bible had begun to frame the American experience. In his farewell sermon to the intrepid English adventurers who were departing for America, Rev. John Cotton identified the Puritans' journey with the exodus of the Israelites from Egypt. On board the *Arbella*, John Winthrop reassured his uneasy companions that "the God of Israel is among us." Certain that they comprised a holy community, the new Israel, the Puritans arrived in the "howling wilderness" of Massachusetts Bay, a "desert" that must be transformed into "a land of milk and honey." As Puritan ministers incessantly instructed their congregations, "The Historie of the Old Testament is Example to us." Accordingly, "*Jerusalem* was, *New England* is, they were, you are God's own, God's covenant people." Cotton Mather succinctly proclaimed: "You may see an Israel in America."

In the New England wilderness, Edenic fantasies of biblical antiquity quickly yielded to the harsh realities of hunger, disease, and war. But the dream of a promised land for God's newly chosen people endured for centuries—and, for many Americans, arguably still does. In time, even before factories and railroads spewed the fire and smoke of progress upon the bucolic American landscape, old dreams were relocated to new frontiers further west. Driven relentlessly by their quest for personal salvation, whether they defined it in spiritual or material terms, Americans remained faithful to their special mission. Indeed, as literary historian Richard Slotkin has written, "to a people nourished on the lore of the Puritans, . . . the association of anything American with the biblical Promised Land and Chosen People was virtually self-evident." From the earliest colonial settlement, "a special relationship" with the land of the Bible was an article of American belief: biblical metaphors, endlessly reiterated, "explained the United States as a new Israel, a New World promised land."[1]

During the struggle for national independence, biblical metaphors were refurbished to suit revolutionary purposes. As Israel was remade from a holy community into "a commonwealth of liberty," George Washington became the American Moses, sent by God to deliver "the posterity of Jacob" from the "*worse* than Egyptian bondage of Great Britain." King George III, predictably, was variously compared to Pharaoh and Haman. Americans were reassured that "the star which rose from Judah lights our skies." When the revolutionary struggle faltered, a New Haven minister blamed the people for their own unrighteousness, which led them to "act over the same stupid vile part that the Children of Israel did in the wilderness." With independence assured, biblical parallels were even more stridently asserted. Just as David had prevailed in his struggle against Goliath, so "by a series of providential wonders have the Americans emerged from oppression and risen to liberty and independence." The Constitution was the "covenant" that secured divine favor for the new nation. As a "heavenly charter of liberty," according to Harvard president Samuel Langdon, it indicated that "God hath . . . taken us under his special care, as he did his ancient covenant people."

Biblical allusions came easily to the Founding Fathers. For the new national seal, Benjamin Franklin suggested Moses lifting his arms to divide the Red Sea, while Thomas Jefferson proposed the children of Israel in the wilderness, following pillars of cloud and fire. In his response to inaugural felicitations from the Hebrew Congregation of Savannah, President George Washington expressed his belief that the same God who had liberated the Israelites from their Egyptian oppressors had once again demonstrated his "providential agency . . . in establishing these United States as an independent nation."[2]

Biblical metaphors and Holy Land references were sufficiently ingrained in American consciousness to reemerge episodically throughout the nineteenth century. The Mormons understood themselves as a covenant people, spiritually descended from the Israelites, whose journey through the wilderness was replicated in their own cross-country trek. Finally settled in their American Zion in Utah, they instantly recognized the resemblance of the Great Salt Lake to the Dead Sea. The Mormon town of Moab affirmed the geographical connection (just as Canaan in Connecticut and Salem in Massachusetts had done for previous generations of Americans). The Mormons hardly were unique in their reliance upon biblical typologies. African-American slaves found in the Exodus narrative a powerful source of inspiration in their struggle for freedom. Identifying themselves as a chosen people, they assumed divine favor in their journey toward emancipation. So, too, Mordechai Noah decided to build his biblical commonwealth of Ararat in upstate New York, while John C. Fremont described California as "the modern Canaan, a land 'flowing with milk and honey.'" And why not? As Herman Melville wrote evocatively: "We Americans are the peculiar chosen people—the Israel of our time."[3]

After the Civil War, however, amid the turbulence of social change in an emerging urban industrial society, biblical analogies seemed increasingly tenuous. Cities and factories could not fit easily into a biblical paradigm, nor did hordes of new immigrants inspire confidence in a chosen American people. Religious orthodoxy began to yield to principles of modern criticism and scientific truth. Yet just when biblical imagery had begun to fade, travel abroad became more feasible, affordable, and safe, enabling Western visitors seeking exotic adventure and spiritual rejuvenation to visit the actual Holy Land. They were often disappointed. Mark Twain found it difficult to retain his sense of humor in so "desolate and unlovely" an outpost of the Ottoman Empire as Palestine, a land of "poverty, dirt, and disease," where ubiquitous beggars and lepers, eager for handouts, testified to the modern degradation of once sacred space. But Christian tourists to Palestine could still experience tremors of connection from their contact with an ancient, if sadly corrupted, incarnation of themselves. Travelers, observed a French visitor, "can always find in the retarded races" of the East "the living types of disappeared societies." After all, as Dr. Samuel Johnson suggested, "almost all that sets us above savages"—religion, law, the arts—came from the shores of the Mediterranean.

No matter how bleak Palestine might be in contemporary reality, it remained a "homeland of imagination" for Western visitors, stimulating nostalgic yearning for the "spirituality, wisdom, contemplative life, metaphysics, and emotion" of biblical antiquity. With the increasing popularity of photography in the second half of the nineteenth century, tourists could easily transform holy sites and local inhabitants into "the living traces of biblical times" to be preserved on film for showing and sharing. Three-dimensional stereographic images brought the Holy Land to Americans at home, stoking their yearning for holy places and images. In sporadic outbursts of "geopiety," elaborate replicas of Holy Land sites were constructed for public entertainment.[4]

By the 1870s, Jerusalem and Bethlehem had become favored venues for Holy Land photography. Christian pilgrims along the Via Dolorosa, Orthodox Jews at the "Wailing" Wall, Arab street life in the Old City souk, and Bedouin nomads riding camels were familiar images. Rachel's Tomb competed in popularity with the Tower of David and the Church of the Holy Sepulcher as attractions for the photographer's lens. The renowned Bonfils Studio in Jerusalem popularized an emerging staple of Holy Land imagery: Arab women with their clay pots aesthetically displayed, lovingly touched, or gracefully balanced on their heads. To anyone familiar with the biblical narrative, these images instantly evoked Rebecca, so compelling a symbol of the innocence and purity of antiquity now irretrievably lost amid the poverty and squalor of Ottoman Palestine. Might the United States, "where freedom has fashioned a nation that is a suitable heir to the Holy Land," be an even more appropriate repository for biblical fantasies than the Holy Land itself?[5]

So it was, far from Palestine, at twilight on a September evening in 1879, that Frank Hamilton Cushing, member of an expedition sponsored by the U.S. Bureau of Ethnology to gather information about the Indians of the Southwest, arrived on horseback at the edge of Zuni Pueblo in western New Mexico. His gaze was riveted by the sight of women emerging from the well, "a picturesque sight, as, with stately step and fine carriage they followed one another up into the evening light, balancing their great shining water-jars on their heads." As he watched, the focus of his reverie sharpened: "A little passageway through the gardens, between two adobe walls to our right, led down rude steps into the well, which, dug deeply in the sands, had been walled up with rocks, like the Pools of Palestine."

For this awestruck twenty-two-year-old explorer, it was a stark moment of cultural encounter: a young man descended from the venerable Cushing family of New England that traced its origins in America to the pioneering settlers, extracting from virtually his first contact with the native peoples of the Southwest an instant evocation of the Bible and Holy Land imagery. Cushing's account of his introduction to Zuni, published in *Century Illustrated Monthly Magazine*, was accompanied by an evocative sketch of the pastoral scene that he described (fig. 1).

In the lush foreground, three women, two with water-jars on their heads, emerge from reeds by the well. A small flock of goats grazes nearby.

FIG. 1

Pool of Zuni and Water-Carriers by Henry F. Farny from Frank Hamilton Cushing, "My Adventures in Zuni," *Century Illustrated Monthly Magazine* 25 (December 1882): 194.

Behind them, in the distance, is Zuni Pueblo, an enclosed village accessible only through a narrow gate. The drawing, entitled "Pool of Zuni and Water-Carriers," invites comparison to those sketched by David Roberts or William H. Bartlett, artists whose languid depictions of Holy Land scenes stoked the nostalgia of nineteenth-century Anglo-Americans for the spiritual nourishment of sacred antiquity.[6]

Cushing's encounter at Zuni revived the faded dream of America as an Edenic paradise, ancient Israel renewed. If not in the teeming cities and fiery factories of the East, then in the pueblos of the Southwest, among native tribes of whom most Americans were completely oblivious, might the biblical promise to the American people still flicker? Indeed, for the next sixty years an intriguing cohort of American explorers would discover in the pueblos, or imagine there, the deep spiritual allure of biblical antiquity converging with American history. Among the Pueblo Indians, they found an elixir for their discontent with the world of modernity they yearned to escape, a source of inspiration for their Edenic fantasies of regeneration.

Sylvester Baxter, a Boston journalist who visited Zuni and became Cushing's enthusiastic publicist, also was captivated by the biblical resonance of the pueblo. "The street scenes of Zuni," Baxter wrote, "seem thoroughly Oriental." Throughout the day, he noted, "there is an unceasing carrying of water, the women passing and repassing through the streets on the way to and from the springs with the large ollas, or water jars, so nicely balanced on their heads as not to spill a drop, and walking with a fine, erect poise." Especially toward sunset, the gatherings of women at the well offered "a Scripture-like scene," in which "crowds of girls come and go, dipping up the water, and pausing to gossip as they meet in the path or beside the well. Their soft voices fill the air like the chatter of swallows . . . and their figures are bathed in a mellow glow."[7]

Cushing imagined that he had entered a time warp in Zuni, a community governed by tradition and custom expressed in sacred rituals unchanged for centuries. In these religious ceremonies, Cushing observed, "the Zunian throws off everything foreign," retaining only what was indigenous to the tribe. Like so many of the Anglo explorers who followed him to the Southwest, Cushing failed to comprehend how much of indigenous Pueblo culture had been penetrated and transformed by Spanish conquistadores and missionaries during nearly three centuries of occupation. He could imagine that he was the first Westerner since Cabeza de Vaca to gaze upon these pristine communities, so isolated from modernity that they might even inspire dreams of return to an imagined biblical past. Yet Cushing had barely arrived before he perceived the vulnerability of Pueblo culture. "My anxiety would not be so great were there not a probability that I am among the last who will ever witness all this in its purity," he explained to his supervisor at the Smithsonian Institution. "The proposed advent of the Rail Road next fall, will, with its foreign inflow, introduce all sorts of innovations."[8]

Indeed, Cushing had arrived in Zuni when the Southwest was on the cusp of discovery, exploration, and development by Anglo Americans. Within another year, precisely as he anticipated, the Atchison Topeka & Santa Fe Railroad cut across New Mexico, inexorably linking the pueblos to the new economy and society of Gilded Age America. Before the century ended, Pueblo Indians were discovered and popularized as inspirational and marketable symbols of "America's ancient, unspoiled past," a past whose spiritual antecedents were located in the Bible. In Zuni and Acoma, in Taos and Laguna, and in the Hopi pueblos of Walpi and Oraibi in northeastern Arizona, time had apparently stood still for centuries. Here was the world of premodern virtue—with self-contained villages, sacred rituals, self-reliant farmers, and skilled craftspeople—doomed to imminent oblivion by the relentless materialism of an encroaching urban industrial society. "As exemplars of a natural life thought to be pure and unchanging," historian Philip Deloria writes, "Indians were among the most important symbols used to critique the modern." Especially in the pueblos, they were invested with the power to evoke "a nostalgic past more authentic and often more desirable than the anxious present."[9]

The Zuni of Cushing's imagination, historian Eliza McFeely has observed, was "frozen in time, caught in a moment before contact with the culture of the United States changed it forever." But the arrival of the railroad, a streamlined symbol of the new American industrial colossus, destroyed the imagined purity of Pueblo culture. Reaching Gallup, just north of Zuni, in 1882, it brought a "foreign inflow" to the pueblos. Many of these new visitors, like Cushing himself, were eagerly in pursuit of that elusive "lost moment in the American past" before modernity intruded. But Cushing understood, better than most, that their very presence—and, by implication, his own—would relegate it to oblivion.[10]

The discovery—or, more precisely, creation—of the Southwest as an American Eden was the spontaneous response of many people at a particular historical moment. In the 1880s, Americans were conspicuously ambivalent about modernity, every bit as unsettled as they were inspired by its machine-made wonders. Amid late Victorian optimism about the new industrial society, there were "undercurrents of doubt and despair" among the members of older professional elites with reason to fear their own diminishing power in the new world of industrial tycoons, political bosses, and foreign-speaking immigrants. Many educated, middle-class Easterners, predominantly Protestant males, felt squeezed by concentrations of economic and political power, and demographic changes, over which they had no control. Confronting what historian T. J. Jackson Lears has aptly called "a crisis of cultural authority," these "antimodern dissenters" searched in memory and geography for alternatives to modernity, taking refuge in the past, in exotic lands, and among native peoples.[11]

The American Southwest, and the Pueblo Indians who lived there, could satisfy these yearnings. Here was an unexplored land, the last vast "empty" space within American continental boundaries, inhabited by peaceful tribes who lived completely isolated from modernity, enclosed by languages and rituals that only a handful of Anglo-Americans had ever encountered, no less penetrated. An American aesthetic sensibility that was sufficiently eclectic toward the end of the nineteenth century to embrace Gothic architecture, Japanese art, Buddhist spirituality, and artisan craftsmanship—indeed almost anything that expressed what Lears calls "the healing wholeness of primitive myth"—could not help but be enchanted by Pueblo Indians. They seemed to retain precisely what many Americans had lost and wished desperately to recapture: the (imagined) organic unity, spiritual wholeness, and moral integrity of premodern society.[12]

Just a few years after Cushing visited Zuni, the "barren magnificence" of New Mexico evoked for writer Susan Wallace (whose *The Land of the Pueblos* became an early compendium of Pueblo lore) "the land once the glory of all lands," biblical Palestine. There was "much," she insisted, "to remind us of Bible pictures; the low adobe houses, the flocks with the herdsmen coming to drink at the shallow stream, the clambering goats in scanty pastures high up the rocks." In the arid Southwestern desert, she saw abandoned villages that reminded her of "the desolation of Zion." Pueblo men, she observed, used farming tools that resembled "the oriental implement in the days of Moses." Like Cushing and Baxter, she was captivated by women "carrying water-jars on head or shoulder, like maidens of Palestine." In these Pueblo women, Wallace saw "the veiled face of the gentle Rebecca."[13]

But a "deep sense of foreboding" afflicted many Americans at the end of the nineteenth century. As Frederick Jackson Turner declared at the Chicago Exposition in 1893, reading a paper that redefined the writing of American history for decades to come, the frontier—and with it the meaning of the American experience as a promised land—had vanished. Modernity and "progress" meant that the promise of a second chance on the Western frontier, the shimmering possibility that lay at the core of the American dream ever since the earliest settlements, was gone forever. From John Winthrop's vision of the "City on a Hill" to Turner's lament over the closing of the frontier, Americans—and those who aspired to become Americans—had been prepared to leave their homes to strike out for new, and seemingly limitless, possibilities. As long as there had been virgin land to explore, to conquer, to settle, and to develop, that dream endured. Until the 1890s, Americans had never confronted geographical boundaries that closed off the timeless future of hope and possibility. Now, with evident uneasiness, they did.[14]

Like the closing of the frontier that Turner popularized, the "vanishing" American Indian was a staple of *fin de siecle* nostalgia. In the Southwest, photographers and artists discovered a new "Eden," a place of extraordinary beauty where Pueblo Indians lived as Americans imagined their own spiritual ancestors had lived, in an Arcadian golden age before modernity intruded. As a Taos artist explained, "the manners and customs and style of architecture are the same today that they were before Christ was born. They offer the painter a subject as full of the fundamental qualities of life as did the Holy Land of long ago." Pueblo Indians wrapped in blankets were even more artistically evocative than Arabs wearing *keffiyas*, and easily interchangeable with them.[15]

To those Americans for whom progress meant decline—whether defined as the loss of community to urban sprawl and anomie, or the submission of workers to factory discipline—Pueblo culture offered an enticing leap backward in time, a return to what was indigenously "American," in a place settled long before the first colonists reached New England and the inexorable corruption of "civilization" began. Longing for a recoverable past, Americans would discover in the Southwest "a special American precinct—the nation's exotic, the faraway nearby." Pueblo Indians, still untouched by modernity, epitomized the primitive virtues that have always retained their appeal to overcivilized peoples. "It is through communication with the primitives of past and present, and with our own primitive possibilities," writes Eric R. Wolf nostalgically, "that we can create an image, a vision, a sense of a life once led by all men and still lived by some, a life richer and more intricately human than their own."[16]

Unlike the Plains Indians, those "noble savages" whose defeat in battle and confinement to reservations served the greater glory of American manifest destiny, Pueblo Indians were perceived as settled and pastoral, law-abiding, and self-governing—a gentle people who remained "devotees of peace and order." They were promoted to a receptive public as "Indians who are neither poor nor naked; Indians who feed themselves and ask no favors of Washington; Indians who have been at peace for two centuries and fixed residents for perhaps a millennium; Indians who were farmers and irrigators and six story house builders before a New World had been beaten through the thick skull of the Old. They had nearly a hundred republics in America centuries before the American Republic was conceived." Reviving the promise of American life, they seemed even more genuinely American than modern Americans themselves. Might they become a vital source of American rejuvenation, even salvation?[17]

Visitors encountered the Pueblo peoples through the lenses of their own fanciful projections. A provincial American might experience a pueblo "as foreign of atmosphere as Egypt is," where even horses treading grain resembled "the unmuzzled oxen of Scripture." And "Rebecca at her well was not a fairer sight, we fancied, than some of those Indian maidens in their picturesque pueblo dress." To Anglo men, the appeal of Pueblo culture might be found in the clarity of its gender divisions at a time when the "proper" roles for men and women in American industrial society had become problematic and contested. In the pueblos, wrote Charles Francis Saunders, "the old-fashioned partition of life's labors between male and female is as it was in the days of the ancients." In an era of heightened gender fluidity, it could be reassuring to discover a place where men worked in the fields and women baked bread, where men hunted for meat and women cooked it, where men built homes and women plastered them, where women were potters and weavers while men were free to be men.[18]

Early photographs of the Southwest conveyed these stereotypical images to Americans who were just beginning to perceive the world through the camera eye. That land, as Christopher Lyman wrote in his study of the photography of Edward S. Curtis, was "the Garden of Eden which many wanted to believe existed, a magnificent panorama of 'views' seldom marred by the mundanities of everyday life." Curtis was pre-eminent, but hardly alone, in transmitting Edenic vistas through his camera. Other contemporary photographers shared his sense of an Indian population verging on imminent disappearance, whose lives must be preserved—at least on film—lest they be forever lost. "In a remarkably short time," warned Frank A. Rinehart (who learned his photographic technique with William Henry Jackson, perhaps the foremost Western landscape photographer of his time), "education and civilization will stamp out the feathers, beads and paint—the sign language, the dancing—and the Indian of the past will live but in memory and pictures."[19]

In what has come to be identified by contemporary scholars as the "construction" of the Southwest—from a barren desert wasteland into a major tourist attraction—the intrusive Santa Fe Railroad found an eager partner. Fred Harvey was an immigrant from England whose business acumen, perhaps more than anything else, stimulated public interest in the Southwest and its native peoples. By the end of the century, his aesthetic vision and entrepreneurial genius had all but transformed the Southwest into the last repository of American promise, an Edenic paradise populated with indigenous Americans whose lives exemplified the lost virtues of premodern America. "Inventing" the Southwest as a marketable commodity for tourists, Harvey introduced Pueblo Indians to eager American travelers and propelled native crafts—and the women who made them—to national attention.

An emerging urban middle class, with money to spend, leisure to enjoy, and cultural ambitions to satisfy, embraced rail travel to newly accessible exotic places. Once the Santa Fe Railroad opened isolated pueblo villages to the outside world, the Fred Harvey Company did the rest, enticing travelers with comfortable accommodations, quality food, and attentive service. It shrewdly capitalized on the growing popularity of the arts and crafts movement, with its emphasis on human creativity rather than machine-made products, to make Indian crafts both desirable and accessible to American consumers and collectors. The Fred Harvey Company and the Santa Fe Railroad cultivated relations with an expanding circle of artists in Santa Fe and Taos who were eager for freedom from traditional aesthetic constraints and promoted tourism with paintings of the natural beauty of the region and its exotic native inhabitants.[20]

As the Fred Harvey Company stimulated the burgeoning ethnic arts and crafts markets of the Southwest, pueblo dwellers confronted the inexorable commercialization of their culture. As tourism to New Mexico increased in popularity, "exotic but docile Indians proved profitable." Lorenzo Hubbell, owner of a trading post at the gateway to the Hopi pueblos in northeastern Arizona, brought the potter Nampeyo to Harvey in 1904 to demonstrate her talent. Harvey installed her in his Grand Canyon lodge, where she gained national renown as the most artistically creative Hopi potter. The convergence of craft and commerce, native artisan and Anglo merchant, inaugurated the successful marketing of the Southwest, which has flourished ever since.[21]

After World War I, for an array of cultural and personal reasons, women began to discover the possibilities of self-redefinition in the Southwest. Amid postwar disillusionment with American society and deepening feminist consciousness, women dramatically transformed the pueblos from places of missionary and teaching opportunity into feminist utopian communities. Pueblos attracted Anglo women, especially from the East Coast, who were seeking to elude the class and gender constraints of their upbringing, while gaining recognition for their intellectual abilities, cultural sensitivity, and entrepreneurial skills. They, too, used Pueblo culture as a projection screen for their own yearnings and struggles.

Elsie Clews Parsons, an outspoken feminist and anti-war pacifist, was attracted to anthropology as an instrument of social reform and personal liberation. She would abandon New York, she told her husband, for "Negroes and Indians." Especially Indians, she conceded, for the "tangle and fusion" of cultures in the Southwest intrigued her. Accompanied by Professor Franz Boas of Columbia University, the foremost American anthropologist of the early twentieth century, Parsons journeyed to the Southwest. Their experiences blazed a trail for a cohort of Boas's most talented female graduate students—including Ruth Benedict, Ruth Bunzel, and Esther Schiff—whose landmark studies emerged from their pueblo fieldwork. Their efforts to elude the constraints of family, gender, and culture made the distant and remote Southwest—with its natural splendor, tri-cultural (Native, Spanish, and Anglo) population, and matrilineal patterns of pueblo life—uniquely appealing to young professional women coming of age in the postwar era.[22]

Aspiring anthropologists were not the only women to become enthralled with Pueblo Indians. Mabel Dodge, born into a wealthy Buffalo family that prepared her for high society, marriage, and motherhood, had rebelled at an early age to redefine herself as a New Woman. After a seven-year sojourn abroad, she returned to the United States in 1912 to discover the sordid ugliness of American capitalism. Retreating to her Fifth Avenue townhouse, where she hosted her famous salon, she attracted disaffected artists and intellectuals who shared her despair about American society. In 1917, shortly after she married Maurice Sterne, a medium predicted that she would soon find herself surrounded by Indians.

In the Southwest, where she was drawn to the "quietude and nobility and wisdom" of the Pueblo Indians, she imagined "a garden of Eden, inhabited by an unfallen tribe of men and women." Taos represented her last, best hope to escape the torments and constraints of modern civilization. There she was attracted to Tony Luhan, a Taos Indian who looked "like a Biblical figure." The religion of white people, Tony told her, was machinery; but the religion of Indians was "Life." Choosing life, Mabel settled in Taos with Tony, immodestly offering herself as a model of "cultural renewal for the dying Anglo civilization." There she would live out her life as a "tourist" in "the Garden of Eden," generously supported by her trust fund and eagerly sharing the allure of the Southwest with legions of disaffected visitors from various decaying precincts of Western society.[23]

Amid the hard times of the 1930s, Edenic fantasies about the pueblos began to wane. Ruth Benedict's *Patterns of Culture*, based upon her research in Zuni, was published in 1934 to rave reviews. Georgia O'Keeffe painted the Southwestern landscape, and Laura Gilpin photographed Pueblo Indians. But utopian dreams were deflated by the grim realities of the Great Depression, when fewer Americans could afford the luxury of travel. An Indian arts and crafts movement remained centered in Santa Fe and Taos, but the Fred Harvey Company, like other businesses, fell on hard times. The romance of the pueblos faded.

In recent years, however, the pueblos have attracted attention from a new generation of feminist scholars. Whether studying their predecessors who did fieldwork in the Southwest, exploring the "construction" of the Southwest by rapacious American business interests, or analyzing the "fetishization" of Pueblo women by patriarchal photographers, artists, and salesmen, these scholars have restored the pueblos to a conspicuous place in the literary imagination. "Something about the Southwest," writes one of them, has "attracted independent, unconventional women." The Southwest offered "sexual and intellectual freedom" that could not be found elsewhere in the United States, and a strategic vantage point for cultural criticism. For these academic women, working with Pueblo Indians provides "an escape from mainstream society and an active political statement."[24]

Ever since Cushing's arrival in Zuni first provoked interest in Pueblo Indians, explorers and visitors have brought their own cultural assumptions—along with their personal frustrations, aspirations, and yearnings—to the Southwest. Largely oblivious to the deep penetration of Spanish culture in the pueblos, they imagined a pristine people untouched by foreign influences. For many of them, Pueblo Indians symbolized the last, best opportunity to discover, if not actually preserve, something indigenous and vital in American life—or, at least, in their own lives—before the inexorable corruption of "civilization" destroyed it forever. Longing for an unrecoverable past, or a revitalized future, they discovered in the Southwest new possibilities, for their nation and for themselves, that could not be found elsewhere in the United States. In their imaginations—whether framed by the Bible, their frustrations with American society, or their own gendered aspirations—Pueblo Indians became inspirational symbols of personal salvation and cultural redemption.[25]

From the moment when Cushing's exploits first captivated the American public, Southwestern pueblos offered an enticing alternative to modernity—the Garden in its innocent purity, just before the corrupting intrusion of the Machine. Determined to explore, understand, document, market, or merely encounter Pueblo culture before it disappeared forever, adventuresome Americans who went to the Southwest have much to tell us still, not only about Pueblo Indians but about themselves—and who we are as a people.

PART ONE

A Man's World

CHAPTER ONE

Cushing in Zuni

In the fall of 1875, John Wesley Powell, an experienced explorer of the Southwest, conducted a geological survey for the United States government. He journeyed through the Grand Canyon to the isolated Hopi pueblos in Arizona. In Oraibi, where he encountered "unsightly" homes and "filthy" streets, the people were "very hospitable" and women demonstrated "great skill in ceramic art." In this "desert land," he realized, the Indians possessed "a vast store of mythology, and an elaborate ceremonious religion." Evidently intrigued as he heard tales drawn from their "unwritten bible," Powell wondered: who is this "strange people," whose origins were shrouded in mystery? Noting how "Bible stories are compounded with native stories" in Pueblo lore, he found it understandable that Americans might believe that Pueblo Indians were "descendants of the lost tribes of Israel."[1]

Powell remembered his pueblo visit. Several years later, as chief of the Bureau of Ethnology, a new branch of the Smithsonian Institution, he authorized Col. James Stevenson, his former associate in the geological survey, to lead an expedition "to make as careful a study as circumstances will permit of the Pueblo ruins and caves." It should include collections of artifacts representing "the arts and industries of the inhabitants"; photos and drawings of the Indians with scenes of daily life; and an investigation of their language, customs, habits, myths, governance, and architecture. Powell believed that government sponsorship of such an expedition would be an important contribution to the "new science" of anthropology, while simultaneously providing a persuasive rationale for national Indian policy.[2]

The director of the Smithsonian, Spencer F. Baird, supervised a young protégé who seemed destined for just such an expedition. As a precocious and independent boy growing up in western New York, Frank Hamilton Cushing's early interest in Indian artifacts was stimulated when a Cushing family plowman unearthed an arrowhead, telling him, "Indians made that." This formative experience inspired young Cushing to explore Indian history and culture in his own way, seldom attending formal school. With his brother, Cushing built a wigwam, which the boys inhabited for days at a time while they foraged for Indian artifacts, gathering arrowheads, beads, and pottery shards. To better understand the techniques of Indian craftsmanship, Cushing even attempted to reproduce by hand the artifacts that he found. "If I would study any old, lost art," he later explained, "I must make myself the artisan of it." Baird, who learned about Cushing's adventures from a mutual family friend, invited the teenage explorer to publish a paper on his collection of artifacts in the *Annual Report* of the Smithsonian Institution. Three years later, after a brief sojourn as a student at Cornell, Cushing joined the Smithsonian staff. Despite his ethnographic work for the Centennial Exposition in Philadelphia, it did not take long for him to feel stultified by his "socially dead, morally dead, intellectually dead" life in Washington.[3]

"One hot summer day in 1879," Cushing recalled, "as I was sitting in my office in the ivy-mantled old South Tower of the Smithsonian Institution, a messenger boy tapped at my door." Professor Baird asked to see him. "Haven't I heard you say you would like to go to New Mexico to study the cliff-houses and Pueblo Indians?" Baird inquired. Hearing Cushing's enthusiastic reply, Baird told him to be prepared within four days to join the Stevenson expedition to Zuni. "I want you to find out all you can about some typical tribe of Pueblo Indians." Baird advised him: "Use your own methods; only get the information."[4]

Photographed just before he left Washington, Cushing was every bit the effete Easterner indulging his Western frontier fantasies (fig. 2). With his hair neatly parted and combed, wearing a fine shirt, silk cravat, and gaiters, his belt-knife and rifle (resting on neatly folded gloves) seem more like props for a performance than genuine weapons. Posing against a leafy studio backdrop, holding a note pad and pen, he was the embodiment of a young Eastern gentleman primed for the challenge of his journey into manhood. If this photo

FIG. 2. "Frank Hamilton Cushing Before His Departure to Zuni,"
National Anthropological Archives, Smithsonian Institution (80–9479).

captured Cushing's "cultural point of departure," as Jesse Green suggests, "its pale and Eastern manner" also reveals how far Cushing would travel on his journey to Zuni and self-transformation.[5]

Relieved at his escape from the bureaucratic confines of the Smithsonian, Cushing was instantly enchanted by the harsh and spacious beauty of New Mexico. Impatient for a glimpse of what awaited him in Zuni, he rode out from Santa Fe on a mule to visit nearby Tesuque Pueblo. The moon was high on a clear starry night when he spotted "the blocks and ladders which books and pictures had taught me were peculiar to Pueblo dwellings." He also saw, "gracefully outlined against the sky, the silhouettes of three women and a little girl," who had been drawing water from a spring. One of them had a clay pot balanced on her head. Cushing called for directions to the pueblo, but the "frightened creatures" remained silent, "still as statues." Spurring his mule, he rode toward them. Startled, they "dropped ollas and dippers and scattered among the tall weeds which covered the bank."[6]

It was a memorable experience for the young ethnographer from the East, confronting for the first time native peoples of the Southwest who would prompt his impulsive decision, a few weeks later, to learn about them by living among them. Whatever the Pueblo women may have experienced went unrecorded. Unable to gauge the intentions of this determined Anglo intruder, who suddenly appeared out of the night, hollered in a strange language, and then charged toward them on his mule, they likely would have been terrified. Cushing, however, was exhilarated, a feeling that returned when his expedition was encamped outside Zuni. Invited to visit the pueblo by the governor, whose profile reminded him of "an Egyptian cameo," Cushing mused: "How strangely parallel have been the lines of development in this curious civilization of an American desert, with those of Eastern nations and deserts."

Cushing spent his early days in Zuni wandering around the pueblo, exploring, taking notes, sketching, and attempting—with little success—to communicate with the natives. In his letters, he repeatedly framed Zuni within Middle Eastern images. A distant procession of farmers on burros resembled "a caravan crossing a desert waste." Women at the well reminded him of "the Pools of Palestine." During his first visit to a Zuni home, he was delighted by the presence of "a beautiful young girl [who] had just come in with a water jar on her head, and, still balancing it, stood gazing at me through the part in her hair." For Cushing, still a stranger in Zuni, Pueblo Indians and biblical figures instantly became interchangeable people in strikingly similar exotic locations. For the duration of his "scientific" investigations, he never lost his powerful fascination with his new Indian companions.[7]

After days of frustrated attempts at communication, amid palpable hostility from the Zunis, Cushing sensed that he would fail in his mission to understand them. When the other expedition members prepared to journey to the Hopi pueblos in Arizona, Cushing impulsively decided to stay behind and move in with the Zunis. "I one night bore my hammock, blankets and a few possessions and took up my abode"—choosing the governor's house for his new home or, perhaps, directed there by the governor to assure proper surveillance. "How long will it be before you go back to Washington?" his host inquired. "Two months," Cushing replied confidently. Convinced of his "youthful folly," the other members of his expedition departed without him.

Cushing's decision expressed his intuitive understanding that he would learn about the Zuni Indians only by "actual experience and experimentation, endeavoring always to place himself as much as possible in their position, not only physically but intellectually and morally as well, [to] gain insight into their inner life and institutions." His strategy for unlocking the mysteries of Zuni culture was implicit in his method: "becoming one with the Zunis, learning their language and living with them." With this insight, Cushing made history, becoming the first American ethnographer to live among his subjects as a participant observer. Despite his assurance of a two-month visit, he remained in Zuni for nearly five years.[8]

Cushing's Zuni experience endures as one of the great journeys of discovery and self-transformation in American history. With seemingly boundless tolerance for "isolation and martyrdom," he exposed himself to prolonged privation and danger at the risk of serious impairment to his physical and emotional health. But he would not be deterred from exploring the mysteries of Zuni culture and, in the process, the depths of his own identity. Cushing, as Eliza McFeely has written, "found a variety of ways to blur the line between himself and the Zunis." Imagining that "he could think and act like a Zuni," that he was "becoming Zuni while remaining himself," Cushing became a fascinating self-study of "the capacity of civilized man to recover, almost physically, his ancestral past"—and, indeed, to enter imaginatively into it. By "Playing Indian," Philip Deloria has suggested, his "cross-cultural boundary hopping" enabled him to discover sources of personal identity and cultural authenticity that modernity had all but destroyed. In Zuni, Cushing could return to a golden age of Edenic innocence.[9]

With the departure of the Stevenson expedition, Cushing "woke to find myself alone among the Indians. Of provisions I had almost none; of money, almost none, as it chanced; of resources aside from these, none whatsoever." Understandably despairing, he "wandered dejectedly about the town or stayed within the doors of the empty council chamber." Unable even to speak to his hosts, he regressed to virtual helplessness. Driven by hunger, he nearly set his room on fire trying to cook, until Patricio Pino, the governor—taking pity on such an inept "barbarian" as this effete Easterner—came to his rescue. Insisting that Cushing decide whether to remain a fool or become a Zuni, Pino prodded him to make the choice upon which his very survival depended.[10]

But it was not easy. Cushing lived "in constant discomfort"; Indian food was "disgusting"; communication, mostly in pidgin Spanish, was difficult and stressful. Cushing wrote plaintively of his personal sacrifices: "It is *solely* with the wish to make my visit to the Pueblo of a little scientific use that I would consent even to remain here." Undaunted by adversity, he appealed for an extension of his stay. Indeed, by the end of October, his plea gained special urgency. "My anxiety would not be so great," he explained, "were there not a probability that I am among the last who will ever witness all this in its purity as the advent of the Railroad next fall through the valley will, with its foreign inflow, introduce all sorts of innovations." Zuni life, he predicted, "which is to-day substantially what it was before the Spanish conquest, cannot fail soon to be modified by American civilization, and it must be recorded soon or never."[11]

A fast learner, Cushing persisted relentlessly, immersing himself in the intricacies of Zuni language, customs, ritual, and lore. By day, he moved with increasing ease throughout the pueblo. "Everywhere I wandered," he wrote, "the little children, shy as prairie dogs, would dodge in and out of the sky holes or scamper away far ahead, calling to one another so that the chance of seeing a man of such strange race and costume as we Americans then were to that people should not be missed." It took time and patience, reinforced by enticements of sugar and beads, before the children would approach him; and some ointment applied to a youngster's wounds before Cushing could win a mother's trust. Gradually, he noted proudly, his walks through town had become "a sort of triumphal march, leading a procession of shouting, laughing, expectant children." Cushing, the Pied Piper of Zuni, was heartened.[12]

But Zuni men remained understandably wary of the Anglo stranger in their midst. Inevitably, Cushing's presence aroused suspicion, hostility, even threats. Charmed at first by his sketches ("They would pass their fingers over the figures as though they expected to feel them"), the Zunis became angry when he drew scenes from their sacred dances. He tried to remain circumspect, but he was constantly monitored. "Day after day, night after night, they followed me about the pueblo, or gathered in my room," Cushing recorded. Not until he finished writing up his notes at night would the governor finally leave him. Even while sleeping he was not alone; the governor, a relative, or a tribal member slept sprawled across the doorway, lest he try to leave. Despite warnings that he might be thrown off the mesa, or condemned for sorcery and executed, Cushing persisted.[13]

Cushing's insistence upon sketching sacred dances finally provoked a decisive showdown. Instructed to leave his notebooks and pens behind, Cushing refused. Warned of their confiscation if he brought them along, he pulled out his knife and threatened: "whoever cut my books to pieces would only cut himself to pieces with my knife." His bluff succeeded, at least temporarily. Not long afterward, however, while sketching another dance, he was surrounded and accused of being a Navajo spy. Again drawing his knife, he "waved it two or three times in the air so that it flashed in the sunlight, and laid it conspicuously in front of me," adjacent to his notebook. Backing off, the Zuni men decided to sacrifice a dog instead. Impressed by his courage, other Zunis in attendance applauded. "Some of the old men even came up and patted me on the head, or breathed on my hands," Cushing wrote. He had passed a critical test; never again would he be physically threatened. That night, with praise from the tribal chief, Cushing understood that "the fate of my mission among the Zuni Indians" had been decided.[14]

Cushing needed more than tolerance; an outsider, he yearned for inclusion. How could his government in Washington extend friendship, he shrewdly asked the governor, if it knew nothing about the Zuni people and their tribal secrets? Persuaded that benevolence toward this stranger served their own self-interest, Zuni leaders drew upon tribal history to accommodate him. Centuries earlier, the Zunis had learned to align themselves with Spanish invaders against their local Indian enemies. Now, the Zunis were confronting new dangers: they needed protection from Anglo penetration, Navajo invasion, and Mormon intrusion. They probably anticipated that Cushing's influence in Washington, which they surely exaggerated, could be parlayed to their advantage.[15]

To win their confidence, Cushing believed that he must shed his Anglo ways. He began to dress like a Zuni; or, at least, according to their version of a white man dressed like a Zuni. "By appearing in the ancient national costume (at my Zuni friend's instigation)," he informed Baird, "I have succeeded in lulling their new born suspicions." He replaced his hat with a red silk handkerchief; his English walking shoes gave way to buckskin moccasins. "Heartily ashamed of my mongrel costume," Cushing nonetheless wore it as a significant sign of Zuni acceptance. Before long, he was outfitted in recognizably Zuni breeches, a woolen blanket shirt, and a striped serape. With the gift of a stone-beaded necklace from a friendly Zuni priest, and a copper bracelet, his sartorial transformation was complete. "The first time I appeared in the streets in full costume the Zunis were delighted," Cushing wrote proudly. As he quickly learned, he had no choice. Returning to his room, he discovered that his "civilized clothing" had disappeared in his absence. "I want to make a Zuni of you," the governor informed Cushing.[16]

With measured steps, carefully calibrated by his hosts, Cushing was drawn deeper into the Zuni tribal circle. At the governor's insistence, his room was refurbished in Zuni minimalist style. His hammock gave way to blankets and sheepskins suitable for sleeping on the floor, the better to have his "meat hardened." He was advised not to visit the local Anglo missionary or trader, who would encourage his regression by serving him American food. An old Zuni priest who befriended him told him that to become a "complete Zuni," he must not only dress authentically, but have his ears pierced. "I steadily refused," Cushing wrote; "but they persisted, until at last it occurred to me that there must be some meaning in their urgency." Cushing reluctantly complied; after an elaborate religious ceremony, he was symbolically reborn as a "Child of the Sun" and received his Zuni name. For the first time, Cushing referred to the Zuni governor as "my father."[17]

Cushing's initiation into Zuni culture was a carefully choreographed encounter between uneasy partners with different agendas, engaged in an uncertain process whose outcome neither could precisely anticipate. Cushing might boldly assert his independence when he felt threatened, but he yielded submissively when enticing new opportunities for inclusion were offered. The Zunis insisted that he could best serve his own ethnographic purposes by identifying himself with their tribal needs. Cushing made it clear, in return, that he would demand considerable personal autonomy, even authority, as fair exchange for his representation of their interests.[18]

Writing to Baird after barely a month in Zuni, Cushing was most impressed with how a Zuni Indian "throws off everything foreign"—that is, modern—precisely as Cushing himself was attempting to do. "His dress, where not fantastic, is primitive; his axe and knife are of stone; his gorgeous scarves and feather ornaments are much as Cabeza de Vaca saw when first he climbed the mesa and saw the city which afterward was Nica's Cibola." Determined to learn their ways, Cushing was prepared to "dominate myself with their needs, surround myself with their material conditions, aim to do as they did." He would rely upon his "eyes and ears," not books, to instruct him. He believed that "my *method* must succeed. I live among the Indians, I eat their food, and sleep in their houses. . . . They love me, and I learn."[19]

Cushing imagined that the Zunis retained a completely indigenous native culture, uncontaminated by outside influence. In fact, the impact of Spanish occupation was deep and enduring. It was hardly accidental that the most conspicuous structure in any pueblo was (and still is) likely to be its Catholic church, a telling symbol of Spanish religious authority. Over time, Pueblo Indians had learned how to preserve their native religion by channeling priestly rule and ritual into underground kivas, even as they worshiped in church on Sunday mornings. But any sense of a completely autonomous Pueblo culture, untouched by outside influence until the Santa Fe Railroad delivered its first trainload of tourists, was illusory.

Reality constantly intruded. Cushing's "self-inflicted degradation to the daily life of savages," as he described it, exacted its toll. Visiting Fort Wingate, he was humiliated to be assigned quarters in the henhouse, although "plenty of clean and comfortable rooms" were available for the night. He drew slight solace from the reassurance of his Pueblo companion, "Well, you see, *we* are Zunis." But Cushing was nothing if not persistent. By Christmas, he proudly reported to Baird: "With the partial acquisition of the Zuni language, and the entire adoption of their costume and habits of life, I have . . . overcome that superstitious prejudice with which all observers of savage life have most to contend."[20]

Two months later, after Cushing dressed like a Zuni and participated in their rituals, they counted him as "one of their people." This "closer intimacy," he realized, conferred "the most important advantages" because Zuni religious, social, and political life was "rigidly ruled by instructions," contained in prayer, song, and "ancient talks" that had remained "unvaried from a remote period of prehistory." It was, Cushing insisted, "the *duty* of some one to record, word for word, in the original language, and with faithful translation, these prayers, ancient instructions, and formulae." He alone could do this, because he had finally "won the confidence and esteem of the Indians, as no other man can, without equal sacrifices." In return, the Zunis became "very free with their information regarding the meaning of certain plumes and prayers."[21]

Cushing realized that the more welcoming the Zunis were, the more they would demand of him. To his considerable dismay, he learned that his hosts wished to strengthen his tribal attachment through marriage to a Zuni woman. (In Washington, Emily Magill, his fiancée, patiently awaited his return.) His adamant refusal to marry a Zuni caused "the only drawback I have had since my adoption." He tried to compensate by participating in "one of the greatest dances of the season." He seems to have been successful, for he wrote to Baird and Powell that he had received "a much coveted costume, and admission into the sacred houses [kivas] during religious ceremonies." This glimpse "revealed to me a mysterious life by which I had little dreamed I was surrounded."[22]

As the Zuni Indians became his "adopted people," Cushing meticulously documented his experiences in long, detailed letters to his superiors at the Smithsonian. "My living is simply horrible, unmentionable," he continued to complain. He despaired over "the superstitious character of these natives," "the desert character of this country," and "the utter absence of all vegetable substance from my diet." But his fierce dedication to his ethnographic work, even at considerable personal cost to his health, sustained him. He remained unwavering in his conviction that "there is no Ethnographic field in America, if in the world, as rich in uncollected material and fact, as in the Pueblos, of which I have come to regard Zuni as the highest representative."[23]

Cushing's "prodigious task" of collecting "the psychologic material of savages" both exhausted and exhilarated him. His acceptance in Zuni always felt precarious, and his personal relationships remained a source of stress. "I hold my friends from doing me violence by a bond of brotherhood which, you have but to be conversant with the Indian character to appreciate the strength of; and my enemies I have equal power over from their absolute dread of me." Because of his "absolute fearlessness," he had become "pretty much master of my situation," although "the superstitions of these fellows and the things they ask me to do in compliance with them are, at times exhasperating [sic] in the extreme."

Cushing conceded that "however full my life be of hardships (from the civilized standpoint of view) and my work of discouragements (from the savage), yet, both have their bright sides; and the only actual depression I ever suffer from is when I see my health failing, and sometimes recognize my inability to fill the time properly with work." Despite "longings for my Eastern home," and complaints about "the isolated and at times intensely suffering life which I lead here," his work—and "the love, ever increasing, of the studies which I have chosen for life"—sustained him. Indeed, Cushing's experience in Zuni gave him pleasure that he described as "so fairly intense that I forget how I live."[24]

Describing his life in Zuni "in one sentence," after nearly a year, he told Baird, "physically, so far as the appetites are concerned, paralysis; socially, exile; ethically and theoretically, a constant feast and peace of mind such as I have not known in all my previous experience." Summarizing his experiences for an old family friend, he referred to "this paradise of ethnography, the great Southwest." He conceded, "for many months my suffering and loneliness were dreadful." The Indians were "my masters" and they were "tyrannical." But, he concluded proudly, "by policy and patience I won, in long months, their confidence, respect and esteem, gained authority over them . . . so that at present the table is turned and I am *their master*."[25]

The decisive moment for Cushing came with his initiation into the Bow Priesthood, a secret religious society located at the apex of Zuni tribal power. "I bent all my energies toward this supreme order of the Zunis for more than a year," he acknowledged. Membership in the Bow Priesthood "would secure at once standing with the tribe and entrance to all sacred meetings," where innermost tribal secrets would be revealed. The final obstacle to his inclusion was removed after a dangerous journey through Apache country. "I returned from that expedition, at the end of a hot day," he laconically recalled, "with a scalp, sole remaining requisite for my initiation into the Priesthood of the Bow." His initiation rites, spread over several days, were arduous. While fasting, "I was set at sunrise on a large ant-hill of the red fire ants of the Southwest, so named because of their bites, and there all day long I had to sit, motionless, speechless, save to priests in reply to instructions." After an evening procession through Zuni, involving the ritual killing of dogs, came "more fasting, more sleeplessness, purifications, vomitings each day, sacrificial pilgrimages, then silent motionless meditation again."

It was an experience that Cushing described as "more amazing than anything I could relate." To Baird, he confided, "it is the greatest of all the achievements of my life perhaps; for it breaks down this last shadow of objection to my gaining knowledge of the sacred rites, not only of this but of the Moqui [Hopi] tribes and others as well." His ordeals comprised "the grandest, most interesting, weird and terrible experiences and days my life has ever seen, and open up the sublimest depths of meaning to my researches in Zuni."

Cushing's initiation as a Bow Priest completed his absorption into tribal society; his time of testing was over. He would recall a dream in which a stranger told him: "you are an Indian, truly an Indian, disguised as it were in the flesh of an American." He might accuse the Zunis of "tyranny," but he understood that without their acceptance his own ethnographic work would be severely impaired—and his dreams of self-transformation shattered. In Zuni, he acknowledged, he had discovered his own "long-sought-for social utopia." Now he could proceed with his work while serving, with no small measure of pride, as "vindicator of the legal rights of the Zuni Nation" to government officials in Washington. Whether the Zunis were "my Indians," as he audaciously boasted, he had come to believe, after one year in the pueblo, "I am Boss here just now." In Zuni, Cushing discovered internal sources of power, authority, and self-fulfillment that his work in Washington never could provide. Stripped of the vestments of civilization, he encountered himself.[26]

In May 1881, Sylvester Baxter, a *Boston Herald* journalist, accompanied by Willard Metcalf, a staff artist for *Harper's Weekly*, came to Zuni to visit Cushing. In an article for the *Herald*, Baxter recounted the "Wonderful Achievements of Frank H. Cushing," identifying him as "a young gentleman whose name will soon rank with those of famous scientists." His description captured Cushing's dramatic—if carefully tailored—appearance: "a slender, light complexioned young man—he is not yet 24 years old—with long, flowing blonde hair, confined by the Indian head band, and dressed in the picturesque costume of the tribe—every article of native manufacture, from the cloth of the dark blue woolen serape-shirt, the buckskin knee breeches, long dark blue stockings, leather moccasins, and artistically embroidered sash, to the rows of silver buttons and other richly worked silver ornaments, and the precious ancient necklace from a mysterious cave of relics up in the mountains." As an army officer at Fort Wingate told Baxter: Cushing "can not stand contemplating his subjects from the outside, like a spectator at a play. He must go on to the stage, and take his own part in the performance."[27]

Cushing's performance engaged Baxter, who recognized a compelling feature story when he discovered it. Although the Pueblo peoples, to Baxter's dismay, had been "callous to all attempts to Christianize them," he was convinced that Cushing had discovered a strategy to unlock their secrets: "that of becoming one with the Zunis, learning their language and living with them." Cushing, in characteristically American fashion, had achieved his objective "by the use of pluck, tact and adaptability." Noting that this dashing figure came from "the old Cushing family, so well known and highly honored in Massachusetts," Baxter interlaced his account of Cushing's adventures in Zuni with romantic glimpses of Montezuma and the Aztecs, the lost cities of Cibola, and "the mystery of the magnificent ruins of the Yucatan." For "a man of such powers" as Cushing possessed, Baxter predicted, the opportunities for scientific discovery and personal fame seemed boundless.[28]

Baxter described Zuni, in all of its romantic allure, as "Oriental." There, he wrote, "We were away back in the centuries, and living the life of the remote past." Children raced through the winding alleys "in cherubic nakedness"; women, who went up and down ladders with water jars on their heads, walked "with a fine, erect poise." Toward sunset, when crowds of girls gathered by the spring for water, it evoked for Baxter, as it had for Cushing, "a Scripture-like scene." With their "startling resemblances to the familiar civilizations of the East," Zuni religious ceremonies seemed to be "strangely like those of the ancient Egyptians and Greeks."[29]

By the time of Baxter's visit, Cushing had reason to be proud of his achievements. As he had recently reported to Baird: "I am making more rapid progress in the study of the *inner life* of these wonderful savages during the past few days than ever before." But it was not easy, and it exacted a toll on Cushing's health. "I am terribly weary, terribly cast down," he confessed. "It does not seem at times as though I could endure longer this terrible work." Yet Cushing knew that he had "laid open a field which without presumption I can say is the richest ever within the reach or sight of an American investigator." To abandon his work prematurely, he wrote, "would seem not short of sacrilege to me." Melodramatically, but with evident passion, Cushing described his ethnographic interest as "an instinct—a deathless enthusiasm, an ever present, silently urging voice, which I follow because I cannot resist."[30]

Cushing had arrived in Zuni just when the pueblo was beginning to experience increasing contact with outsiders: Anglo missionaries, Mormons, traders, land speculators, government agents, ethnographers—and even the first trickle of tourists. It was precisely this constellation of developments, early in the 1880s, that gave Cushing his unique opportunity in Zuni, enabled him to play multiple roles in the pueblo, and determined his place in American ethnographic history. "Literally and figuratively denuded," as historian Curtis Hinsley writes, Cushing had learned Zuni ways to survive. Yet he also needed to maintain his link to the Smithsonian, upon whose financial support and encouragement from Baird he depended. With one protective "father" (the governor, Patricio Pino) in Zuni, and another (Baird at the Smithsonian) back East, Cushing pursued his dual life as government ethnographer and member of the Zuni tribe.[31]

Cushing experienced both the precariousness and rewards of his dual identity. He became the consummate "outside-insider," from whom much was expected and for whom the risks were high. Placed on trial for sorcery during his first year in Zuni, he nonetheless emerged as "First War Chief," with a wide array of responsibilities as ambassador and advocate for the Zuni people. With tribal consent, for the Zunis surely expected a return on their investment in him, he came to be recognized as a leader, the better to protect Zuni interests from those who were eager to exploit native peoples for their own benefit. Yet the perception of Cushing in Zuni as a "government" agent, empowering though it was, simultaneously exposed his vulnerability. As he explained to Baird, "The Indians having named me one of their chiefs and regarding me as a 'child of Washington,' look forward to me being able to relieve them." Were he to fail, however, "I fear that I shall lose all standing among them."[32]

To preserve his status in Zuni, Cushing had been persuaded to return East with a tribal delegation. "I must do one of two things," he told a friend: "either marry a Zuni girl or make a tour East with some of the principled men of the Pueblo. I infinitely prefer the latter." Cushing knew that his reputation would precede him, for Sylvester Baxter had stirred considerable interest in his exploits. "There is a large body of gentlemen—and ladies—in various Eastern cities, of great culture, wealth and position," he noted, "who are anxious to have me bring my Zunis forward." The benefits from the trip, he predicted, would be "inestimable." At the very least, increased Zuni respect for his stature in government circles might facilitate his acquisition of valuable sacred artifacts for the Smithsonian. Cushing also noted, with commendable candor, "the natural desire to have attention called to my work . . . and to its purity of purpose and singleness of aim," especially since his "moral character and earnestness have often been questioned and slandered."[33]

FIG. 3. "Frank Hamilton Cushing Returns to Washington, D.C." Photographer unknown.
Courtesy Museum of New Mexico, Neg. # 9147.

Cushing made an eloquent plea for the benefits of his trip to the Zuni people, to whom "I owe a lasting debt of gratitude." He hoped "to establish pleasant feelings between them and Americans, to solicit aid for them in times of trouble, and to show them the wisdom of consenting to education—*not* innovation." Here was a native tribe, after all, that was "born in ancient times to the hardships of savage invasion and warfare." The Zunis had "struggled up to their little incipient civilization, receiving aid from no human agency and asking nothing save the good will of their deliverers, ourselves." All the more reason, therefore, for Cushing to convince them "that I *am* what I have always claimed to be, their *friend*."[34]

Cushing and his Indian delegation left Zuni for the East in February 1882. Attentive to Cushing's emerging role as a performer, Hinsley observes that they "brought rich traveling theatre eastward." Provided with free railroad passes, and accompanied by considerable journalistic fanfare, the Zuni delegation arrived in Washington, eager to see the "great cacique's house" (the White House) and to visit the Smithsonian, where their artifacts were exhibited. After meeting President Chester A. Arthur, they departed for Boston (fig. 3).[35]

In Massachusetts, "where the ladies of Boston have extended cordial invitations," Cushing and the Zunis had cultural encounters surely as quixotic as any that Cushing had experienced in Zuni. Baxter had done his work well, lining up the Brahmin elite to celebrate Cushing's visit. He assured Cushing that the Rev. Edward Everett Hale, the renowned minister and author, "feels a great interest in your work and is interesting others in you." Cushing would be welcome at the Old South Church "with your Zunis," and he should also plan to address the American Antiquarian Society in Worcester.[36]

Boston's Brahmins were enchanted with Cushing and his Zuni companions. The delegation received a special tour of Harvard's Peabody Museum, with its rapidly expanding collection of Indian artifacts. At the Paint and Clay Club, they met Francis Parkman and William Dean Howells, the Brahmins' favorite historian and novelist. Cushing was introduced to philanthropist Mary Hemenway, who befriended him and generously offered to sponsor an expedition once he decided to leave Zuni. On Deer Island in Boston Harbor, accompanied by officials from Harvard and MIT, "civic dames and learned ladies," and jostling reporters who got their feet wet in the rising tide, the Zunis filled vessels with water for ceremonial purposes from the "Ocean of Sunrise." In nearby Salem, one of the Zuni chiefs thanked the local people for the efforts of their ancestors to eradicate witchcraft. In Worcester, they were astonished by the wonders of factory technology. As "souvenir fetishes of magical industrial power," the Zunis received bits of snipped iron from the largest wire manufacturer in the country. Years later the journalist Charles F. Lummis, not reticent about promoting his own pueblo adventures, wrote appreciatively, "Never was [a] tour more skillfully managed. Perhaps never was another quite so curiously mixed between genuine scholarship and the arts of the showman."[37]

Cushing and his Zuni companions even visited Wellesley College, the newest outpost of Boston evangelical culture and female refinement, only recently opened on the Durant estate ten miles west of the city. After Cushing's lecture and a Zuni dance performance in the chapel, a reception was held in the Centre of College Hall, where Cushing, Zuni chieftains, and Wellesley College students had an incongruous, yet delightfully revealing, encounter with each other.

In Willard Metcalf's evocative drawing of the reception, two Zuni Indians with dangling earrings and feathers in their headbands are seated at the center of a circle of perhaps a dozen attentive (and appropriately refined) female students, some with flowers in their hair, others holding fans. One young woman leans forward intently, her chin resting on her hand just inches from the Zunis, all but obliterating the cultural chasm that separated them. Between them, civilization and savagery converged beneath the tropical fronds that graced the Centre of College Hall (fig. 4).

Everyone, according to the *Boston Herald*, had a wonderful time. Students played the piano, sang, and tried to teach the words of "Little Brown Jug" ("Hah, hah, hah, you and me/Little brown jug, don't I love thee?") to the Zuni chiefs. During the reception, Zunis frequently repeated "E-lu!"—their word for enchantingly beautiful—while the students found them "so handsome that they reminded us of [James Fennimore] Cooper's heroes," those fabled noble savages of nineteenth-century literature studied by Wellesley students in their literature classes.[38]

By any measure, however, it must have been a curious encounter. Lucia Grieve (Class of 1883) left what may be the only surviving firsthand account of the visit by a Wellesley student. "Some Indians came to visit the College, and we saw them in the chapel," she noted laconically, before analyzing Cushing with a sharp eye and tart pen: "This Mr. Cushing has gone to the homes of these Indians, for scientific—especially ethnological—investigation. He wears their dress, has been adopted into their tribe and initiated into their

FIG. 4. *The Reception at Wellesley College* by W. L. Metcalf, Wellesley College,
from Sylvester Baxter, "An Aboriginal Pilgrimage,"
Century Illustrated Monthly Magazine 24 (August 1882), 533.

secret orders, and is next to the head man in civil authority. But I don't alto-
gether like the way he has done all this; it shows sharpness, but does not seem
very honorable."

The Indians, Ms. Grieve continued, "are not the down-trodden Indians
of the North, but an independent, comparatively civilized tribe, the cave-
builders, or Pueblo Indians, or Zunis." They live, she noted (inaccurately), "on
the bank of the Rio Grande, in the face of a cliff, in one house holding 1600
people." She conceded, "They dress well, are an agricultural people, and possess a fine literature and an extremely complicated religion." Concluding, she
wrote, "They amused the girls immensely at the Reception, so I heard."[39]

Lucia Grieve carefully distanced herself from the Wellesley students who
gazed adoringly at Cushing with such rapt admiration. Clearly, something
about his successful insinuation into Zuni culture troubled her. Perhaps he was
too flamboyantly—or artificially—"native" to suit her taste. His very success
as a participant observer, after all, collapsed boundaries between "civilization"

and "savagery" that she, like many of her contemporaries, may have preferred remain inviolate. By venturing into liminal space, neither Anglo nor Indian but a blend of both, Cushing seemed to have displayed the "sharpness" that struck her as dishonorable. Whatever her reasons, Miss Grieve reproved Cushing for precisely what made him so magnetically appealing to many of their American contemporaries—his determination, and evident ability, to transgress cultural boundaries.[40]

Many years later, critic Edmund Wilson observed that Cushing, like the Zunis themselves, preferred to live in "an alternative world in which he was more at home than in that of Anglo-Saxon America." Cushing's reference to his own "queer dual life" illuminated, for Wilson, "the struggle between white and red man, not in the forest or on the plains, but in one dislocated human spirit." Yet precisely when the sanctification of Zuni as a utopian alternative to corrupted American modernity began to take hold among beguiled Eastern audiences, it was already too late; Zuni society, debilitated by alcoholism, disease, and factionalism, was anything but paradise. Yet Cushing was hardly the last adventurous American to discover (or imagine) in Pueblo culture, especially in Zuni, an Edenic utopia that modernity had stifled elsewhere.[41]

Cushing lingered in the East for several months before returning to Zuni. He worked at the Bureau of Ethnology, transforming his extensive notes into a study of Zuni fetishes and writing a series of articles, published in *Century Illustrated Monthly Magazine* as "My Adventures in Zuni," that gained him an enthusiastic national audience. With or without Zuni approval, he married Emily Magill. (In a tender letter, written before his journey east, Cushing had told her: "I am one of those flowers you have picked up—and people call me a weed? Never mind! They do not see all of me—and I am growing. Only one among them knows that.") Accompanied by two Zuni chiefs who remained behind (perhaps to monitor his advocacy on their behalf), Cushing and his bride vacationed with his parents in upstate New York before leaving for the Southwest.[42]

Cushing was noticeably relieved to return to Zuni. "It seems more like home than any other I have seen," he wrote in his journal shortly after his arrival. Highly respected as a tribal chief, he enjoyed enhanced credibility as an influential "Washington man." By then, however, there was "a considerable little American community" in Zuni, comprising the Cushings, Emily's sister Margaret, a "negro cook brought from Washington, and trained in an old Virginia family," artist Metcalf, and the local trader and government teacher.

When Baxter came to visit, he immediately noticed that Emily's "charming artistic taste" had transformed Cushing's room from spare Zuni space into "a luxuriant little boudoir." He admired the "civilized furniture," the "rich and varied hues" of the Zuni and Navajo blankets hanging on the walls (which reminded Baxter of "Oriental tapestry"), and the "excellent oil paintings" set out on easels. He noticed "rare and curious pieces of pottery" on the mantle-piece, along with the books, magazines, Japanese screens, and "a handsome lamp" that produced a "cozy, homelike effect." To Baxter, "the refining touch of a woman's hand was everywhere manifest." Civilization, personified by Emily Magill Cushing (as by Wellesley student Lucia Grieve), had reasserted its claims over (male) savagery.[43]

But Cushing's domestic Victorian haven in Zuni was precarious. A journalist observed that although Emily had converted Cushing's mud house into "a pretty little paradise," she "does not enjoy life in Zuni as her husband does. . . . She hates the uncouth women and the naked children, and despises their filthy ways." Nor would she permit Zuni visitors "to intrude into her apartments without permission," making "frightful examples of some of them" in her efforts to teach them to knock before entering. Before long, Cushing was complaining about "the constant crowd of visitors which the unfortunate popularity of Zuni has attracted."[44]

The more publicity that Cushing received, the more sharply he was criticized. Already suspect for his reversion to "savagery," he was rebuked for "sensationalizing" his own exploits. His former expedition colleague Matilda Stevenson, with evident annoyance, wrote on the back of a photograph of Cushing dressed in full Zuni regalia: "Frank Hamilton Cushing in his fantastic dress while among the Zuni Indians. This man was the biggest fool and charlatan I ever knew." Senator John Logan of Illinois, whose son-in-law was involved in a land dispute with the Zunis in which Cushing intervened on their behalf, dismissed him as a "white Indian" who, treasonably, was "disrobing himself of citizen's clothes."[45]

Allegations of Cushing's misbehavior accumulated from government agents, missionaries, land speculators, and even from Zunis who disapproved of his activities. With his personal and professional credibility under attack, Cushing became increasingly vulnerable. Forced to delay his writing because of frequent illness—and inclined to act boldly, even impulsively, as a Zuni "war chief"—he began to lose the confidence of his superiors in Washington. Strongly rebuked by Senator Logan and others for helping "savages" assert claims against American interests, he was finally recalled by Major Powell. His idyll shattered by the unwelcome attention that his own flamboyant behavior had attracted, Cushing left Zuni at the end of April 1884, nearly five years after his arrival as an unknown ethnographer in a remote Indian village that few Americans even knew existed.

Cushing has remained an enigma ever since. His disregard for the conventional cultural boundaries of his era, which sharply separated Anglos from Indians, made him simultaneously intriguing and suspect. He was, as Jesse Green suggests, "a straddler between two cultures." In the end, he was incapacitated by the contradictions between them, and within himself. Yet Cushing was also a creature of his time, drawing all the conventional stereotypical distinctions between (Anglo) "civilization" and (Indian) "savagery," while never forgetting on which side of the boundary he ultimately stood. As he explained to a cousin: "I have to have knowledge of savage life, and it matters less to me where I find it, than it does in what measure I find it. Zuni, therefore, while I confess it to be a patch of thorns in the side of a civilized being, is attractive to me because of the satisfaction it gives to my craving after knowledge of savage lore and life."[46]

Cushing was powerfully drawn to explore the tenuous evolutionary boundary between savagery and civilization, and inclined—according to the standards of his time—to transgress it. "Exploration," he wrote not long before his untimely death in 1900, "is the breath of my life. It, far more than study work, is the line of all my tendencies, and has been, ever since the runaway days of my boyhood." Just as a bee needs honey, Cushing explained, "I have to have knowledge of savage life." Why study "savages"? Because, he insisted, it was impossible to understand "our high state of civilization" without comprehending its development from "a barbarous unlettered condition very like that in which we find savages today." In the end, "we cannot understand this civilization of which we partake without understanding what it springs from and how."[47]

Cushing's conventional distinction between "civilized" and "savage" never blunted his sensitivity to the plight of his adopted tribe, shared by all the Native peoples of the United States. "By thoroughly studying and revealing the life and traits of the Indian," Cushing insisted, "we cannot fail, if happy in our mission, of exciting interest in him where none existed before; we cannot fail of showing him to be more human than we had supposed him, more capable of being made usefuller and better than it has been supposed possible." Yet the more deeply that Cushing explored Zuni culture, and the more closely that he identified with it, the more elusive it remained to him. Their "seclusiveness and reserve," he explained to a newspaper reporter, were all but impenetrable. "Although I have lived among them for years, . . . at times I feel that I have hardly commenced to learn anything about the Zunis."[48]

Cushing's deep identification with the Zuni Indians nourished his fervent determination to help and uplift them. His "unconscious sympathy," according to a friend, was "the keynote" to his personality. It accounted for his remarkable "gift," as Jesse Green describes it, "for entering imaginatively into other identities." Cushing's ethnographic method, he once explained, required that he "place himself as much as possible in their position, not only physically but intellectually and morally as well." It was not only a method for Cushing, but a powerful emotional attachment. Yet he could also be dismayingly patronizing toward the Zunis. Someone must "teach lovingly, teach them right ways of living, right ways of working," he wrote. Only when they were "transformed gladly (not unwillingly)" would their ancient patterns finally fall away "like dead leaves or worn-out garments." Then the Zunis could finally emerge, "enlightened according to our lights."[49]

Cushing's empathy for the Zunis, and commitment to them, could hardly be doubted. "I love the Zunis and would save them with my very life if I could," he insisted. Indeed, his impassioned defense of their land claims against Anglo speculators, which aroused the political antagonism that embarrassed his Smithsonian supervisors, finally cost him his place in Zuni. Looking back on his experiences there, he harbored nagging doubts about its benefits to the people he had so unequivocally embraced. "I opened the door of Zuni," he noted proudly. But, he continued remorsefully, "Would that I never had, or would that some noble souled man or woman had entered the door I thus opened as I did—through the hearts of the people." In the end, although vigorously defending his method and himself, Cushing seemed to realize that once the Zunis were confronted with the very dilemmas of modernity that tormented him, they would be as powerless as he was to resolve them.[50]

Indeed, Cushing's remarkable identification with the Zunis surely had its source in his own intense feelings of displacement from American culture. A social renegade ever since boyhood, he abandoned the modern world of cities, factories, and offices to find his place in the wilderness of the past, living among another people whose remoteness from modernity exceeded his own. As Mary Austin wrote in her introduction to his monumental *Zuni Folk*

Tales, Zuni became his refuge because there he could experience life "before it was contaminated with modern Americanization." The dominant American values of his time—progress, profit, patriotism, Protestant piety—defined precisely what he was determined to escape. He did not belong, as Joan Mark observes, to "the optimistic, progressive and civilization-celebrating current in late nineteenth-century America." Indeed, he fled as far from it as he could, to the very frontiers of American society and his own personality.[51]

Not only did Cushing transgress cultural boundaries during his lengthy sojourn in Zuni; he simultaneously lived in another era, the mythical Before. His regression through time enthralled journalist Sylvester Baxter, who was drawn to the same disjunction between American modernity and Indian antiquity (whether real or imagined) that attracted Cushing. Baxter posed the obvious, and sharp, contrast between the pueblo and the railroad. As competing symbols of past and present, they created "a strong tension and sense of counterpoint between change and stasis" that defined the allure of the Southwest to Anglo-Americans. They provided an updated expression of that most jarring, yet revealing, American cultural image, "the Machine in the Garden," which had long been a literary theme of American disaffection with modern civilization. For Baxter, as for Cushing and so many of their contemporaries, "Southwestern nostalgia" became, as Hinsley suggests, "a central and revealing trope for ambivalence and powerlessness." Revealingly, Baxter's first description of Cushing—"with long, flowing blonde hair, confined by the Indian head band, and dressed in the picturesque costume of the tribe"—vividly captured the romantic appeal of his bold regression to the past, and the profound contradiction inherent in the attempt.[52]

Cushing not only located himself at the cultural divide between savagery and civilization, but at the temporal divide between primitive antiquity and enlightened modernity. He became "anthropology's pioneer modernist," yet he was trapped, as Green suggests, in the very contradictions that he explored so imaginatively. A renegade from Anglo-American civilization, he was nonetheless convinced of its cultural superiority as the measure of evolutionary progress. That, in turn, justified his self-imposed responsibility to lead the Zunis along the path to civilized enlightenment. Drawn to the primitive past, he nonetheless mingled easily in Washington and Boston social circles. The effete Easterner who posed as the "gentleman leatherstocking" before his departure for Zuni would be renowned—and pilloried—as a "white Indian." Somehow Cushing combined—in uneasy, yet creative, tension—Victorian certainty of Anglo superiority with a modern sense of cultural relativism. An insider-outsider in two cultures, he embodied "in his own polarities a conflict in the spirit of his generation."[53]

At times, Cushing displayed discernible confusion over what it meant to be a man in modern American society. His changes of clothing—of costumes, really—and his "long, flowing blonde hair" not only brought him closer to the Zunis, they enabled him to redefine his own understanding of maleness in opposition to the prevailing standards of his era. That, in turn, contributed to some gendered uneasiness among women, expressed in Matilda Stevenson's biting criticism, Lucia Grieve's wariness over his cultural transgressions, and Emily Cushing's determination to redecorate their Zuni home in proper Victorian style.

What, indeed, did manhood mean toward the end of the nineteenth century, a time of acute uncertainty and anxiety over gender identity in an over-civilized society? Older attributes of manhood, resting upon physical power and personal independence, were diminished in an urban industrial society whose business was increasingly conducted in offices, bureaucratic hierarchies, and corporate boardrooms. The rugged, confident, self-made man of frontier lore was in danger of emotional emasculation in the modern era. Amid Victorian domesticity and decorum, which could not entirely conceal emerging female assertiveness in the public sphere, maleness seemed to have become more precarious. To regain true manliness, white American males often tried "to seize the 'primitive' strength, freedom, wildness, and eroticism" that they attributed to darker-skinned, primitive peoples.

Cushing was hardly alone among young men of his era to head west to escape the confinements of "civilization" and elude the debilitating feminine softness that infused it. "The whole generation is womanized," complained Basil Ransom in Henry James's *The Bostonians*. For men such as Cushing, Theodore Roosevelt, Frederic Remington, and Charles F. Lummis, civilized refinement was a curse of modernity that could only be overcome by recovery of the "savage drives and instincts" possessed by more primitive peoples—who, paradoxically, remained inferior. Middle-class Anglo men struggled resolutely to discover, and if need be, to invent, "a pure, lost powerful masculinity in primitive prehistory."[54]

Cushing, like Roosevelt, was a puny Eastern youngster who reached robust manhood on the frontier, the place of choice for rejuvenating "the flagging manhood of modern civilized men." As a Zuni, McFeely notes, Cushing—who arrived as a cultured, rational ethnographer—could express "other forms of masculinity that seemed to have faded" amid civilized modernity. The obviously less civilized Zuni men were nonetheless unmistakably masculine in their tribal roles as leaders, farmers, hunters, and, if need be, fighters. In Zuni, Cushing "could be a man as he never could be in Washington or Boston." Indeed, by his transformation into a Zuni warrior, even displaying a scalp to demonstrate his manly prowess, Cushing finally achieved manhood that was stifled in effete Eastern circles.[55]

Cushing's conspicuous fondness for costumes, for trying on clothes to display his new roles, suggests the malleability of his identity even before his arrival in Zuni. The "gentleman leatherstocking" in stylish Eastern dress (and a knife and gun as props for his aspirations) made much—as did Baxter—of his sartorial transformation into a Zuni, despite its contrived flamboyance. It did not stop there. The summer after his arrival, when Cushing was taking on a larger role as protector of the Zunis against Navajos and Mormons—"my special enemies," he told Powell—he made yet another clothing change befitting his changing identity. The officers at Fort Wingate, he reported, had advised him "to fully equip myself, for effect, if for nothing more," for asserting the authority of his country in his dealings with hostile Indians. So Cushing had purchased a government-issued military uniform and began to identify himself as an agent of the United States government. By the time of his return to Washington as leader of the Zuni delegation, his transformation completed, Cushing was dressed virtually indistinguishably from his Zuni companions. And, suggestively, photographs of Cushing once he finally left Zuni are virtually non-existent, as though the identity he had worked so assiduously to cultivate had evaporated with his departure from the Southwest.[56]

Cushing certainly tested and extended the boundaries of his Anglo manhood, instinctively realizing that he must become a Zuni to even hope to understand his Pueblo hosts. In the end, however, he could not elude his own cultural identity. He pushed its boundaries as far as he could, but his return to the East with the Zuni delegation marked the end of his creative period of cultural transgression and transformation. In Washington and Boston, he undermined his new identity even as he displayed it. Fascinating Eastern audiences, and securing a philanthropic patron for his continuing research, he was easily recognizable among his own people and clearly distinguishable from his Zuni companions. Appreciated and honored, he was pulled back—now as a celebrity—into the world he had abandoned. Indeed, his marriage to

Emily Magill expressed his attachment to that world, his place in it, and his determination not to abandon it.

Undeniably, his Zuni experience was the highpoint of Cushing's life. Although he returned to Washington in 1884 as a celebrity, still a young man in his twenties, the arc of his career, indeed of his life, had begun to turn downward. Pressed by Smithsonian officials to prepare a report on his explorations and discoveries, he worked himself into a frenzy of frustration and poor health, requiring leave from the Smithsonian to recover in his father's home. During his recuperation, he and Emily were invited by Mary Hemenway to spend time in Manchester-by-the-Sea, north of Boston, where she provided them with a cottage on her estate. Eager for Mrs. Hemenway's financial support, Cushing spun wondrous tales of the ancient cities of the Zuni and Hopi that still remained undiscovered in the Southwest. With her sponsorship, the Hemenway Expedition left for Arizona in 1886, but Cushing's health remained precarious and, despite a respite in California, he was finally compelled to return to Washington. It was a sorrowful anti-climax to his Zuni years.[57]

If Cushing was among the first Anglo Americans to find an alternative to civilized modernity in a pueblo paradise, he was hardly the last. Once his exploits were popularized and romanticized, and after the railroad opened the Southwest to tourism, the pueblos became a continuing source of fascination for Americans who were eager to discover islands of primitive antiquity and cultural stability where they might, if only temporarily, find sanctuary from the turbulence of modernity. Until well into the twentieth century, Zuni remained an American Eden—an imagined utopia—irresistibly appealing to disillusioned Americans who yearned for a garden where their romantic fantasies could blossom.[58]

Zuni was what Americans could imagine their country had once been, even before the first settlers from England reached its shores, but never could be again. Driven by nostalgia for a lost America, the attachment of culturally confused Americans to the pueblos expressed a profound ambivalence over the meaning of progress. From the early 1880s, Cushing's time in Zuni, into the 1930s, Pueblo Indians served as "a therapeutic Other for a machine-driven civilization." In the Southwest, where the trappings of civilization so easily fell away, the primal authenticity of a people rooted to its land, ruled by the harmonious rhythms of nature and the seasons while still attentive to its ancestral past, remained an inspiration and an escape.[59]

Just a few years before Cushing's arrival in Zuni, historian Hubert Howe

Bancroft, writing about "the native races" of the Southwest, distinguished the Apache and Navajo tribes—"American Arabs" and "American Bedouins" who plundered and killed strangers—from "the semi-civilized townspeople of New Mexico and Arizona." The pueblo dwellers, Bancroft wrote, were "industrious, honest, and peace-loving." Emerging from "the ruder phases of savagism," they were approaching "civilization." The Pueblo peoples encouraged dreams of a recoverable past that would fulfill American destiny as the newly promised land.[60]

Framing the American experience ever since its seventeenth-century Puritan origins was the inspirational theme of Christian regeneration within an American Israel. Precisely when it had become difficult to reconcile God's favor with teeming cities, smoke-belching factories, and strange foreigners, Pueblo Indians revived the promise, reminding Americans of their pioneering forebears and their own chosenness. At the moment when Frank Hamilton Cushing saw a Zuni maiden at the well, and was reminded of "the pools of Palestine," the dream of return to a vanished paradise was reborn. With men herding flocks like their Old Testament forebears, and women at the well who resembled the biblical Rebecca, it is hardly surprising that Sylvester Baxter would attentively record Cushing's observation, at an inn where animals huddled in an interior courtyard: "Oh, Palestine."[61]

From Zuni emerged the mythical Southwest as an Edenic alternative to Gilded Age America. Baxter, with Cushing's eager cooperation, was the first to spin this myth, but it was not long before Zuni, along with the other pueblos, became "the special property" of romantic artists, photographers, journalists, and ethnographers who shared Cushing's dream of escape and transformation. In their imagined idyllic community, which bore little resemblance to the complex reality of Zuni Pueblo, disaffected Americans passionately wanted to believe that they had discovered the elixir for their discontent with American modernity.[62]

CHAPTER TWO

Visitors and Visions

If Cushing was unique, he was nonetheless accompanied to Zuni Pueblo, and then followed to the Southwest, by a fascinating array of Americans who were engaged in their own personal, professional, and entrepreneurial quests. Matilda Stevenson, a fellow member of the Zuni expedition, was Cushing's formidable adversary and a conspicuous exception to male dominance of Southwestern exploration in the nineteenth century. Charles F. Lummis, directly inspired by Cushing to make his own remarkable odyssey to the Southwest, developed a romantic attachment to the pueblos, their people, and the Southwest that transformed his life and promoted a new regional identity. Fred Harvey, an English immigrant with a taste for good food, an insistence upon efficient restaurant service, and a keen eye for entrepreneurial opportunity, did more than anyone else to popularize Pueblo Indians and attract tourists. The "Southwest" that so enchanted tourists was in large part Harvey's creation and became his legacy. Very different from each other, they were nonetheless bound by their shared fascination with Pueblo culture. While Stevenson and Lummis found opportunities to elude, at least temporarily, the confines of civilization and the constraints of gender, Harvey was determined to bring the comforts of civilization to this American frontier, enticing Americans to enjoy its undiscovered pleasures.

A child of the antebellum South, Matilda Coxe seemed unlikely to become a woman who, by shattering gender boundaries, would behave more like a man.

Born a dozen years before the Civil War into a Virginia family of economic means and polite conventions, she was taught by a governess before attending Miss Annable's Academy, where girls were prepared for their future as wives of successful husbands. Matilda enjoyed her girlhood of "culture and refinement" (as she later described it), but she declined to remain confined within its genteel gendered norms. After studying law by clerking for her father, she married Col. James Stevenson, an officer with the United States Geological Survey. She dutifully accompanied him on a series of Western explorations, where she not only helped him with his work but prepared the foundation for her own transformation into a pioneering female ethnographer.[1]

Matilda Stevenson made her first visit to the Southwest in 1879 as a member of the expedition led by her husband. The Zuni experience changed her life—in different, but no less dramatic, ways than it did for Cushing, her irritatingly eccentric young colleague. After leaving Cushing behind in Zuni, the Stevenson group journeyed to the Hopi pueblos for an exploratory visit. Returning to Zuni, they established their base in the local mission. Like other Anglo visitors, Matilda Stevenson believed that the Pueblo Indians, on the verge of being overwhelmed by American culture, were fated to disappear imminently. She, too, was determined to document Indian life before it vanished forever. She realized, as Cushing did, that "the environment of the railroad is doing more to upset the autochronic institutions of the Zuni than all other influences." Time was short and precious, and she threw herself into her work with extraordinary energy, ferocious determination, and an astonishingly cavalier disregard for the customs, traditions, and proprieties of Zuni culture.[2]

Like other pioneering women entering male-dominated spheres of work, Matilda Stevenson demolished gender barriers even as she accommodated herself to the social stereotypes that sustained them. Responding with fierce assertiveness to any restrictions based on assumptions of female docility and intellectual limitations, she proceeded in her work with arrogant certainty that her identity as a woman afforded her the necessary insights to understand the Zunis better than any man. Indeed, John Wesley Powell, who appointed her to her husband's expedition, anticipated precisely such benefits from her participation: she "would have access to Native American women whose knowledge was crucial to anthropology but inaccessible to male researchers."[3]

Matilda Stevenson became the first American ethnographer to pay careful attention to the lives of Native women and children. Her focus on pueblo domesticity, considered (by Powell and perhaps also by her husband) the proper preserve of a woman, assured her unusual autonomy. Enjoying privileged access to Pueblo women, she carved out an unconventional professional career in government service that replicated the patterns of male achievement. By "working like a man," ironically, she became an enduring inspirational model for younger women who would follow her into the emerging—and uniquely female-friendly—professional discipline of anthropology.[4]

Despite her ambitions, Stevenson arrived in Zuni enclosed in Victorian stereotypes that were as restrictive as her long dresses and tight corsets. She accepted the prevalent notion of women as "the repositories of civilization," bearing responsibility to "elevate" native peoples. These "children of nature" and "barbarous people," after all, were still mired in "a primitive stage of evolutionary development." To a refined Southern lady, "a civilized woman," Zuni Indians were dirty, ill-mannered, and astonishingly superstitious. So she supplemented her professional work with efforts to instill proper Victorian standards—which included washing clothes in a tub, eradicating the "vice" of abortion, and abandoning religious rituals that were "shocking." Throughout her stay in Zuni, Mrs. Stevenson behaved very much as a Victorian mother determined to civilize her unruly children.[5]

Even for a Victorian woman, however, Mrs. Stevenson was uncommonly candid—indeed, outspokenly brusque—in expressing her cultural priorities and prejudices. "Primitive man," she wrote in her massive study, *The Zuni Indians*, "is less happy in his philosophy than enlightened man, because the latter has left behind many of his superstitions." For the primitive, "all that his untutored mind fails to comprehend is associated with some occult power." Religious conviction, she assumed, must be grounded in "superstition." Pueblo witchcraft both fascinated and repelled her as a misguided ritual of ignorant primitive people who were "still mired in that stage of culture where superstition is the prime factor in their lives."

The evident sexual component of Zuni witchcraft startled prim Mrs. Stevenson. She had "never seen anything else in aboriginal life which so thoroughly aroused her indignation," she wrote, as when a twelve-year-old girl, "suffering from a severe case of hysteria," was placed on trial as a witch. (The likeliest source of the girl's upset was a seventeen-year-old boy, with whom she had been seen "romping.") Trial procedure was rife with sexual overtones; Stevenson described how the girl's body was rubbed with medicine water before the presiding official "placed his lips to her breast, pretending to draw material from her heart." It is little wonder that she concluded her account by intoning: "Those possessing superior intelligence and a love for humanity, and only such, may lead our Indians from darkness into light." Stevenson, of course, was describing herself.[6]

Given the cultural baggage that Matilda Stevenson brought with her to Zuni, it is hardly surprising that she became notorious for her brazen disregard of Pueblo mores. If a witchcraft trial offended her, she felt free to interrupt it to state her objections. She did not hesitate to barge into a kiva, the holiest and most private ritual space in any pueblo, during a secret religious ceremony. Disregarding repeated warnings against photographing religious rites, she had dirt thrown at her by angry pueblo residents when she persisted in taking pictures. Her unrelenting intrusiveness made her an unwelcome presence almost everywhere she visited. In Zuni, as elsewhere, she was often forced to do her work outside pueblo walls, with Indian collaborators who risked punishing ostracism if their status as informers was exposed. When criticized, she threatened to summon soldiers from Fort Wingate to protect her flagrant behavior. Like other ethnographers (including Cushing) who worked in the Southwest, she justified her actions, which included theft of religious objects and transmission of tribal secrets, as the "salvation" for posterity of the remnants of a vanishing people.[7]

Matilda Stevenson's experiences in Zuni exposed some of the gender contradictions of her era, which—paradoxically—both constricted and expanded her opportunities. As Powell had anticipated, she was able to participate in "the daily lives and rituals" of Pueblo women as only a woman could. Encountering a tribal society that carefully apportioned male and female power, with separate gender roles and precisely defined exceptions to them in most aspects of pueblo life, Stevenson managed to carve out her own independent sphere of ethnographic competence.[8]

Her work in the pueblo depended upon extensive collaboration with the only person—We'Wha, a berdache or "man-woman"—who was as little bound by Zuni conventions as she was by Victorian proprieties. Each, in their own way, transgressed gendered norms. Stevenson, doing work that was all but impossible for a woman back East, developed a life in Zuni within male and female realms simultaneously. Occupying space "between the two genders," she combined feminine and masculine attributes that gave her the freedom to be a professional woman. What Cushing did with his sartorial innovations and role changes, she did with the sheer force of her personality, "taking on the persona of scientist, invader, adventurer, trader, nurse, friend, and bully, sometimes all at once"—and, in the process, redefining what it meant to be a woman. It is little wonder that she confused, and annoyed, defenders of established gender norms, both within and outside Zuni, or that We'Wha became her friend and confidant. Perhaps, Eliza McFeely suggests, We'Wha recognized in Stevenson "a kindred spirit, a metaphoric man in woman's clothing."[9]

A memorable, if scathingly caricatured, cartoon in the *Illustrated Police News* captured the gender confusion and hostility that Matilda Stevenson's behavior elicited (fig. 5). Easily identifiable as a formidable Victorian lady by her full-length dress and hat, she cornered a terrified Indian against a pueblo house, with her fist under his nose and her umbrella pointed like a spear at his midriff. In the background, helpless Zuni men (and her docile husband) observe her behavior with evident astonishment. This depiction

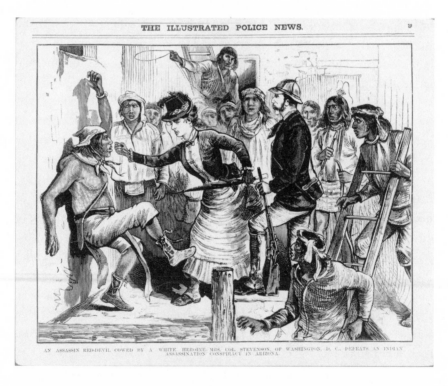

THE ILLUSTRATED POLICE NEWS.

AN ASSASSIN RED-DEVIL COWED BY A WHITE HEROINE. MRS. COL. STEVENSON, OF WASHINGTON, D. C., DEFEATS AN INDIAN ASSASSINATION CONSPIRACY IN ARIZONA.

FIG. 5. Matilda Stevenson in Zuni Cartoon in *The Illustrated Police News* (March 6, 1886), National Anthropological Archives, Smithsonian Institution (53-516).

of Mrs. Stevenson—the refined Victorian lady as aggressive bully—displayed the contradiction between conventional gender expectations and defiant possibilities. Defending her intrusive ways by intimidating and humiliating a cowering Zuni, Stevenson became a woman with the attributes of a man, while the "real" man cringed in feminine submission. She was a fearsome and threatening figure, in Zuni as among respectable Americans.[10]

Gender identity in Zuni may have been confusing, at least by conventional Victorian standards. But Matilda Stevenson seemed most enraged by Cushing's "Zuni" adaptations, which challenged her own refined Anglo sense of gender propriety. In acerbic, hand-written comments on the back of the photograph of Cushing in his Zuni regalia, she noted: "He even put his hair up in curl papers every night. How could a man walk weighted down with so much toggery?" To Stevenson, Cushing—acting like a woman—was insufficiently masculine. Yet Stevenson herself, with her deserved reputation for aggressive belligerence in her dealings with Zunis, did not hesitate to act like a man: "what she couldn't obtain through respect or friendship she got by buying, demanding, or simply taking it, going where she pleased and observing what she wished." Yet true to maternal fashion, she persistently referred to the Zunis as "children of nature [who] are like civilized beings of tender years." To Cushing, however, there was nothing childlike about them; they were "savages" who were "preeminently men of war and the chase." Cushing stripped the Zunis of civilized attributes, the better to compel their compliance with his expectations, while Stevenson infantilized them, the better to "mother" them into civilized behavior.[11]

If Cushing seemed too feminine for Matilda Stevenson's tastes, she aggressively combined "feminine and masculine attributes that allowed her to do what she wanted to do." We'Wha was her Zuni counterpart, engaged in both male and female economic activities: farming (male) and weaving (female), potting (female) and housekeeping (male). In the religious life of Zuni, however, We'wha assumed the male roles that were the prerequisite for participation. Very much the gendered "outsider" in Zuni, Stevenson was drawn to We'Wha, who seems to have occupied "a third gender status," neither male nor female. A close companionship seems to have developed between these incongruously allied deviant individuals, each of whom defied the established gender boundaries of their respective societies. Indeed, evidently feeling upstaged by Cushing's trip East with his Zuni delegation, she invited We'Wha to live in the Stevenson home in Washington, where he resided for six months in 1885. He was described in the press as a Zuni "princess" (although, one newspaper noted, "rather masculine" in appearance).[12]

We'Wha may even have confused his hostess as to his true gendered identity. For many years, Matilda Stevenson—if only to observe marital proprieties—claimed that he was a woman. Upon his death, We'wha was buried in Zuni wearing white cotton trousers (male), while otherwise dressed in female attire. His hair, she observed approvingly (in contrast to her scathing comment about Cushing), was "done up with the greatest care." If We'Wha represented the "possibilities of male identity and gender reconciliation," as his biographer Will Roscoe observes, then Matilda Stevenson may have symbolized its female equivalent in Victorian America.[13]

Stevenson made annual visits to Zuni during the 1880s to gather additional material for her comprehensive tribal study. After her husband's death in 1888, she was employed by the Bureau of Ethnology as the first, and for some time the only, woman serving as a paid government ethnographer. But she never completely eluded the gender boundaries that she managed, if brusquely, to transcend during her early years in Zuni. Later in her life, she asserted to friends the duty of a wife to assist her husband in his work and expressed her appreciation for the opportunity this had afforded her to elude the constraints imposed by her conservative Virginia family. But, as Nancy Parezo observes, "She could not escape her Victorian upbringing." It is unlikely that she could have worked in the Southwest when she did had she not been married to a male ethnographer. Once she arrived, however, Mrs. Stevenson became a woman of formidable independence—even as she became curiously dependent for her access to Zuni lore upon We'Wha, whose independence from the conventional gender norms of his society conspicuously mirrored her own.[14]

Matilda Stevenson may have been the first woman to confront in the pueblos of the Southwest the conflicts between her gender identity and professional status, but she was hardly the last. An Anglo-American outsider, she intruded upon Pueblo Indians not only to document their lives but to instruct them in what was best for them according to her cherished Victorian standards. As an Anglo woman, she was a double outsider in Zuni, where her disregard for the conventional gender norms of her own society enabled her to blend her ethnographic skills and personal idiosyncrasies to carve out a rewarding professional life.

A woman could discover in Zuni, as Matilda Stevenson did, "other possible ways of being female." Female ethnographers, Deborah Gordon has astutely suggested, "both created and were caught within a historical problem of trying to change inequality but preserve difference"—and with it, their own cultural superiority. There might indeed be strong emotional ties between Anglo and Pueblo women yet, in the end, it was a relationship among "political unequals." Matilda Stevenson struggled to escape her provincial past, finding new freedom in Zuni while embracing gender contradictions that she could never completely resolve. Identifying strongly with Pueblo women, she nonetheless used her extraordinary access to assert, at times quite forcefully, the superior values of her culture and her class and her special sensitivity as a woman to aspects of domesticity that men could not be expected to comprehend.[15]

∼

When Cushing and his Zuni entourage visited Boston, they gave a public performance in Harvard's Hemenway Gymnasium. In the audience was an attentive Harvard drop-out, Charles F. Lummis, who was riveted by Cushing's "magnetism" and found "the undoubted romance of his life of research among 'wild Indians' of the frontier" to be "contagious." So contagious, in fact, that it inspired him to leave the cultural constraints of New England behind, redefine his life as a new man of the Southwest, and do more than anyone else to popularize its romantic appeal.[16]

Lummis was born in Lynn in 1859 and raised by his father, a Methodist minister who was also principal of the local women's seminary. At age eight, when the youngster (like Cushing) refused further schooling, his father became his teacher until Lummis decided to attend Harvard, "because it was the cultural convention of New England—to which I acceded as I did in most things." Early in his freshman year, he encountered a voluble and engaging student, a year ahead, who became his lifelong friend. Like his new companion Theodore Roosevelt, Lummis had become "an obsessive body-builder" who constantly needed to test and enhance his physical prowess to demonstrate his manliness. He most fondly remembered his Harvard years not for what he learned but for instilling "the most useful form of athletics, boxing, wrestling, walking and running."

Despite strenuous efforts to build his strength by relentlessly climbing nearby New Hampshire mountains, Lummis fell ill shortly after his secret marriage to a medical student, failed two courses, and did not graduate. Leaving his new wife behind in Boston, he moved to Ohio to manage her father's farm. There he also became editor of the Scioto *Gazette*, which claimed to be the oldest newspaper west of the Alleghenies. In his spare time (again like Cushing), he searched for local Indian artifacts, memorably discovering a flint knife embedded in the breastbone of a skeleton. After three years of increasing restlessness with his life (and his wife), Lummis once again became ill, this time with malaria. Confronting his own mortality—and, perhaps, marital sources of his unhappiness and frequent illnesses—he chose a radically new life course.[17]

Yearning for "the exhilarant joy of living outside the sorry fences of society," Lummis decided to "tramp" to California. Devising this "colorful and athletic stunt" to test his physical mettle and his spiritual resolve, he set out with high spirits, his dog, and three hundred dollars in gold quarter eagles stashed in his money-belt. Leaving Eastern domesticity and culture behind to test his male assertiveness, he covered his expenses by wiring stories of his adventures back to his local newspaper and ahead to Harrison Gray Otis, publisher of the *Times*, who promised Lummis five dollars for each letter and a job upon arrival. Reaching Denver, Lummis decided to detour south to New Mexico. After 112 days and 2,202 miles (by his own calculation), he arrived in Santa Fe, "a flat little town of dry mud," which he laconically described as "the New Jerusalem."[18]

With an Easterner's characteristic confidence in the superiority of Anglo-Saxon culture, laced by occasional touches of racism, Lummis dismissed the Mexicans he encountered along the way as unpleasant "Greasers" and "poor specimens." Only slightly more impressed by his first glimpse of Indians in Española, he described "Bucks, with bottles of whiskey or plugs of tobacco in their hands, squaws with their big papooses slung across their backs." Santa Fe, however, charmed him: "once I had reached Spanish America, I realized that this was where I belonged." (Despite his "Puritan" conscience, he wrote, "my whole imagination and sympathy and feeling were Latin.") Enchanted by "the exhilarant twang of this high, dry, champagney atmosphere," he decided that Santa Fe, "a quaint old town [that] holds on like Potiphar's wife," must be "one of the most interesting places on the continent." Safely removed from "the repressive influence of my birthplace," Lummis rediscovered the "bubbling boyish impulses which had been considerably frosted in New England." He began to revise his views of Mexicans, coming to see them as "a simple kindly people" who were able to eradicate his "silly prejudices."[19]

But in nearby San Ildefonso, the first pueblo that Lummis visited, he was unimpressed with the "poor savages" he encountered. At their best, they might become "good Christians," but he lamented their tendency to absorb commercial skills "from the Jews, who trade with them." Because Pueblo culture, ruled by elders, "naturally sticks in its ruts," he thought it advisable for Pueblo children to be sent away to training schools, "entirely removed from the home influence and customs." After these patronizing first encounters, however, his tone once again began to moderate. In Tesuque Pueblo, he encountered Indians who, he conceded, were "intelligent, rather neat, and industrious after their own funny fashion." Especially in comparison with the Navajos, who were "still savages," Pueblo Indians were "cleanly (for Indians), honest, hospitable, and chaste"—in a word, "civilized." By the time he reached Isleta Pueblo, he conceded that they were "peaceful, well-to-do, happy farmers," who live in a "quiet town" as "members of the church." He described their "uncommon merits": morality, respect for property, neighborliness, hospitality—even cleanliness. ("I don't believe it possible to find a dirty, shiftless-looking room in all the 19 pueblos of New Mexico.")[20]

Lummis began to spin out his fantasy of pueblos as the enduring repository of national virtue, miraculously still intact amid the sordid corruption of modernity. By the time he had completed his initial round of pueblo visits, he rapturously described "Indians who were as industrious as any class in the country, and tilled pretty farms, and had churches of their own building, and who learned none of these things from us, but were living thus before our Saxon forefathers had found so much as the shore of New England." Delighted to discover this hidden corner of the old world embedded in the new, he remained in New Mexico for ten weeks. Enjoying nearby Santa Fe, he understood why the ancient Israelites "were 30 years in the wilderness": it was because "they struck some Arabian Santa Fe, where all the inhabitants nearly paralyzed them with good dinners." Leaving the decadent East behind to find personal salvation, he had discovered in the Southwest what he would endlessly popularize as a "land of enchantment"—both geographical and spiritual—that could rejuvenate the American promise.[21]

In 1885, Lummis moved to Los Angeles, where he endlessly exalted the Spanish colonial heritage of New Mexico and California. But after three years as city editor for the *Los Angeles Times*, with the strain of work increasing and his marriage disintegrating, he suffered a paralytic stroke. Escaping to New Mexico to recuperate, he moved into Isleta (which he had found only "tolerably interesting" during his previous visit). There he lived for four years, extensively photographing pueblo life and writing stories and books about the Southwest. His reputation spiked with a lengthy essay of photojournalism published in *Cosmopolitan* which described a curious band of Hispanic locals, called Penitentes, who annually reenacted the crucifixion of Jesus by binding each other to crosses. Encouraged by the enthusiastic public response, he transformed his travel letters into *A Tramp Across the Continent* (published in 1892), an elegy to the wonders and virtues of Pueblo culture.[22]

With romantic ardor, Lummis described the "little kingdom" of pueblos strung along the Rio Grande. Their "well-tended farms, orchards and vineyards, herds of cattle, sheep, and horses" made them "very different in every way from the average eastern conception of an Indian." He praised Isleta as "one of the strange little city-republics of that strange Indian race which has achieved this quaint civilization of their own before Columbus was born." In the pueblo, "better neighbors I never had and never want." The people, he wrote, were "kindly, thoughtful, and loyal, and wonderfully interesting." Even the ancient pueblo ruins that he explored impressed him as testimony to these "patient, industrious, home-loving farmers." Amid these wonders he found noble remnants of "our new-old land"—a phrase that curiously anticipated, while inverting, Theodor Herzl's *Altneuland*, a fantasy of revived Jewish statehood that was published several years later. [23]

Returning to Los Angeles after his lengthy sojourn in Isleta, Lummis became the self-appointed popularizer of the Southwest. In *The Land of Poco Tiempo*, a paean to New Mexico, he identified the Southwest as "the United States which is *not* the United States." Contrasting the "hurrying world" of the "haggard states," he found New Mexico to be an anomaly where "poco tiempo," not fast-paced progress, defined the good life. Among its native peoples, "there is no unseemly haste, no self-tripping race for wealth." Indeed, in Acoma Pueblo, perched at the top of a high mesa jutting above the vast desert landscape, Lummis encountered "hints and flashes of the unknown and the unknowable." There he discovered a dreamlike, mysterious, and alluring alternative to "civilization." With his popular essays and books, Lummis brashly took credit for having "christened the Southwest."[24]

As editor of *Land of Sunshine*, a magazine filled primarily with promotional advertisements, Lummis portrayed Southern California as paradise West. (California's image, to some, as "a failed promised land," suffering from drought and lagging population growth, dismayed him.) Attentive to its Spanish heritage, he spun "a monumental edifice of Southwest romantic imagery," filled with fantasies of escape. Living what he wrote, Lummis, in the style of a Spanish don, built a grand house named El Alisal for the sycamore trees that surrounded it. Never a man of modest ambition, he envisioned something "even more massive and varied" than the Alhambra. Its rock-faced turret occupied a prominent hilltop location, high above "the smoke and dust and noise of metropolitan streets," assuring that it would "See and Be Seen." Importing a team of Isleta workers to assure the authenticity of construction, he filled it with his extensive collection of Navajo blankets, ethnographic artifacts, Indian photographs, and Pueblo pottery. There he lived for thirty years, serving lavish Spanish dinners to his guests, enjoying "his version of the Spanish American myth." An adjacent building, with his overflowing collections (Lummis admitted to "the Collector's Fever"), became the Southwest Museum, the first museum in Los Angeles. It endures as a monument to his irrepressibly romantic vision.[25]

As enamored as he was of Spanish-style splendor, Lummis never lost his fondness for the pueblos. In his later years, he accepted an invitation from the Fred Harvey Company to serve on its advisory board, receiving in return free travel and accommodations at Harvey hotels in Albuquerque and Santa Fe. Returning to New Mexico in 1926, shortly before his death, he wrote longingly of "my Pueblo Indians, that ancient Aristocracy which was ripe a thousand years before Columbus." This unusual people had "no politicians, no newspapers, no taxes, no graft, no spoiled children," and, Lummis took pains to emphasize, "no ladylike men & roughneck women." Considering "the bedlam we welter in," Lummis was easily captivated by the tranquility, harmony, and gendered certitudes (whether real or imagined) of pueblo life.[26]

Lummis, like Cushing, was a disenchanted refugee from Eastern modernity. A "bourgeois Yankee" in lifelong flight from New England, he found spiritual nourishment in the Southwest. Disconcerted by the gender fluidity and confusion of his era, as his pointed reference to "ladylike men & roughneck women" suggests, Lummis needed to test his manhood and try on new identities that were independent of Eastern definitions. He followed his dream to the land of sunshine and "poco tiempo," whose virtues he, more than anyone else, identified and exalted. Yet he seems never to have resolved the personal contradictions that propelled him restlessly across the continent. Touting pueblo simplicity, which he experienced during his prolonged recuperation, he nonetheless preferred to live in California splendor as a Spanish aristocrat at the edge of Los Angeles, high above the bustle and din of urban sprawl.

There he remained "a savvy salesman" of the Southwest, simultaneously proclaiming its simple virtues while enjoying the conspicuous luxuries that his promotional talents afforded.[27]

~

For Americans with the leisure and money for travel and a taste for adventure, the widely publicized experiences of Cushing in Zuni and Lummis in Isleta helped to popularize a Southwest that was romantic, exotic, and—beginning in the 1880s—accessible. The Atchison Topeka & Santa Fe Railroad not only made tourism possible but promised an enticing cultural experience wrapped in streamlined comfort along the way. Before long, a virtually unknown, unexplored, inaccessible, and barren wasteland had become an American Eden, whose Pueblo peoples symbolized a pure, if primitive, way of life that "civilized" Americans had abandoned in their relentless pursuit of progress and profit.

An appetite for travel to the new Southwestern frontier was stimulated by the Wild West shows that recently had become a staple of popular entertainment. If provincial and apprehensive Americans were uneasy about leaving civilization behind, then William F. Cody would bring the Western frontier to them. Tapping into deep cultural ambivalence about Indians, "Buffalo Bill" shrewdly mixed fear of their savagery with respect for their nobility, at least in defeat and subjugation. He orchestrated sham battles—filled with chases, races, Indian ambushes, and cavalry charges—for the entertainment of enthusiastic audiences. Simulating the bygone Indian menace, he simultaneously provided assurances that it was already consigned to the dustbin of history. With Sitting Bull in virtual captivity as a performer, there no longer was any fear—only pathos for the vanished warriors. Buffalo Bill's Wild West shows affirmed the triumph of American civilization over native peoples, "living anachronisms whose societies verged on extinction." The message was clear: "the future belonged to those Indians who abandoned their past."[28]

That very moment of triumph, however, encouraged nostalgia for what was now forever irretrievable. "The tourists' frontier," Earl Pomeroy's felicitous phrase to describe the sudden spurt of interest in railroad travel westward, brought "a trainload of Eastern excursionists peering through Pullman cars" at the newest wonders, both natural and human. Americans familiar with biblical stories were explicitly reminded of exotic places from their childhood reading. California was the American "Palestine" (and, simultaneously, our Riviera); hot springs offered reminders of the "pools of Silwan" (and Karlsbad). The favorite biblical accolades were reserved for the Southwest, where pueblos evoked "the villages of ancient Egypt and Nubia, Ninevah and Babylon," inhabited by people who resembled "the descendants of Rebecca of Bible fame." As one New Englander wrote on his journey, "We must cross deserts and scale mountains till we reach the Eden of the West." So long scorned as a menacing emptiness to be avoided, the Southwest was promoted as the "last refuge" of uncorrupted purity and a "living museum of the nation's past."[29]

New travel possibilities stimulated entrepreneurial ingenuity and innovation. With its monopoly of the Southwestern route to California, the Santa Fe Railroad, escaping from bankruptcy as it attracted flocks of eager travelers, promoted the allure of Pueblo culture and such nearby natural wonders as the Grand Canyon. It celebrated "the exotic and simple life of an earthly paradise," where tourists, stimulated by "the powerful narcotic of nostalgia," could find "a prototype of preindustrial society. Simplicity. Freedom. Nobility." The railroad, symbolically as in reality the engine of national progress after the Civil War, could return Americans, if only for the duration of a vacation, to their bucolic, Edenic past.[30]

In promoting the Southwest to tourists as the American Eden, the railroad found an ideal partner in Fred Harvey, a prototypical self-made American entrepreneur who had arrived in the United States from England as a teenager in 1850. Working as a busboy in a New York café for two dollars weekly and meals, he lived the American dream, prudently saving his skimpy earnings until he could afford to move west to open his own restaurant. He shrewdly chose St. Louis, a major railroad junction for transcontinental travel, as his preferred site. From a bout of dyspepsia, Harvey quickly grasped the benefits—to himself no less than his customers—of providing quality food and efficient service to weary travelers.

Dreaming of a chain of Harvey restaurants at major tourist destinations, he took his proposal to the Burlington & Quincy Railroad, which summarily rejected it. Undeterred, he approached the Atchison Topeka & Santa Fe, whose line then extended only as far as Pueblo, Colorado. Eager to penetrate the Southwest and willing to take chances, the railroad encouraged Harvey. Beginning with a simple lunchroom above the railroad depot in Topeka, Harvey began to stimulate the American appetite for travel to the Southwest with his entrepreneurial ingenuity and energy combined with the old-fashioned virtues of integrity, respectability, and service.

More astutely than any of his contemporaries, Harvey seized the opportunity to package and sell the breathtaking natural beauty and exotic native peoples of the Southwest. He provided structured and safe encounters between Anglo tourists and Pueblo Indians, who appeared as their curiously twinned primitive Other from a bygone era for which Americans were becoming increasingly nostalgic. Harvey's business acumen, combined with his shrewd eye for evocative cultural symbols, enabled him to present an idealized Southwest to tourists, with a carefully arranged, highly sanitized display of Pueblo culture for their enjoyment and consumption.[31]

Harvey was remarkably attentive to the cultural nuances and mores of his adopted country. To reassure tourists who preferred the culinary comforts of home to sleazy local diners, he imported morality and refinement from the farms and towns of the Midwest. Advertising for eighteen- to thirty-year-old women "of good character, attractive and intelligent," he hired waitresses to work in Harvey restaurants under his strict supervision. In the 1880s, employment in such remote places was still considered highly risky for young women of good character who needed reassurance that "their status as ladies would be protected." Harvey was determined to provide it.

"Harvey girls," as his female employees came to be known (in the 1940s, Hollywood made a movie with that title), signed six- to twelve-month contracts that required them to abstain from marriage during their term of employment. Disciplined "with the regimentation of an army boot camp," they were housed in supervised company residential facilities that were "as respectable as their own homes back East." Harvey's rules required clean bathtubs, "no loud talking and laughing" in rooms or halls, "neat and clean clothing," and "no spitting on floors"—all designed to encourage "a tidy and homelike" environment. Crisply uniformed in black and white dresses (to resemble nuns, it was suggested), and trained to be "motherly, sisterly helpers," they served patrons under Harvey's rigorous supervision. It was hard work, but it enabled them to satisfy their own ambitions by acquiring financial resources, self-esteem, and unrivaled travel opportunities.[32]

Demonstrating in Topeka that he could fulfill his promises to provide good food and efficient service while turning a profit, Harvey received first option from the Santa Fe Railroad on all hotel and restaurant sites along its line. Within a decade, fifteen Harvey hotels and nearly fifty Harvey restaurants served railroad travelers according to his meticulous standards. These "islands of American culture, linked to the 'homeland' by the Santa Fe rails," brought tourists to the Southwest and made Pueblo culture accessible to them. Shrewdly attuned to marketing techniques in the new consumer culture of the Gilded Age, Harvey and the Santa Fe jointly promoted the region as "an exotic destination" that was "a last refuge of magic, mountains, and quaint ancestors."

It took Harvey, an immigrant, to appreciate the yearning of Americans for the comforts of fine hotels and restaurants amid the rigors of travel. He promised an indigenous, authentic American "wonderland" in which tourists could discover "our last frontier . . . of . . . picturesque people." Long ago, in "the days of romance and chivalry" (an attractive Fred Harvey Company publication noted), the Southwest had been invaded by Spaniards and Mexicans, then by Jesuits and Franciscans. Finally, at the apex of civilization, the "heroic pilgrimage" of Americans led to "the march of Western progress." Travelers were reassured that "centuries of contact with the white race have not materially changed the Pueblo Indian." Remaining "independent, self-supporting and contented," these Indians were the ancient exemplars of enduring American values.[33]

The Fred Harvey Company rode a rising tide of interest in American Indians that peaked in the 1890s, after the battle of Wounded Knee brought an end to centuries of Indian warfare. In the Chicago Exposition of 1893, Indians were exhibited for public appreciation as skilled craftspeople, rather than the vanquished warriors of the Buffalo Bill shows. Depicted as a "vanishing" people who were "entertaining but not threatening," they appeared as simple primitive artisans who made and sold blankets, jewelry, pots, and baskets. Their ersatz pueblo, located on the Midway, was nestled between equally exotic street scenes from Cairo and Constantinople. Presented as "an oriental curiosity" to be discovered right here in America, the pueblos were, after all, only a train-ride away.[34]

Working in tandem with the Fred Harvey Company to promote Southwestern tourism, the Santa Fe Railroad retained photographer William Henry Jackson to take scenic landscape photographs and cultivated relations with a growing circle of artists in Santa Fe and Taos. In return for courtesy travel opportunities, they photographed and painted the exotic wonders of the region and its native inhabitants for promotional purposes. Artists were sent on excursions at the railroad's expense, first to capture the wonders of the Grand Canyon and then throughout New Mexico and Arizona.

Fred Harvey Company patronage served art and profit for native and

Anglo artisans alike. The company purchased more than six hundred paintings—mostly Indian portraits and landscapes—for promotional purposes. In its hotels, adjacent to railroad stations, the Fred Harvey Company adopted the world's fair formula of displaying live artisans demonstrating their skills. An appreciation for native crafts was stimulated among newly affluent middle-class travelers, whose aesthetic tastes could now include "Indian corners" for the display of their Southwestern artifacts in the parlors of their fashionable Victorian homes. Shrewdly and skillfully, the company and the railroad collaboratively "constructed a version of Indian life that reflected and spoke to American middle-class desires and anxieties."[35]

With tourists attracted to the Southwest, the Fred Harvey Company and the Santa Fe Railroad could offer a packaged travel experience that included safe and efficient transportation, comfortable hotel accommodations, quality dining, and welcoming encounters with Pueblo Indians—the perfect blend of commercial and romantic impulses. In 1902, when the splendid new Alvarado Hotel opened in Albuquerque, adjacent to the railroad platform, travelers encountered Fred Harvey's idealized Southwest. Departing from the train, they were ushered to their meal at the Harvey restaurant, and then directed into the Harvey Indian Building, designed to stimulate their appreciation—and purchase—of Pueblo crafts, before they exited to the elegant Harvey Hotel for a comfortable night's rest. Harvey's efforts created a flourishing new arts and crafts industry for tourist consumption.

The Fred Harvey Company was remarkable for its era, not only for its innovative vision of Southwestern tourism as an entire package of pleasurable exposure to another region and culture, but for the people Harvey chose to implement it. Mary Colter, the interior designer of the Indian Building at the Alvarado Hotel (and Hopi House at the Grand Canyon), was trained as an architect at a time when few women passed through professional portals. Colter was selected to express an "authentic" regional style of interior decorating, attentive to the Southwestern landscape and Indian motifs. Harvey's daughter Minnie, an avid art collector, suggested that the sale of Indian crafts become part of the Harvey business operation. Accepting her advice, Harvey hired Herman Schweizer, a German Jewish immigrant, to acquire artifacts for the Indian Department, which quickly became a highly profitable adjunct of its flourishing restaurant and hotel business. Relying for his success on the aesthetic ideas of a Jewish immigrant and two women, all of whom were outsiders to the culture of American entrepreneurial opportunity, Harvey sold their design of the Southwest to tourists who eagerly embraced it as genuinely American.

Schweizer cultivated a network of Pueblo artisans whose work he showcased for sale, not only to tourists but also to museums, which had only recently begun to compete avidly for American ethnographic objects. Collaborating with Lorenzo Hubbell, another bold entrepreneur whose trading post at the edge of the Hopi pueblos became an important source of native crafts, Schweizer stimulated and guided the market for Indian pottery and weaving. Carefully monitoring sales patterns in the Harvey shops, it was not long before he began to stipulate the sizes, shapes, and colors of the pots, baskets, blankets, and jewelry that he would purchase from Pueblo artisans. Relying upon Hubbell, who dealt directly with local native craftspeople, Schweizer displayed the work of favored artisans, such as weaver Ellie of Ganado and potters Nampeyo and Maria Martinez, whose work has adorned galleries and museums ever since.[36]

Before long, Harvey's Indian Department functioned simultaneously as a salesroom, a museum, and a work habitat for native craftswomen. Schweizer brought Pueblo artisans to Albuquerque, providing room and board and retaining their services for months at a time to work in Harvey's simulation of their home environment. New and profitable opportunities developed, especially for female artisans who were accustomed to working for a pittance of what the Fred Harvey Company paid. Perhaps because he was an immigrant who had created his own business model, Harvey's instincts seemed impervious to established hierarchies of status and gender within the American corporate economy. He attracted talented outsiders into his expanding network of company operations, rewarded them generously, and profited from their collaboration with Indian artisans.

Schweizer also had a talent for discovering wealthy patrons and educating them in the pleasures of acquiring native crafts for their private enjoyment. He played William Randolph Hearst's acquisitive urges like a fine musical instrument, assuring the California publishing magnate that he was the "only exception" to the company's no-discount policy, and that especially rare objects were available "only to you." Under Schweizer's flattering tutelage, Hearst became a major collector of Indian crafts, and the Fred Harvey Company profited handsomely from the newly acquired taste that Schweizer shrewdly cultivated.[37]

So it was that within two decades after Cushing had arrived in Zuni, precisely as he had anticipated, the Southwest had been dramatically transformed.

With the completion of the Santa Fe Railroad line and the arrival of the first waves of intrepid tourists, Pueblo artisans were swept into the vortex of American commerce. Their crafts, until then "the picturesque subjects of artists and photographers," were "transformed into works of art," eagerly acquired and displayed in American homes. With fortuitous timing and entrepreneurial acumen, the Santa Fe Railroad and the Fred Harvey Company capitalized on a rising surge of *fin de siecle* nostalgia, expressed in the arts and crafts revolt against factories, mass production, and the dislocations of the new industrial age.[38]

Indeed, Pueblo Indians themselves had become objects for popular admiration and consumption. In sharp contrast to impersonal, menacing modes of factory production, native artisans embodied "craft ideals." They belonged to a domestic economy where women worked at home, with nature's own ingredients, to create aesthetically pleasing objects. As the American workplace became ever more mechanized and corporate, the allure of Indian crafts increased as "an antidote to the alienated labor of industrial production." In an age of factories and machines, Leah Dilworth suggests, Pueblo artisans could be appreciated as "primitive craftspeople" who were "bound by nature and tradition." Among all the pleasing images of Pueblo culture that the Santa Fe Railroad and the Fred Harvey Company encouraged and marketed, none was more ubiquitous—or reassuring—than the Pueblo artisan herself.[39]

Already by the turn of the century, the Pueblo potter had emerged as an iconic figure, symbolizing the gendered distinctiveness of Southwestern culture and crafts (fig. 6). As an exemplar of "authentic primitive labor," she appealed to deepening anxieties about work at a time when more of it than ever before was taking place in factories and offices, increasingly perceived "as alienating and meaningless, separated from ethical and moral rewards." For many Americans, as Dilworth notes, work had already become "mechanized, urban, repetitive, mindless, proletarian, centralized, and unskilled." By contrast, artistic creativity in the pueblos was "rural, traditional, classless, satisfying, local, and skilled." The Pueblo artisan provided "a fantasy of authenticity and autonomy," which had strong appeal to Americans for whom work had become ever more detached from its idealized preindustrial antecedents. Pueblo artisanship, Dilworth concludes, evoked "a time before modernity and all its attendant problems, when 'tradition' prevailed, when the authority of the father was unquestioned, when men were men and women were women, . . . and when people knew the value of an honest day's work."[40]

Returning from a two-week journey in 1899 to "Hopiland," the remote and isolated Pueblo communities of northeastern Arizona, George A. Dorsey, curator of anthropology at the Field Columbian Museum in Chicago, described the Southwest that Harvey was energetically promoting. "We may hope to discover among the pueblos," he wrote, "that richness and completeness of aboriginal life," unspoiled by "foreign influence," which had all but vanished elsewhere. Traveling west of Santa Fe, "we may easily imagine ourselves transported beyond the confines of the United States"; indeed, there is a feeling "that one has left this modern world." In the pueblos, Dorsey encountered native peoples who were "conservative, proud, independent, mysterious" and "intensely religious." Men worked in the fields and spun their own clothes, while women were the "house builders and owners" who, in their spare time, made pots and baskets. Dorsey admired these "sober, industrious, patient toilers." In a thinly veiled swipe at urban reformers of his era, he praised a people "absolutely independent . . . contented and beyond the needs of alms from the nation." Lest travelers be apprehensive about their contacts with these primitive people, Dorsey reminded them that at Harvey hotels, "one is assured excellent meals, the luxuries of a bath, and other comforts which are greatly appreciated on the return from a desert journey."[41]

FIG. 6. "Nampeya, Hopi Pottery Maker,"
Harry Herz, Phoenix, n.d. Postcard provided by author.

John F. Huckel, Harvey's son-in-law and supervisor of the Indian Department, embellished the romance of Pueblo culture in his *American Indians: First Families of the Southwest*. Huckel reminded his readers that "even in the days when Christopher Columbus was a boy playing about the streets and docks of Genoa, there were little republics scattered through a portion of the America he was to discover." In these pueblo villages, Indians had already "recognized property rights"; they "chose men to make and administer laws"; and women "had rights beyond the hopes of the most enthusiastic suffragettes of our time." They shared "a regard for law and observed a code of broad morals." Indeed, Huckel wrote reassuringly, Pueblo Indians "retain the customs of four centuries ago to a degree equaled by no other people, excepting the Bedouins of the Far East."

In a time of heightened anxiety over the consequences of industrialization, immigration, urban poverty, and the changing role of government in the newly emerging welfare state, Huckel touted the Pueblo peoples for virtues that modern Americans seemed to have lost. Pueblo Indians, he pointedly observed, "feed themselves and ask no aid of Washington." Their women seemed significantly more privileged than the white women who agitated militantly for gender equality. "No other Indian women, and few of the gentler sex among the white peoples, possess the rights of the Pueblo women," he asserted. In their matrilineal tribes, property passed "through the maternal branch of the family." Divorce was "easy," and "if she wills it she may dismiss her husband on the slightest pretext."[42]

Huckel's location of the pueblos in the broader context of American history, romanticized and distorted though it surely was, suggested to his contemporaries that what was most genuinely American still survived in the Southwest. If Americans wanted to discover who they once were, before the corruptions of modernity intruded, they need only encounter Pueblo Indians. The Fred Harvey Company, unstinting in its efforts to promote the romantic possibilities and exotic rewards of Southwestern travel, relied heavily upon Huckel's pueblo imagery in its promotional literature (figs. 7A–D). His comforting scenes of pueblo domesticity recurred in Harvey brochures, postcards, and playing cards: a Hopi mother holding her two naked children; a young girl carrying her brother on her back while climbing a ladder (captioned "Taking the Elevator, Hopiland"); a mother braiding her daughter's hair in characteristic Hopi squash blossom whirls; women baking bread in outdoor ovens; olla maidens returning from the well; women weaving and potting ("Where Woman is the Perpetuator of the Arts").

FIG. 7A–7B. Pueblo Domesticity, Fred Harvey Postcards: "Pueblo Women Making Bread," "Hopi Basket Weavers," Heard Museum, Phoenix, AZ. Postcards provided by author.

FIG. 7C–7D. Pueblo Domesticity, Fred Harvey Postcards: "A Woman of
Pueblo of Isleta Decorating Pottery," "Hopi Hair Dressers,"
Heard Museum, Phoenix, AZ. Postcards provided by author.

These reassuring domestic images of women offset glimpses of exotic, even menacing, ceremonial activities (the repulsive, yet ever-fascinating, Hopi snake dance conspicuous among them). A handsome company book, *The Great Southwest*, featured equally benign color photographs of trains winding through mountains, the famed Alvarado Hotel in Albuquerque, the adjacent Indian Building where Schweizer's acquisitions were tastefully displayed, and familiar views of pueblos and potters. Souvenir decks of Fred Harvey Company playing cards, intermingling scenic vistas with pueblo cameos, were popular with rail travelers. (The ace of clubs displayed a husky Pueblo man identified as "an Indian Samson.")

More Americans, in all likelihood, gained their first and formative glimpses of pueblo life from Fred Harvey Company postcards than from any other source. Picture postcards had first made their appearance during the 1870s as mailings for hotels and other businesses. Harvey, keenly alert to the promotional potential of visual material, bought out the pioneering Detroit Photographic Company, whose "Photostint" cards—photographs for writing and mailing messages—became "one of the era's crazes." Harvey's keen eye for images, and his recognition of the advertising potential of postcards, enlisted virtually every tourist as his own promotional agent for Southwestern travel.[43]

A popular postcard enticingly displayed the encounter that the company and the railroad collaboratively cultivated (fig. 8). A cluster of Pueblo women, several with pots on their heads, are gathered by the steps of a Pullman car to greet tourists and sell their wares. They surround a train conductor, who evidently mediated the contact between strangers, while a white-uniformed waiter from the dining car stands by. Outside the circle of native women is a conspicuously affluent male tourist, dressed in a suit and vest, who sizes up the situation, deciding whether and what to buy. All the ingredients of the tourist encounter are evident: the elegant train, the efficient crew, the tourist from far away, and the local native women. It is an inviting arrangement, certain to pique the interest of its recipient. One of these cards, mailed by "Aunt Rosa," reads: "This is the way the Indians come down to the train. There are not so many today, but several are here, including some little tiny ones. I am writing this at the beautiful big [Harvey] hotel at Albuquerque." The partnership between the Fred Harvey Company and the Santa Fe Railroad, like the meeting of Indians and tourists that it facilitated, provided reassurance of a safe and comfortable journey to an exotic destination, filled with the pleasures of cross-cultural encounters in a safely controlled setting.

FIG. 8. Cultural Encounter. Fred Harvey Postcard: "Pueblo Indians Selling Pottery," Heard Museum, Phoenix, AZ. Postcard provided by author.

The obverse of Harvey postcards often included a description of some exotic yet reassuring aspect of pueblo life. Description and judgment were indiscriminately mixed: Isleta, with its "well-kept and clean" houses and streets; "quaint" San Ildefonso, with its large plaza and cottonwood trees; "primitive" Taos, where four hundred Indians lived in "many-storied adobe communal houses . . . white-robed like the Arabs and very conservative"; Laguna, whose residents belong to "an intelligent, industrious and independent race"; and Tesuque, where women "still prepare their meals on the primitive metates." An olla maiden, bearing a pot on her head, wears a costume that "is in a degree picturesque." An unmarried Hopi girl, her mother setting her hair in whorls to symbolize her purity, is one of many maidens with "a great wealth of hair . . . of striking attractiveness."

Occasionally, the postcards offered explicit commentary on Pueblo mores. A scene of three girls perched on a ladder at Santo Domingo prompted the observation that Pueblo men "are very jealous of their women and keep them in the background as much as possible and seldom permit them to leave the confines of the pueblo." The text for another card, quoting Huckel, was even more expansive: "The Pueblos are picturesque anywhere and always, but particularly in their dances, races, and other ceremonials. These are Indians who are neither poor nor naked; Indians who feed themselves and ask no favors of Washington; Indians who have been at peace for two centuries and fixed residents for perhaps a millennium; Indians who were farmers and irrigators and six story house builders before a New World had been beaten through the thick skull of the Old." The lengthy description left little space for a tourist's message, but no patriotic American, solidly grounded in traditional values, could fail to appreciate Pueblo virtues: attachment to the land, self-reliance, and independence.

Harvey offered Pueblo Indians as an antidote to turn-of-the-century confusion and uneasiness about national and personal identity. Amid the turbulence of social change, the Southwest was presented as a self-contained region of indigenous and timeless truths, where stability coexisted with tranquility and harmony in an unspoiled natural setting. Here was the "promise of redeeming spiritual and traditional values through contact with nature and people who lived in the natural world," still following the ways of their ancestors. Not long before, Indian savages were conquered and confined on reservations; now, Pueblo Indians might inspire the restoration of traditional spiritual values that were so conspicuously absent from contemporary American society. In a stroke of entrepreneurial and promotional genius, the Fred Harvey Company and the Santa Fe Railroad collaborated in juxtaposing "the progress and comfort of modern life with a reproduction of the premodern past." Riding the sleek, powerful, engine of progress, Americans could rediscover the world they had lost. As Charles F. Lummis wrote: "There is no railroad in the world . . . which penetrates such a wonderland of the pictorial in geography and in humanity." Returning home, newly enlightened and invigorated by their past and eager to display its artifacts, they faced a future of infinite promise and progress.[44]

If the Santa Fe Railroad and the Fred Harvey Company exposed Pueblo Indians to the intrusiveness of Anglo culture, they also made its material rewards more available to these native peoples than ever before. The new economic relationships that were first established with the collaboration of Hubbell, the potter Nampeyo, and Harvey facilitated contact between artisans and buyers, building the foundation for the modern ethnic crafts markets that attract Indian artisans by the hundreds and Anglo buyers by the thousands. As the popularity of the arts and crafts movement demonstrated, the sense that work had been separated from craftsmanship was widespread among

Americans at the end of the nineteenth century. The allure of the Southwest—and the collaboration between the railroad, the Fred Harvey Company, native artisans and Anglo artists—evoked admiration for Indian crafts that mass production might otherwise have stifled. If anything, the "selling" of the pueblos by the Santa Fe Railroad and the Fred Harvey Company deepened awareness and appreciation for the aesthetic virtues of handcrafted work, and heightened respect for native people who still practiced it.

As foreign as Pueblo Indians surely were to other Americans, they nonetheless escaped the negative, often vicious, stereotyping of new immigrants that was so common around the turn of the century. Jacob Riis, writing about "the other half," the immigrant population that he encountered as a police reporter in New York City, casually referred to Jews, for whom "Money is their God"; "John Chinaman," who suffered from "ages of senseless idolatry"; and Italians, "lighthearted and ... inoffensive as a child." There was no romance in their poverty, only squalor; their religious rituals were displays of ignorance, not curiously intriguing; they were foreigners, not indigenous survivors of an imagined past of peaceful harmony. An immigrant woman with a bundle of clothes on her head was not nearly as exotic or enticing as a Pueblo woman carrying a pot; nor was an immigrant seamstress in a squalid urban sweatshop the moral equivalent of a Pueblo weaver whose hands spun wool from a primitive loom. Assaulted by the pace of modern life in the cities where they swarmed, immigrants lacked the moral stature of Pueblo Indians, still living close to nature, enclosed in a "mythological American past" whose "primeval exoticism" reminded Americans of their long-vanished bucolic way of life.[45]

By the 1890s, liberal reformers—Riis only one among many—began to confront the social malfunction and personal dislocation that seemed endemic to urban industrial society. For some, European models offered plausible solutions: Jane Addams's Hull House, for example, owed its origins to the settlement house movement in London. Others, such as Jacob Coxey, marched on Washington to protest the passivity of the federal government to unprecedented unemployment. And some found inspiration in exotic native cultures. As "primitivism" became what Dilworth aptly calls a "cultural cure" for modernity, Pueblo Indians attracted attention from an array of Americans who yearned for new possibilities based upon venerable traditions of community and domesticity. The imputed spiritual authenticity of Pueblo Indians, derived from their fidelity to ancient values, offered an appealing contrast to the worship of science, progress, and money. Living in harmony with nature, tradition, community, and each other, they offered new possibilities to Americans whose lives seemed anomic, fragmented, and incomplete. Collaborating with the Santa Fe Railroad in creating an appealing new identity for the Southwest, with Pueblo Indians as its picturesque center-piece, Fred Harvey's visions of progress and comfort converted primitivism into mesmerizing—and profitable—images of national redemption.[46]

CHAPTER THREE

Representing the Southwest

Nowhere else in the United States at the end of the nineteenth century were Indians as evocative of a lost American paradise as in the Southwest. Here was the last vestige of an American Arcadia of small villages and hard-working people, living close to the power and wonder of nature, inexorably slipping away. In the pueblos, anthropologist Barbara Tedlock writes, Americans could discover "a vast psychic oasis" removed from the spreading wasteland of modern civilization. To rescue Pueblo Indians from the imminent oblivion that many Americans assumed was their inevitable fate, photographers and artists documented their lives with compelling images of a vanishing people. In the process, ironically, these image-makers became ever more deeply enmeshed in the very commercial society that they so often fled to the Southwest to escape.[1]

By then, artistic nostalgia for the ever-vanishing Indian hardly was a novelty. Even before the Civil War, it was famously expressed in the simple yet compelling paintings of George Catlin, who worked in a frenzy of energy to depict "the living monuments of a noble race" and save them for posterity before they disappeared from the stage of history. During the war, for the first time, cameras preserved the present moment for the instruction of future generations. With his brutally memorable shots of the bloody carnage of war, Matthew Brady "shaped the role of the photographer as national historian." Even before Cushing's arrival in Zuni, William Henry Jackson had photographed the abandoned sites in Mesa Verde of ancient cliff dwellers, the presumed ancestors of Pueblo peoples. Jackson, like so many of his contemporaries, saw "a trajectory of decline" for native peoples, who were "fast passing away or conforming to the habits of civilization." By 1890, with the conclusion of the Indian Wars and the closing of the frontier, it became possible—indeed, urgently necessary—to locate all the surviving Indian tribes and preserve them on film for posterity. With the spreading popularity of the Kodak camera, photography suddenly became "a truly ubiquitous part of American culture."[2]

As Indians were transformed from a dangerous menace into a vanishing species, none were better suited for romantic preservation than the Pueblo tribes. Their growing popularity as the living remnant of the lost American Eden was irresistible. For photographers, Martha A. Sandweiss writes, the Southwest quickly became a land of "idealized beauty with a storied and romantic past." Here was "another civilization," indisputably foreign yet genuinely American. In New Mexico, according to a photographer's advertisement, "one feels as in a foreign land." In the paradox of familiar foreignness, and the captivating discovery of the past in the present, photographers and painters found their opportunity for artistic creativity.[3]

A trio of Californians—Charles F. Lummis, A. C. Vroman, and George Wharton James—was among the first to attract a national audience with their pictorial representations of pueblo life. As a *Los Angeles Times* reporter, Lummis had been dispatched to cover the Apache wars in southern Arizona, where he accompanied a photographer to the battlefield. When he returned to Isleta Pueblo in 1888 to recover his health, he took hundreds of pictures to record "types that are dead, buildings that are destroyed, ceremonials that are no more." Needing money for his living expenses, he began to sell the photographs that accompanied his writings. Lummis's photography, stark and unembellished—in contrast to his rhapsodic prose—captured the bleak harshness and simple humanity of pueblo life.

Even before Pueblo ceremonial dances had begun to attract droves of Anglo spectators, Lummis provided revealing glimpses of the ordinary domestic rituals of a simple people living close to the land. His camera eye was attentive to Pueblo children (at play, with their parents, guiding a blind elder); young women with pots on their heads; primitive agricultural tools (carts, hoes, brooms); public entertainment (a game of chance); "an aboriginal toilet" (a woman brushing a man's hair); a Pueblo girl incongruously (at least to Lummis) holding metal kitchen utensils that were not indigenous to the pueblo. He simultaneously conveyed the simplicity of pueblo church architecture and the stunning beauty of Acoma and Walpi, perched atop mesas high above the desert flatlands. His photographs provide unembellished glimpses of the timeless patterns and rhythms of pueblo life.[4]

Adam C. Vroman, the proprietor of a popular Pasadena bookstore, had moved to California from Illinois for his wife's health. After her death in 1894, he made his first pueblo visit, taking photographs that were published by Lummis in *The Land of Sunshine*. Vroman, preferring to carry fifty pounds of equipment for his traditional view-camera to the newer, streamlined Kodaks, discovered in the Southwest "the long looked-for land of opportunities" for a photographer. Accustomed to the "trim lawns and durable Victorian mansions" of Pasadena, when he ventured to the pueblos it was "hard for him to believe he was in America."

Drawn by Lummis's vivid description of Acoma Pueblo, near "the enchanted mesa," four hundred feet high, where the pueblo had once stood, Vroman became an avid photographer of Southwestern native culture. His stunningly beautiful landscape vistas were balanced by riveting portraits of Pueblo artisans, several of which appeared as Harvey postcards. He patiently won the confidence of his subjects: "The Indian must always have plenty of time to think over anything he has to do, and you cannot rush him a particle; sit down with him, show him the camera inside and out, stand on your head (on the ground-glass) for him, or anything you want him to do, and he will do the same for you."

Vroman was captivated, as many (male) photographers were, by Hopi maidens with their squash blossom hairstyle. Whether he photographed a Hopi mother nursing her baby or arranging her daughter's hair, or the potter Nampeyo at work, his encounters with his subjects were direct and unadorned. His photo of a farmer with a hoe, tending an isolated stalk growing from the arid desert floor, offered a stark vision of agrarian hardship in the Southwest; his portraits of old men and women simultaneously conveyed the ravages of age and the timelessness of Pueblo culture.

Witnessing the Hopi snake dance, a riveting ritual that Vroman was among the first to photograph, he had "a religious experience" that returned him to Arizona every year for the next decade. His annotated photographs from his visit in the summer of 1895 convey his fascination with what he encountered. Vroman was stunned by the "high dark buttes," rising up from the desert floor "like sentinels, placed there to see that man did not control the world." (They also prompted him to wonder how Mrs. Low, an obese member of his traveling party weighing 260 pounds and barely able to walk, would reach the top of the mesa.) The steep ascent was arduous, but exhilarating: "I shall never forget that climb in the faint light of a new moon, winding around among the great pieces of rock up and up." (Seven Indians were required to carry Mrs. Low.) After daybreak, wandering around the pueblo, he encountered hospitable Indians who "would pose for us when asked to do so." Pueblo houses, "built one above the other, each having distinct stairways or ladders," appealed to him. Constructed of stone and mortar, they "have stood as they appear today as far back as we have any record."

The snake dance was held on a Sunday evening, at twilight, "when the sun had dropped below the buildings so the top of the 'Sacred Rock' was in shadow." The entire population of the pueblo, and several dozen Anglo visitors, gathered for the ceremony (fig.9). Vroman, eager to secure "a favorable position" for his camera, "was in readiness an hour before [the] dance was to commence." (So, too, were other photographers, who occasionally appear in his prints.) In the fading light, the constant motion of the dancers made photography difficult, but Vroman's notes display his attentiveness to the ritual performers: the snake woman who "stirs the sacred broth"; girls with "baskets of sacred meal"; Thunder Man, "whirling a small piece of wood on [the] end of string which makes the most weird sound one can imagine"; the Snake Chief, "a magnificent looking fellow." Vroman calculated that "70 snakes of all kinds were used. . . . Probably one fourth of all were 'Rattlers.'"

With everyone in place, "Now commences the chanting of their prayers, swinging to left and right in a kind [of] slow motion." As they marched around the Sacred Rock in pairs, "perhaps three or four snakes in their hands and one or two hanging from mouth[s]," the dance unfolded "in all its weirdness." After each circuit around the Rock, the snakes were dropped for others to pick up. As many as a dozen snakes might be crawling about until someone came to gather them, often with "half a dozen in his other hand, and all he can hold in his mouth." Vroman realized that "words cannot picture it all. The location, the surroundings, the costumes which are beautiful. The bodies of Dancers [dyed] a rich brown with the entire chin white, making face[s] look almost hideous." Despite his evident revulsion at some aspects of the snake dance, Vroman was profoundly affected by what he had seen. "I felt I could spend a year right there, be one of them and learn their ways and beliefs."[5]

FIG. 9. Fred Harvey Postcard: "Hopi Snake Dance,"
Heard Museum, Phoenix, AZ. Postcard provided by author.

Instead, his pueblo visits converted Vroman into a social reformer, determined to protect Indians from government intrusion and tourist exploitation. Eager to encourage respect for their religious life and attachment to
their land, he portrayed "a people strong, vigorous, proud, eternal." In his
photography, "there is no sensationalism, no deliberate portrayal of squalor,
no sentimentalism, no propaganda." He believed that Pueblo Indians, isolated
from modernity for so long, were "the dwellers at the source from which we
all came and to which we all shall one day return."[6]

More unrelenting and obtrusive (and far less subtle) than either Lummis
or Vroman, George Wharton James bullied his way into the pueblos after his
career as an itinerant preacher was devastated by scandal. An English immigrant who had settled in Nevada for health reasons, he lectured throughout
the Southwest on an array of subjects, including India, the Paris Exposition,
Queen Victoria, astronomy ("The Glories of the Heavens"), and social purity.
Hailed as "a God-fearing Christian gentleman," his lectures were praised as
"the best entertainment ever given in the West."

Venturing to Chicago in 1891, James vividly described its "dark places,"
where "the poor and vicious live"—or, worse yet, "'exist' in misery and filth
and squalor unspeakable." Much like Jacob Riis (whose photographic images

he borrowed to enhance his descriptions of Chicago), James was palpably revolted by the degradation of urban life. Struck by the numbers of immigrant women "with an immense sack of paper or rags on their heads" (who never were as romanticized by photographers as Pueblo women with pots on their heads), he described "a new world of horror and black despair" that must offend "those who think of womanhood as necessarily implying all that is tender and gentle and good."[7]

James, evidently, was not among them. Charged by his wife with adultery and incest, he lost his pulpit in 1889 and fled to the Southwest. There, he reminisced, "I saw no one but Indians. . . . There I regained purpose and that outlook on life that has ultimately brought peace, serenity and joy . . . here my real spiritual birth occurred." The Pueblo Indians, he imagined, lived "a perfect life, in harmony with nature, untouched by the problems of civilization" that had so distressed him in Chicago, where "money-mad" America displayed its "commercially cursed, bargain-counter, curio-living, showy, shoddy civilization." If only Americans could adopt Indian virtues, James wrote in *What the White Man May Learn From the Indian*, "the evils of the Industrial Age" could be eradicated. But, he concluded, "I sadly fear that the knell of his doom has sounded, and that a few generations hence he will be no more."[8]

Despite his claims of spiritual rebirth in the Southwest, James behaved like an avaricious Easterner. He bullied and bribed Indians for pictures, intruded (much like Matilda Stevenson) into sacred kivas, and plundered Pueblo artifacts while collecting and selling Indian crafts and religious objects. (Whenever he acquired any sacred or ceremonial artifact, he conceded, "it was always at night, and secretly.") At the same time, however, he romanticized the Indians as "the Bedouins of the United States . . . who rival in picturesqueness, if not in evil, their compeers of the deserts of the Nile."

Like many Americans, James was fascinated by the mix of "civilization and barbarism" that he discovered in the Southwest. There, "strange, peculiar, and interesting" peoples engaged in religious rituals that were "more elaborate than those of a devout Catholic, more complex than those of a Hindoo pantheist, more weird than those of a howling dervish of Turkestan." He described Pueblo government "as simple, pure, and perfect as those of the patriarchs, and possibly as ancient." Like other turn-of-the-century photographers of the Southwest, James was captivated by the durability of tradition in Pueblo culture—and dismayed by its imminent demise. His snake dance photographs, like Vroman's, revealed the ubiquitous presence of tourists and other photographers. Even before the turn of the century, the most traditional Pueblo ceremonies had already become a modern American spectacle.[9]

Among all the photographers of Southwestern Pueblo Indians—and Lummis, Vroman, and James, joined by Ben Wittick and Sumner Matteson, were only a prominent handful among many—none exceeded Edward S. Curtis in his fierce dedication or the stunning quality of his work, and the sharp criticism it subsequently elicited. His attentiveness to the world that Americans—and the native peoples—had lost, and his relentless determination to memorialize it, created a matchless portfolio of artistic photography. As James was influenced by the photojournalism of Riis, so Curtis followed in the footsteps of Lewis Hine, whose "photographic social work" (as Alan Trachtenberg has identified it) included immigrants, factory workers, and child laborers among the "illustrious" Americans who were no less worth photographing than the wealthy and famous. What Hine did in tenement districts and factories, Curtis would do in the West and Southwest. Struck by the human plight—and integrity—of their subjects, both photographers attempted "to join art to the science of the camera and the social science of anthropology."[10]

Curtis, a midwesterner by birth, had worked with a photographer in St. Paul before moving to Seattle to establish his own studio. As the result of a chance encounter in 1898, he was invited to join the Harriman Expedition to Alaska, where he left behind his constraints as a studio photographer of portraits and landscapes to work with Native peoples. Two years later, on his first trip to the Southwest, Curtis decided to specialize in Indian photography, intending to leave "a permanent record of all the important tribes . . . that still remain . . . [and] their primitive customs and traditions." In the early years of the new century, the plan for his life's work crystallized. Harriman, pleased with his Alaska photography, introduced Curtis to President Theodore Roosevelt, who enthusiastically supported his determination to record "some of the most picturesque phases of the old-time American life that is now passing away." With financial assistance secured from J. P. Morgan, Curtis began the work that consumed him for the remainder of his life, a multi-volume portfolio of photographs to document for posterity every Indian tribe of North America.[11]

Curtis caught the rising tide of romantic nostalgia that transformed Indians, once they had been conquered and devastated, into "the profoundest of Americans." Vanishing into history, they could be represented as "an ancestor steeped in drama and mystery, of whom the country could be proud." To Curtis, as he wrote in his Introduction to *North American Indians*, all Indians were bound by "their primitive customs and traditions." He wanted desperately, if futilely, to present them in their original purity, as they were "before any 'white contact.'" Acknowledging that "advancement demands the extermination of these wild, care-free, picturesque" peoples,

FIG. 10. "Taos Water Girls." Edward S. Curtis, *The North American Indian* (1926), Library of Congress, Plate #544.

who were "ground beneath the wheel of civilization," Curtis was nonetheless insistent on producing "an irrefutable record of a race doomed to extinction," by memorializing them before they passed into "the darkness of an unknown civilization."[12]

Curtis's pueblo photographs, comprising only a small portion of his work, were scattered through several volumes, erratically published from 1908–26. Introducing Volume XVI was the photograph that most evocatively incorporated the major themes of his work in the Southwest (fig. 10). Entitled "Taos Water Girls," it subtly interweaves biblical tropes with the American dream. Surrounded by unspoiled Edenic nature, two women seem to be emerging tentatively from within its protective shadows. Uncontaminated by civilization, they are eternal symbols of female purity, the premodern innocence of native peoples, and the intertwining of biblical memory with the American experience. Here was Curtis's "Rebecca" in her primitive allure, an unspoiled symbol of receding national virtue. By then, the ubiquitous popularity of "Rebecca" images had already been recognized by the Eastman Kodak Company, which awarded a prize (ten dollars) for "A New Mexican Rebecca," photographed at San Juan Pueblo in 1896 (fig. 11).[13]

Curtis repeatedly photographed Pueblo women with pots: on their head, in their hands, at their side, or in the process of crafting. In an especially compelling sequence at Acoma, girls ascend to the old well, fill their pots in a sylvan pool enclosed by rocky ledges, and descend, clustered together while holding hands. His portraits radiated female innocence. At San Ildefonso he repeatedly photographed the same attractive girl gathering fruit from a peach tree, filling her jar from a pool, and posing for two portraits—one labeled "Flower Girl" ("The regular features of the comely Morning Flower are not exceptional, for . . . most pueblo girls are not without attractiveness") and the other "Girl and Jar" ("Pueblo women are adept at balancing burdens on the head").[14] Through his depictions of female innocence, Curtis's photography testified to the innocence of premodern society.

By the time that the final volume of *North American Indians*, long delayed for lack of funds, was published in 1930, Curtis had suffered a physical collapse and was deeply depressed. Divorced, he lived with his daughter, tirelessly writing books about Indians that were never published. By 1950, barely three hundred sets of the original edition of five hundred had been sold. All but unknown and forgotten, he died two years later, only to be rediscovered during the Sixties. Amid the resurgence of "Red Power," a developing interest

FIG. 11. "A New Mexican Rebecca." San Juan Pueblo, 1896, by Philip E. Harroun.
Courtesy Museum of New Mexico, Neg.# 12422.

in ecology, and the spread of the counterculture into the Southwest, Curtis's native subjects enjoyed renewed interest and admiration.

Just when Curtis's Indian photographs were finally appreciated, however, his integrity was vigorously assaulted. Despite his professed dedication to historical accuracy, displaying the Indians "as they once were," he was sharply rebuked for paying and posing his subjects, for using props, for retouching his photographs to remove evidence of contact with Anglo civilization (wristwatches, clocks, suspenders), and for dressing his subjects to reflect his own romantic nostalgia. He imagined "a precontact, Edenic world, and then snapped its picture." Indians whose clothing seemed insufficiently indigenous were invariably wrapped in a blanket, pinned at the shoulder, to appear (at least to Curtis) "native." Some of the ceremonies he photographed had been staged for his benefit, while others revealed the corrupting presence of tourists.[15]

Cresting a wave of revisionist criticism, historian Vine Deloria Jr. accused Curtis of "obvious fakery and romanticism." Conceding that his Indian photographs symbolized "the survival of human values in a universe gone mad with materialistic greed," Deloria nonetheless insisted that Curtis's work "did not in the slightest degree speak to the reality of the American Indian, either past or present." Rather, it displayed "Curtis's reality," not "the less glamorous substance of history." His work, wrote Christopher Lyman, who edited a volume of critical exposure, was tinged with "racism and ethnocentrism"; in the end, Curtis "was selling images to a popular audience whose perception of 'Indianness' was based on stereotypes." Amid post-1960s ethnic identity consciousness, Curtis became just one more misguided white man too blinded by his own bias even to recognize it, no less accurately represent his subjects. His astonishingly creative, if unabashedly sentimental, achievement—to portray an idealized vision of "America's romantic youth," with the Indian as symbol of the "ancient wisdom" that modernity had destroyed—was all but ignored. Even when Curtis's photographic work was praised with faint damns, the elaborate corporate enterprise that he created to produce and distribute his pictures was cited as if to implicate his work in the evils of corporate capitalism.[16]

The attack on Curtis was part of a withering assault against what Susan Sontag bluntly described as "colonization through photography," in which its "predatory side" was "the most brutal" in Indian photography. To be sure, turn-of-the-century photographers frequently described their efforts in the language of the hunt. "Photographing a native of Santo Domingo," Curtis claimed, "is comparable to hunting big game with a camera." Photographer

Frederick Monsen recalled pre-Kodak days as a time when "the long, murderous looking lens was pointed straight at his heart," with the photographer, at the other end, "about to pull the trigger." He compared his skill in focusing quickly to that of "a rifleman," who "will hit the target when firing from the hip." George Wharton James wrote that the pursuit of a picture "has all the fascinations of the difficult hunt." Like all hunters, "I prize most the game I find hardest to get"—an unposed Indian. In the muscular language of male photographers, the very photos that would "save" vanishing Indians for posterity became "trophies of the hunt."[17]

To postmodern critics, the bias of these pioneering photographers is self-evident. For Lee Clark Mitchell, the camera was the product of an "expansively imperialistic" culture. Indeed, the photograph itself has an "intrinsically imperializing role" that encourages and sustains "colonization through photography." To Marta Weigle and Barbara Babcock, the "imaging" of Indian photographs by the Fred Harvey Company and the Santa Fe Railroad "was part of the continuing campaign to make 'hostile' natives manageable and safe for tourists while 'simultaneously glorify[ing] and domesticat[ing] empire.'" Indian photography, therefore, can best be understood as "a discourse of domination." In its "imperial textuality," it demonstrated "the ability to control and maintain many images of Otherness." At best, its "imperialist nostalgia" expressed "a sense of longing for what one is complicit in destroying or altering."[18]

Yet this critique is no less demeaning to Native peoples than to the photographers it targets. Assuming that all Pueblo Indians resisted photographic incursions as hostile acts, it oversimplifies a more complex reality to sharpen its political edge. Responses to photographers varied, from occasional hostile attacks to requiring admission fees to the welcome that Vroman and Lummis gratefully praised. In Zuni, religious leaders, protective of their rituals and ceremonies, objected to photography far more strenuously than did the governor, who admired the family photographs that Ft. Wingate soldiers carried with them. With a photograph, he reassured a fellow Zuni, "Though your body perish, nevertheless you shall continue to live upon the earth." Suggestions that Curtis invariably "exploited" his native subjects by photographing them were rejected by some of their own descendants, who expressed gratitude for his preservationist efforts. "No one staged the people," insisted a great-grandson, "And we see them at their classic finest."[19]

The photographers at the end of the nineteenth century who delighted in "capturing" Pueblo Indians on film were hardly the rapacious colonizers that contemporary critics have depicted. Confronting stark human reminders of the world that was lost, a loss they felt keenly, they were determined to leave an illuminating pictorial record of their encounters with human symbols of an irrecoverable past. To visit the Hopi pueblos, Frederic Monsen wrote in 1910, is to confront "the unspoiled remnant of a great race, a race of men who have, from time immemorial, lived quiet, sane, wholesome lives very close to Nature." Monsen, like Curtis, was sensitive to the toll that modernity exacted from native culture, perhaps more sensitive than Indians themselves, who often welcomed Western innovations on their own journey into modernity. "Some day when it is too late," Monsen predicted, "we may realize what we have lost by 'educating' the Indian, and forcing him to accept our more complex but far inferior standards of life, work and art." Meanwhile, the photographers' challenge, as they understood it at the time, was to preserve for posterity what modernity had all but destroyed.[20]

~

Artists, no less than photographers, were drawn westward throughout the nineteenth century by the natural splendor of the region and the exotic native peoples who inhabited it. Once Lewis and Clark lifted the curtain of discovery on the West, it was only a matter of time before many thousands of inquisitive—and acquisitive—Americans followed the trail they had so courageously blazed. As early as the 1830s, John James Audubon and George Catlin, sensing imminent danger to the creatures and peoples who inhabited the West, were impelled to illustrate their existence before they disappeared forever. "Nature herself seems perishing," wrote Audubon, who wanted his paintings to "stop time" before it was too late. Catlin focused on Indians, not birds, but otherwise shared Audubon's preservationist impulse. "The noble races of red men," he wrote in 1832, "were melting away at the approach of civilization." Mary Eastman, wife of army artist Seth Eastman, described their own collaborative effort "to depict all the customs, feasts and ceremonies of the Sioux before it be too late. . . . They are receding rapidly, and with feeble resistance, before the giant strides of civilization." Just before the Civil War, Albert Bierstadt, on his first visit to the Rockies, discovered that the Indians were "rapidly passing away, and soon will be known only in history."[21]

During the second half of the nineteenth century, the preservationist impulse was accompanied by the yearning of aspiring artists to escape the values of an Eastern commercial culture that showed little appreciation for their aesthetic sensibilities. The Western wilderness, as historian G. Edward White has observed, existed "in its antipathy to the established customs of eastern civilization." Frederic Remington, perhaps the most popular painter of Western subjects, exemplified the artist for whom urban industrial America represented "a cramped and crowded existence which impinged on a man's freedom." Painters and illustrators, like photographers, expressed "nostalgic wistfulness" for a vanishing America—and for the Indians who symbolized and humanized its disappearance.[22]

Before the turn of the century, artists had begun to discover freedom, beauty, and inspiration in the Southwest, where civilization ended and the wilderness began. They shared the perception of painter Charles M. Russell, for whom "the Red Man was the true American. . . . Their God was the sun . . . their church all out doors. Their only book was nature and they knew all of its pages." Moving west, Remington encountered an alternative to the "heavy-handed God of Progress" that Americans worshiped so devoutly in the East. Yet in one of the curious ironies of American art history, the very artists who fled from sordid Eastern materialism to the pristine Southwest brought commercialism and tourism in their wake. Their newest patrons, who dictated aesthetic standards no less insistently than their effete Eastern counterparts, were the Atchison Topeka & Santa Fe Railroad and the Fred Harvey Company.[23]

Early in the spring of 1898, Bert Phillips and Ernest Blumenschein, experienced illustrators for *Harper's* and *McClure's* magazines, outfitted themselves in Denver, purchased horses and a wagon, and, like Lummis before them, set out for New Mexico. Their destination was Taos, a sleepy pueblo market and festival town described to them euphorically by Joseph Henry Sharp, an art student they had met in Paris. Sharp had raved about the beauty of the Southwest, captivating them with his descriptions of Pueblo ceremonial dances. Indians seemed much more appealing than "the hackneyed subject matter" that preoccupied Blumenschein's contemporaries: "lady gazing in a mirror; lady powdering her nose; etc., etc." Phillips and Blumenschein, soon joined by Sharp and Irving Couse, became the intrepid pioneers who formed the nucleus of the embryonic Taos art colony. Trained in Europe or New York, they felt constricted by the feminization of American civilization and yearned for ruggedly aesthetic, and gendered, alternatives to inspire them.[24]

Recalling his memorable first encounter with Taos, Blumenschein rapturously described "the great naked anatomy of a majestic landscape once tortured, now calm; the fitness of adobe houses to their tawny surroundings; the vastness and overwhelming beauty of skies; terrible drama of storms; peace of night—all in beauty of color, vigorous form, ever changing light." There, he recalled, "I saw whole paintings right before my eyes. Everywhere I looked I saw paintings perfectly organized ready for paint." He was certain that "no artists had ever recorded the superb New Mexico I was now seeing." To Sharp, it seemed almost fated that "a distinctive American art idea" should originate in "the poetic Indian Village of Taos Pueblo."[25]

Couse and Sharp, like Curtis, may have searched for genuine "Indianness," unblemished by American modernity and progress. But they, too, most often found it in their own imaginations. Phillips summed up their inspiration and aspiration when he declared: "Nothing could be more natural than that a distinctive American art idea should develop on a soil so richly imbued with romance, history and scenic beauty as is to be found in the far famed, beautiful Taos Valley and the poetic Indian Village of the Taos Pueblos." Here, he asserted with wonderment, "Father Time laid his hand on an ancient civilization and bade it pause with all its picturesqueness, poetry and romance, until the men who could translate its beauty and charm and forever record for future generations, arrived upon the scene."[26]

Such inflated expectations about the innocence of noble savages confronted the daunting challenge of reality: all too often, Indians were not complicit in such romantic visions. Sharp complained that the Indian, "a slave to superstition," was "not a great success" as a model because he posed with "majestic and often ludicrous stiffness." Couse, whose Indian likenesses became exceedingly popular, was described as a painter of static figures who would "kneel, sit, or squat. They did little else." An anonymous portrayal of Phillips in his studio, painting a nude Indian maiden seated next to a large olla, offered a voyeuristic variation on a familiar theme.[27]

Eager to attract passengers, the Santa Fe Railroad commissioned Taos artists to illustrate its travel literature and calendars. They were avidly courted and generously compensated for their work. For artists Louis Akin, depressed and eager to flee New York to rediscover himself by living among the Hopis, and Frank Paul Sauerwein, suffering from tuberculosis and needing an arid climate, these opportunities were literally lifesaving. Irving Couse produced appealing images of Pueblo Indians for reproduction on Fred Harvey Company postcards and menus; more than twenty of his paintings of Taos Indians, depicting their "smooth flesh, tense muscles, and fine bone structure," appeared on railroad calendars. More than occasionally, Pueblo Indians were portrayed in poses and colors favored by William Haskell Simpson, the railroad purchasing agent.

Inevitably, this partnership empowered the railroad to dictate aesthetic taste. Its advertising director instructed Blumenschein that he preferred Indians "with Taos Pueblo in the [back]ground. . . . Such a picture would have an advertising value apart from its art quality." The railroad made paintings available to the Fred Harvey Company, which displayed them in its hotels and gift shops and reproduced them on postcards. Within a decade, some artists who had come to Taos to escape the sordid commercialism of the East were enmeshed in promotional work for two of the most powerful corporations in the Southwest. Not all Taos artists worked for the railroad or the Fred Harvey Company, but some, clearly, were delighted with their new—and lucrative— opportunities. Blumenschein, with a keen entrepreneurial sense, proposed a society of artists to organize local talent and bargain more effectively with their corporate sponsors. In 1912, the Taos Society of Artists was formed; by the end of World War I, the paintings of its members were being sold and exhibited throughout the United States to appreciative collectors, and Taos had been transformed into a major American art center.[28]

The Taos artists' vision of the pueblos undeniably reflected their own discontent with modernity and their yearning for a more aesthetically rewarding life. Their frequent point of nostalgic reference, as for so many Americans who visited the Southwest at the end of the nineteenth century, was the biblical text. In language resonant of the revelation at Sinai, Phillips observed that the Indians were captivated by "the tales of romance and history from the time when the Great Father called all his people before him and directed them to the lands they were to locate." Their "pastoral scenes of Biblical peace and plenty," inhabited by "happy and noble people," offered a sharp contrast to the less comforting reality of pueblo poverty and disease. Tragedy and sorrow were expunged from Indian history, leaving only a vague melancholy to hover over the native people who endured. These paintings might reflect personal discontents no less than pueblo realities. Artists needed assurance, observed Rina Swentzell, who moved as a little girl from Santa Clara Pueblo to Taos, "that the technological and consumeristic world that was growing around them had not yet pervaded every corner of the globe." But the sources of inspiration were genuine and powerful. As William Victor Higgins, who joined the Society in 1917, wrote: "There is in the mind of every member of the Taos art colony the knowledge that here is the oldest of American civilizations. . . . They offer the painter a subject as full of the fundamental qualities of life as did the Holy Land of long ago."[29]

In Taos, artists experienced closeness to spiritual truths that seemed lacking elsewhere in the modern world. Oscar Berninghaus left St. Louis for New Mexico, where he "became infected with the Taos germ." It promised release from his dreary work for newspapers, a lithograph company, and the Denver & Rio Grande Railroad. The "primitive appeal" of the Indians "urges the painter to get his subjects, his coloring, his tone from real life about him, not from the wisdom of the studios." In art centers such as New York and Chicago, artists were "bound by conventions, ringed round by tradition," but in Taos, by contrast, the artist "takes a chance." Yet it was easy to fall back upon nostalgia and sentiment, while yielding to the aesthetic judgments of patrons. As William H. Truettner has observed, the Taos artists never painted "unpleasant scenes" of pueblo life, preferring "pastoral scenes of Biblical peace and plenty." Artists, after all, brought their own American baggage with them to the Southwest.

Among the Taos artists, there was evident deference to the promotional tastes of the railroad, which strongly encouraged stereotypical representations of Indian subjects, often at the expense of accuracy. One artist was instructed by the railroad to paint a face "a little more like the Indian Chief most of us have in our mind." Phillips depicted a Pueblo flutist wearing the leggings of Plains Indians; Sharp's painting of a Taos girl incorporated a big bowl of zinnias, along with other flowers that were not indigenous to the Southwest. Called by one Society member "unwitting publicists" for New Mexico, they would be accused of becoming accomplices in "corporate image-making."[30]

In the end, Taos artists, like so many other Americans who were drawn to the Southwest at the close of the nineteenth century, discovered in Pueblo culture healing balm for anxieties about their own place in American society. Popularizing Taos as a "Western Walden Pond," they helped to generate the mass influx of tourism that not only propelled one sleepy village, but the entire Southwest, into the consumer culture that signified modernity. In this way, "the discontent of the civilized with civilization" encouraged reverence for primitive simplicity while simultaneously accelerating the conversion of art into yet another form of remunerative commercial enterprise.[31]

By the turn of the twentieth century, the Southwest had emerged as a "New World whose terrain, climate and indigenous peoples offered a model of ecological, spiritual and artistic integration to an alienated and decadent Western civilization." Santa Fe and Taos, as "outposts of avant-garde culture," were becoming a favorite "spiritual and aesthetic resource" for disillusioned critics of American society. But Pueblo culture was trapped within the cruel paradox created by its fervent admirers: the more that natives were studied by ethnographers, described by writers, depicted by photographers and represented by artists as anti-modern symbols, the more they were immersed in modernity, ever more dependent upon the new urban industrial society for opportunities and alternatives that their own culture could not provide.[32]

~

Between the turn of the century and World War I, interest waned in Southwestern Pueblo culture as a remedy for the discontents of modernity. During an era of Progressive reform, Americans glimpsed new possibilities for regulating and redirecting social change. The promise of American life might be realized by engaging with modernity, rather than by fleeing from it. So, at least, Progressive reformers believed, plunging into the politics of liberal reform until disillusionment with the crusade to make the world safe for democracy during World War I finally shattered their dreams. Then, once again, the Southwestern pueblos could emerge as a redemptive force in American society.

In the postwar decade, however, the struggle for personal liberation took new form. The male quest had reached its tragic limits in trench warfare, with so many lives lost and bodies broken. After the war, biblical rhetoric became more the hallmark of religious fundamentalists who resisted the authority of science and the intrusions of modernity. But as the New Woman emerged to assert her place in American society, the pueblos—an arena for testing manhood ever since Cushing's sojourn in Zuni—were recast as female space. There women born in the Victorian era might find ways to shed their personal and social constraints, while young women who came of age during the World War I era could find new opportunities for self-expression and gendered freedom in the Southwest.

PART TWO

A Woman's Place

CHAPTER FOUR

Salon in Taos

One of the first Anglo-Americans to visit the Hopi pueblos, Captain John G. Bourke of the United States Cavalry, had observed that the typical Pueblo girl was "initiated at an early age into the mysteries of the kitchen. . . . By the time she is fifteen, or even at an earlier age, she is considered nubile, and fairly entered in the matrimonial market." Once married, Bourke wrote, her domestic skills enabled her to "hold her own with the most ingenious American housewife." The Hopi matron "makes a dutiful wife and a fond, affectionate mother." Yet for all his conventional Victorian assumptions, Bourke acknowledged that "women have the management, control, and ownership of the house," a Pueblo norm that would have considerable appeal to subsequent generations of feminists. But any "elevated place" of women in Pueblo culture, as far as he could discern, was measured primarily by the absence of nose-slitting and other forms of mutilation that were practiced by the neighboring Apache. Appalled by preparations for the Snake Dance in a Hopi kiva, he wondered, "Could this be the Christian land of America?"[1]

Not long after Bourke's observations were published in 1884, middle-class Protestant women with a refined social conscience trickled into the pueblos to educate and uplift the native peoples with an infusion of Christian virtue. To Mary Dissette, sent to Zuni by the Presbyterian Board of Home Missions, the Indians, living in "gross animalism," were "to be pitied for their ignorance and for the injustice they suffer." Measured by Victorian standards of propriety, Indian family structure posed a serious impediment to Christian moral development. Girls were the "absolute property" of their fathers, while married women were domestic "drudges" at the mercy of their husbands. It was evident that Pueblo women suffered from "intellectual deprivation, domestic oppression, and sexual degradation." Pueblo Indians were described as a "backward, dirty, pagan" people, desperately in need of "uplift" to civilized American standards by dedicated Christian women.[2]

It seems puzzling, therefore, that pueblos would have any allure to modern women. Yet after the turn of the century, amid the currents of artistic creativity, cultural criticism, and personal liberation that crested during the Progressive era, repressive Victorian ideals of moral authority and female purity yielded to a new emphasis on sexual freedom, gender equality, and professional opportunity for women. Along the way, Pueblo culture was refashioned into a feminist utopia where, in writer Mary Austin's phrase, "Mother-rule" prevailed. By the 1920s, Pueblo women were admired by avant-garde feminists as "powerful women whose traditions embodied ideal gender relations." No longer was the Southwest an arena reserved for male adventurers eager to test their manhood; now, women might learn from Pueblo Indians—especially Pueblo women—how to "overcome the psychological fragmentation and alienating isolation" of modern society that left them powerless and vulnerable.[3]

After World War I, the "symbiotic promotion" of the Southwest by the Fred Harvey Company and the Santa Fe Railroad gradually diminished. Their virtual prewar monopoly on travel to the region was eroded by the emerging popularity of automobiles, a spreading network of highways, and the increasing reliance of tourists on road-stop accommodations. The final success of their partnership was the establishment of Harvey's Indian Tours in 1926, a joint venture that offered, as part of the package trip for transcontinental travelers, a three-hundred-mile motor detour "to the new exotic theatre of the Southwest." Indian Tours promised tourists a journey "nearer to the primitive than anywhere else on the continent." Travelers would be transported in elegant touring cars to "a land in which foreign people, with foreign speech and foreign ways, offer them spectacles which can be equaled in few Oriental lands."[4]

Indian Tours was the offspring of a merger between the Fred Harvey Company and its major competitor, Koshare Tours, founded after the war by New Mexico native Erna Fergusson. No less ambitious than Harvey had been to succeed in business by selling the Southwest to new visitors, Fergusson was the prototypical New Woman of the postwar era. She was the granddaughter of a German immigrant who had arrived in New Mexico in 1848 with a wagon train of goods for sale. He conspicuously displayed his success by building an ersatz German castle that became his family home, surrounded by streams, bridges, live peacocks, and Bavarian troll figurines. Fergusson grew up in Albuquerque, studied at the University of New Mexico and Columbia, and served with the Red Cross during the war.

An ambitious woman and an enthusiastic booster of the Southwest, Fergusson described it as a "fabulous land" in which "modern American culture is superimposed on an earlier Spanish civilization, and both of them on a prehistoric Indian mode of life that still survives." She discovered in the pueblos "a complete and extraordinarily beautiful survival of primitive life," with native ceremonies that could be traced back to King David's dances before God. Describing herself as a "woman dude-wrangler," her postwar mission was to lure travelers away from the railroad, accompany them into the wilderness, and enable them to "shake hands with a thousand years." Koshare Tours promised to show visitors "places where the people are going about their primitive—almost Biblical—tasks and pleasures."[5]

Fergusson's entrepreneurial vision suggests that gender identity in the Southwest had changed dramatically since Mary Dissette's time in Zuni. Describing her own "androgyny," or "double vision" as a woman, she adopted a uniform—strikingly different from anything the Harvey girls had worn forty years earlier—that closely resembled the uniform of an American soldier during World War I. As a guide, she wore "high-laced boots, riding pants, military-style jacket, and trooper hat." Challenging gender stereotypes, she displayed her "spiffy forest ranger style" while still adorning herself with native jewelry that any fashionably sophisticated woman might wear.

Rejecting conventional gender constraints, Fergusson declined to be confined to the female role as guardian of morality in the privacy of her home. For guides, she hired "soft-voiced college girls," adorned with Native jewelry and slightly Bohemian in style, who persuaded a *New York Times* writer that "Feminine America is making its mark even in the Wild West." Yet, with the ambivalence that often characterized the struggle of New Women for gender freedom, Fergusson heightened the appeal of Koshare Tours with tea and hospitality for tourists, adding the "personal touch" that she believed only a female guide could provide. After all, she insisted, women "make much more of the little things that mean so much, than men do."[6]

In *Our Southwest,* her testimony to the allure of New Mexico and Arizona, Fergusson praised the Pueblo Indian, who "seems conscious of himself only as one of a group. He has no conception of individualism—no personal ambition . . . His morality is based on the good of the group." Redefining herself as a modern woman, she rejected the rampant individualism of American society. The Southwest appealed to her as an alternative culture, "so much needed by a world weary of getting and spending." It was, she wrote, "a wilderness where a man may get back the essentials of being a man." And, she might have added, where a woman could redefine her own gendered identity.[7]

The quest for a once and future Eden in the Southwest must have seemed quixotic to Pueblo Indians, who again found themselves inundated by Anglo visitors eager to take their pictures and acquire their handmade crafts. Fergusson told the story of a Taos girl who, when asked what she wanted for a wedding present, instantly replied, "a bucket." Fergusson worried that such yearning among the native peoples for modern material objects threatened the symbolic value of the pueblo as "a primitive life away from the world's hurly-burly." She lamented the loss of "the old reverence for life-giving natural things." This, she realized, "is what the ancient pueblo life had; this is what modern life threatens." Yet the Pueblo girl, eager to relinquish her handmade earthen pot for a metal bucket, yearned for an enticing American future, not the "primitive" Pueblo past. Fergusson, like other women who were drawn to the pueblos after World War I, was profoundly ambivalent about the consequences of modernity for the Pueblo girl—and for herself.[8]

Fergusson belonged to a cohort of modern feminists who developed their own gendered revision of Pueblo mythology. What had been, at the end of the nineteenth century, "no place for a lady," would, by the 1930s, become a feminist paradise. At the crossroads of these cultural changes were two formidable women whose early lives of wealth and privilege left them thwarted by Victorian constraints. Mabel Ganson was born in 1879 in the Buffalo mansion owned by her father, a prospering banker whose family ascended to new heights of affluence in the Gilded Age. She grew up to become a flamboyant cultural radical, who was determined to use her Fifth Avenue salon and, after World War I, her new home in Taos, as springboards for changing the world. Elsie Clews, born into a socially prominent New York City family in 1874, spent much of her girlhood moving between an elegant Manhattan townhouse and a sprawling oceanfront mansion in Newport. After the turn of the century, she emerged as one of the most outspoken radical feminists of her time, writing pioneering sociological studies of family structure and gender relations before turning her attention to anthropology, Pueblo Indians, and mentoring Franz Boas's female graduate students at Columbia. In their own distinctive ways, these women—and others—found in the Southwest, among Pueblo Indians, a fulcrum for social criticism and new possibilities for personal transformation and fulfillment.

Mabel Ganson, raised by nursemaids and educated at Miss Graham's School in New York City (where her grandparents lived), was thoroughly prepared for marriage and motherhood, but little else. A European sojourn, and a year of finishing school climaxed by her debut as a debutante, pointed her toward a life of privilege and refinement that was typical for young women of her class. But her emotional life, writes biographer Lois Rudnick, "was invested in romantic longings for an ideal world in which . . . sensuous fulfillment would compensate her for the actively achieving self her family and her society repressed." Her early and hasty marriage to Karl Evans, a "light-hearted, thoughtless boy," seems to have served her contradictory yearning for independence and "her belief that she must derive her identity from men."[9]

Following the exposure of a clandestine affair with her doctor and the torment that accompanied her husband and father's premature deaths, Mabel departed for Europe with her young son John in 1904. In a luxurious villa outside Florence she lived a life of privileged self-indulgence. Newly remarried to Boston architect Edwin Dodge, but still miserable, she described herself as "very stupid, & unhappy, indeed quite desperate, & with no heart at all, nor any brains." Living in grand style as "a Renaissance lady," she cultivated and applied her talents for inspiring the genius, and satisfying the desires, of her many male admirers. Stimulated by an encounter with Gertrude and Leo Stein in Paris in 1911, she recast herself as an exemplar of avant-garde aesthetic modernism and began her lifelong crusade against American philistinism.[10]

Preparing for her return to the United States after nearly a decade in Italy, Mabel Dodge wrote apprehensively: "America is all machinery and money—making and factories—it is ugly, ugly, ugly!" But her arrival in New York in 1913, she marveled, came just when "barriers went down and people reached each other who had never been in touch before. . . . The new spirit was abroad and swept us all together." Settling into an elegant Fifth Avenue townhouse filled with her prized European furnishings, she created her own salon, modeled after Stein's, to attract the "movers and shakers" of avant-garde radicalism. What for Stein was an American home in Parisian exile became, for

Mabel Dodge, the refuge of a woman in exile at home. The salon functioned as a halfway house, where domesticity and liberation converged in creative tension. Her outpost of "the new radicalism" at the edge of Greenwich Village attracted John Reed, Walter Lippmann, Lincoln Steffens, Emma Goldman, and Margaret Sanger, among other luminaries of cultural and political rebellion. There she lived an updated version of the high-society life of her debutante years, while simultaneously serving as cultural godmother to her gatherings of Fifth Avenue rebels. She was a gracious hostess, preserving decorum even as she encouraged radical dissent.[11]

Writing occasionally for *The Masses* and as a syndicated columnist for the *New York Journal*, Dodge and her salon flourished. Her infatuation with the fashionable cultural movements of the day—whether in art (including Indian art, an avant-garde favorite), politics, or psychoanalysis—barely kept pace with her attachments to the various men in her life, John Reed conspicuous among them. She also enjoyed a lengthy affair with Maurice Sterne, an aspiring artist whose odyssey of self-discovery had taken him across Europe, through Russia to Bali, and finally back to his adopted home in New York, where he had grown up as the child of Latvian immigrants. In 1917, just one week after she published an article warning that women who yearn to become "the mothers of men" or "who seek masters" were doomed to frustration, Mabel and Maurice were married. After their wedding, she dispatched him on a solitary honeymoon to the Southwest, while she remained behind in New York to charm and nurture the male guests at her salon.

Maurice, despite the absence of his bride, was smitten by New Mexico. "Do you want an object in life?" he wrote to Mabel shortly after his arrival in Santa Fe. Then she must "save the Indians, their art—culture—reveal it to the world!" He assured her: "you have the energy and are the most sensitive little girl in the world—and, above all, there is somehow a strange relationship between yourself and the Indians." For Mabel Dodge Sterne, the timing of Maurice's epiphany was perfect. His letter, written at the end of November 1917, arrived in the midst of the cataclysm that turned the world inside out for the radicals who gathered in Mabel's salon. Opposed to the war, and inspired by the Bolshevik revolution, they feared the heavy hand of political repression from the American government. As cultural Philistines began to encircle Greenwich Village, the "downtown moderns" in Mabel's salon felt besieged. Despite her transformation from an "ordinary rich woman" into a "fascinating celebrity," New York City had suddenly become unbearable.[12]

But Maurice's "indian mud hut" in New Mexico had little appeal to Mabel. Her impressions of the Southwest, from a previous trip with Reed, had prompted her to conclude: "I'm afraid the West is a man's world & that woman's place is in New York." But she was sufficiently disillusioned with American culture and politics to be intrigued by her new husband's enthusiasm. "Perhaps I too would feel this curious affinity with [Indians] that you do," she responded to Maurice. "Certainly the live heart of me—the inner life, is a life that finds no counterpart in Western civilization and culture." Hesitant to join Maurice, she nonetheless experienced "a sense of renewal and a new awareness" once she arrived in New Mexico.

On their way from Santa Fe to Taos, she caught "a fleeting glimpse of my own spoiled and distorted nature, seen against the purity and freshness of these undomesticated surroundings." There was, she observed, "no disturbance in the scene, nothing to complicate the forms, no trees or houses, or any detail to confuse one." When she heard Spanish spoken outside her room, "it didn't seem possible that we were in the United States." Witnessing her first Indian dance at Santo Domingo Pueblo on Christmas day, she experienced a profound revelation: "I heard the singing and drumming as soon as we reached the Pueblo, and it drew me strongly and I left the others and ran hurriedly towards it with my heart beating . . . I heard the voice of the One, coming from the many." Mabel realized that "the singular raging lust for individuality and separateness had been impelling me all my years . . . when all of a sudden I was brought up against the Tribe, . . . where virtue lay in wholeness instead of dismemberment." Determined to reinvent herself as a woman, she told Maurice that the first thing she wanted to do in her new life was to learn how to cook.[13]

Her burning vision of new possibilities, Mabel explained to Mary Austin, required the transformation of her home in Taos into "a creative center—not just a place for people to retreat into—or to go to sleep in—or to barge in for just a good time. I want people to use it freely but for creative purposes." Leaving the East coast behind (except for occasional visits to her psychoanalyst and, for a time, winters in her house in Croton-on-Hudson), she would entice disaffected writers, artists and intellectuals to the Southwest, there to create a new spiritual center for the rebirth of American culture. A stream of literary luminaries responded to her invitations, transforming her house in Taos into the Southwestern outpost of her Greenwich Village salon (fig. 12).[14]

"My life broke in two right then," Mabel wrote famously in *The Edge of*

Taos Desert, "and I entered into the second half, a new world that replaced all the ways I had known with others, more strange and terrible and sweet than any I had ever been able to imagine." Although she was initially unenthusiastic about her new venue—there was "no law, no reverence, and very little beauty of living"—in Taos Pueblo she experienced "a feeling of home." There she felt "wholeness and harmony," which sharply contrasted to the competitive individualism that fractured American society. Indeed, she discovered in Taos "a garden of Eden inhabited by an unfallen tribe of men and women."

It was, Mabel wrote, "as though the Pueblo had an invisible wall around it, separating the Indians from the world we knew—a wall that kept their life safe within it . . . I *wish* I belonged in there!" The Indians, she observed, were "full of quietude and nobility and wisdom." Enchanted by their self-contained stability, harmony, and spirituality, she felt "more awake and more aware" than ever before. Visiting nearby Santo Domingo Pueblo, and listening to the drumming and chanting that accompanied ceremonial dances, she witnessed the "new communion" that might prevail over the "wistful, sorrowing complaint of individualism." From her pueblo visits, she gained "a sense of new life."[15]

In Taos, as in Florence and Greenwich Village, Mabel created a sanctuary

FIG. 12. "Taos Pueblo." Postcard provided by author.

from the uncivilized excesses of modernity. She realized "that we are ourselves only the tourists in the Garden of Eden!" But the "purity and freshness" of her new environment, she wrote, removed "the waste and sickness of civilization." So breathtaking was the natural beauty of her new home that it left Mabel "without the gesture and response that would adequately fit the scene." Her rapture was considerably enhanced, and more sharply focused, once she met Tony Luhan in Taos Pueblo. In their first encounter, with the sun shining behind him, he appeared to Mabel "like a Biblical figure."[16]

In Tony's presence, Mabel instantly felt liberated from all that she had left behind—including Maurice (fig. 13). Her new husband now "seemed old spent and tragic," while Tony was "whole and young." The two men in her life personified a clash of civilizations: the West, "muffled, stifled, going under"; Indian culture, by contrast, "bare-limbed and free." In retrospect, she realized that her refined Western mind had become "a waste-basket of the world, full of scraps I wanted to throw away and couldn't. I longed for an immersion in some strong solution that would wipe out forever the world I had known." Tony represented the alternative to "a dying world . . . a decadent unhappy world" that she was prepared to leave "to be with someone real at last, alive at last." He was, for Mabel, "a kind of symbol for my having gone over into an 'otherness.' . . . When I left the white people's world I *really* left it—it was not mental attitude or superficial sensational gesture."[17]

Through Tony, Mabel could enter Indian life, "very slowly, a step at a time. I was becoming acquainted with a kind of living I didn't know existed anywhere." As Tony explained to her, the religion of white people "is in machinery to change things," but Indian religion is "Life." Pueblo culture became her model: "to live as a group, and to be part and parcel of a living tribal organism, to share everything." In Taos, she experienced "a spiritual therapy that was cleansing." It was "a difficult and painful method of curing me of my epoch," she conceded, but she savored "this life of natural beauty and clarity" that promised to "wipe out forever the world I had known." Being with Tony "liberated me, freed me from my world, made me *become* myself." Her new life among Indians, she wrote ecstatically, "is not all in the head, with the occasional shriek of an orgasm to break the numb silence of the flesh."[18]

As passionately as Mabel embraced Taos, and Tony, she sensed, deep down, that "lonely atoms like us" could never fully participate in the "rich, shared companioned being" of Pueblo culture. But Mabel was beguiled by the new freedom that her life in Taos afforded. During a brief return to New York

FIG. 13. "Mabel Dodge Luhan." Yale Collection of American Literature,
Beinecke Rare Book and Manuscript Library.

in 1919, she was assured by a medium that Taos was "the beating heart of the world" and "the center of a new birth for Western civilization." Indeed, Mabel had been chosen to become the "bridge . . . between the Indian and white people," by which the "blood consciousness" of Indians, formed in nature, "would merge with the cultural consciousness of the white woman." With this synthesis, Taos would become the new "city upon the hill," an inspiration to the entire Western world.[19]

Instead, Taos became "the Greenwich Village of New Mexico," where Mabel collected art and artists indiscriminately. She was a welcoming hostess to an endless procession of refugees who were in flight from the crassness of American culture: Mary Austin, Carl van Vechten, Georgia O'Keeffe, Ansel Adams, Robinson Jeffers, Thornton Wilder, and Carl Jung among them. (Visiting Taos Pueblo, Jung was told by a native resident that "the whites always want something; they are always uneasy and restless . . . We think that they are mad." At this revelation, Jung apparently "fell into a long meditation," finally realizing that "this Indian had struck our vulnerable spot, unveiled a truth to which we are blind.") "It was a new world," said artist Georgia O'Keeffe, fleeing New York from her marital difficulties with Alfred Stieglitz, "and I thought this was my world." Mary Austin, among the founders of an art colony in Carmel, California, came to Taos yearning to protect Indians from the infection of "Americanism." With their arrival, a new outpost of avant-garde culture was created in the Southwest, which Mabel described as "the land of the new birth."[20]

Although D. H. Lawrence and his wife Frieda resisted her entreaties for a time, Mabel "willed" the Lawrences to Taos, and, after an extended correspondence, they finally arrived in September 1922. Mabel had an ambitious agenda for Lawrence: he must tell "the truth about America: the false, new, external America in the east, and the true, primordial, undiscovered America that was preserved, living, in the Indian bloodstream." Skeptical at first ("Is Taos the place?" he asked Mabel), Lawrence soon was smitten: "In the magnificent fierce morning of New Mexico," he wrote, "one sprang awake, a new part of the soul woke up suddenly, and the old world gave way to the new."

But it quickly proved to be an unstable arrangement, as Mabel paired off with D. H. Lawrence to collaborate on a novel about her (and perhaps more), while Frieda Lawrence hovered uneasily in the background. Before long, Mabel's unrelenting possessiveness—and the glaring contradictions of her life—drove the Lawrences to their own ranch nearby. Lawrence came to believe that "in some curious way, the pueblos still lie here at the core of American life." But it was "a bit too much Mabel Dodge," he confided to a friend. Complaining about "White savages, with motor-cars, telephones, incomes and ideals!" he observed that the Southwest had become "the great playground of the White American," with Indians as "a wonderful live toy to play with." He was acerbically skeptical about Mabel's efforts. She "hates the white world," he observed, "and loves the Indians out of hate." He told her, scathingly, "Somewhere, the Indians know that you . . . would, with your salvationist but poisonous white consciousness, destroy them."[21]

Mabel and Tony, married in 1923, were indeed a bundle of contradictions and incompatibilities. Mabel furnished their Taos home on a grand scale, "with all the past years of my life showing there in Italian and French furniture, pictures from many hands, books from New York, bronzes from Venice, Chinese paintings, and Indian things." She realized that Tony "likes the simple movements of life, like the plaza life, and I don't. . . . If we sit in a room, it is in silence." Her aesthetic tastes, as always, were subsidized by her income from trust funds established by her father and grandfather, generously supplemented by cash gifts from her mother. Her idealized Taos, by contrast, was a wretchedly poor community, where the average annual per capita income was thirty dollars and tuberculosis, trachoma, and venereal disease were rampant.[22]

Mabel rapturously described how being with Tony "liberated me, freed me from my world, made me *become* myself." Yet rather than becoming more "Indian" through Tony, she often regressed into domesticity at his insistence, while he enjoyed the perquisites of her affluence to reemerge as an indulged American husband. Tony, she realized, yearned "to go out in the world & live in it & develop himself up out of the tribe as an individual." Her Cadillac became the symbol of his freedom. Wearing expensive clothes in his new role as chauffeur, he delighted in guiding Mabel's guests to local places of interest, where he could proudly display his affluence to members of his tribe. In the end, Lois Rudnick observes, "Rather than becoming Indian through Tony, Mabel had de-Indianized Tony." Indeed, in one of her more disparaging, yet candid, moments she described him as "the conquered—the subjugated . . . 'a spoiled Indian.'" If Tony had been her passport to liberation from Western culture, she became his passport to the enticing freedom and prosperity that Western culture afforded.[23]

Mabel clung to a vision of Taos Pueblo as "a social experiment," a beacon of light amid the postwar darkness of American civilization. "We want *as a nation* to *value* the Indian as we value ourselves. We want to *consciously* love the wholeness and harmony of Indian life, and to *consciously* protect it." For all her enthusiasm, however, her impulses were profoundly regressive. As she explained to Mary Austin, she wanted to discover "whether their old agricultural system and their other culture cannot be preserved and enlivened ... instead of being fouled as it is by substituted American symbols." Pueblo Indians, she insisted, should be encouraged "to *be* what they have been for so long—real farmers—with a farmer's poetic vision of the land." Imagining a wondrous future, she found her inspiration in the harmony she imputed to a bygone and romanticized agrarian past.[24]

For a time, the spirit of Taos was infectious. *The New York Times* praised the pueblo in 1925 as "the garden of Allah in the New World; an oasis of twentieth-century culture in a vast desert of primitive nature." More than anyone, Mabel Dodge Luhan immersed herself in that culture, molding her new life of liberation within its confines. In her own Eden, her biographer suggests, "the interracial partnership of a restored Adam and Eve" would offer a model of harmony and love to the world. Yet Mabel never could escape her privileged life or her tortured self, to say nothing of the personal and cultural contradictions that blocked her quest for self-fulfillment. Among the cohort of liberated intellectual women of the postwar era to which she belonged, as historian Christopher Lasch wrote perceptively, "The determination to be a 'true woman' forced one in effect to lead a man's life." Yet Mabel never quite reached that point. Her unrelenting dependence upon men to rescue her from herself invariably forced her back on the traditional female roles for which she had been prepared at an early age. In Taos, she remained the ever-genial hostess she had always been who, as Lasch observes, "collected people and arranged them like flowers." Not even in the Southwest of her imagination, nor in the Taos of her Edenic yearning, could she find freedom from the gendered constraints imposed by her Victorian girlhood.[25]

Mabel made enemies along the way. Her relations with Austin and O'Keeffe, infused with jealous rivalries, became strained; she embittered the Lawrences; writer Jean Toomer complained about the "female fascism" of Taos, where "strong resourceful women" were claiming what had once been "man's country." Near the end of her life, Mabel was disparaged by some younger Indians of Taos Pueblo, who envied her affluence and the comforts it provided, and rejected her nostalgic vision of a lost utopia, invariably at their expense. They, too, wanted a grand house with plumbing, electricity, a gas stove, a car, and the opportunities for travel that she enjoyed. As euphorically as Mabel might praise the tribal community, and profess her yearning to belong to it, she always remained a privileged American woman living out the contradictions of her thoroughly American dream of escape and renewal. Despite her proudest boast, she was never able to leave "the white people's world."[26]

Mabel Dodge Luhan finally wearied of her own excessive romanticizing of pueblo life. Taos, she complained in her later years, had become just another American community where "business comes before anything else." No longer was it "a haven that is peaceful and serene"; rather, it symbolized "business, busyness, a lot of activity ending in nothing." Like other redoubts of literary and artistic escapism from postwar Babbitry, Taos could not sustain the weight of expectations that rebels against American society placed upon it. These disaffected Americans, fleeing to the pueblos "to regain a lost sense of community and social intimacy," rarely could elude their own culture—or escape from themselves.[27]

～

One of Mabel Dodge Luhan's favorite guests in Taos, as he had been in her Greenwich Village salon, was John Collier, a former social worker on the Lower East Side of Manhattan. She hoped to interest Collier "in the problem of the pueblo and perhaps saving the Taos Indians from going the way all other tribes have gone." Frustrated with the failure of his Progressive reform efforts, Collier despaired of postwar America. In 1920, he visited Taos, where he was instantly overwhelmed by the intensity and passion of the experience. There he finally found "the genuine community of art, individual, and spirit" for which he had long searched.

Collier, born into a wealthy and prominent Atlanta family in 1884, saw himself at an early age as "a renegade from his caste." Both his grandfathers had been slave owners, who were decorated for driving the Cherokee Indians from Georgia. Following the premature death of his parents, his father's by suicide after a family financial scandal, young Collier vowed to reject the materialism that he blamed for their deaths. He meandered through an assortment of schools; after graduating from Columbia he remained in New York, where immigrant neighborhoods served as his laboratory for applying principles of utopian socialism to modern industrial society, which in its present form, he believed, would hasten "the world's doom." Collier worked for the People's Institute, one of a myriad of municipal institutions created by Progressive reformers to ameliorate the harshness of urban life by restoring a sense of community among uprooted immigrant newcomers. Responsible for its recreational and cultural programs, Collier focused on factory safety and motion-picture censorship, while organizing classes in "citizenship, ethics, social good will, play and aesthetics." His investigations into the lives of slum children framed a book, published in 1913, wryly entitled *The City Where Crime is Play*.[28]

Collier's intellectual stimulation came from the thinkers and dreamers he encountered in Mabel Dodge's salon, where journalist Hutchins Hapgood had provided him with an introduction. (Collier was "full of a reformer's enthusiasm for humanity," Mabel observed.) But burned out by his work, and his own intensity, he abruptly resigned from the People's Institute, moving with his family to North Carolina for spiritual solace. There he recuperated, writing articles about theatre for *Survey Graphic*, until he felt sufficiently renewed to return a year later to establish a training school for community workers. Collier often repeated this pattern of regeneration through withdrawal, periodically escaping from the pressures of his life by venturing into the wilderness for solitude and reflection. Yearning to find, or build, "local communities which are moved by shared purpose," he finally left New York for California in 1919, convinced that "all primitive and ancient cultures were doomed to be swallowed up by the white world."[29]

In California, Collier worked for the Housing and Immigration Commission, teaching an odd assortment of classes on the Russian revolution, St. Francis of Assisi, and Havelock Ellis's theory of sexuality. As the director of community organization, he developed adult education programs to instill principles of citizenship among new immigrants through their participation in community activities. But Collier's laments persisted. "Our Western world way of life"—which he defined as "life lived solitarily by individuals who are divorced from communion with one another toward ends greater than any of them, as individuals"—had become overbearing and destructive.

The "shattering, aggressive drive toward competitive utility" ruled the world that Collier inhabited and he despaired of changing it. In 1920, he again fled with his family from civilization to the wilderness, this time intending to find refuge in the Sonora Mountains of Mexico. "I knew that the Old World was finished," he wrote. In a society that was comprised of "self-seeking individuals" committed to the "traffic and acquisition of goods," human personality was "base, calculating, and shallow." Collier advocated "economic and social revolutions" to shake the United States and Europe "to their foundations" (a wish, when publicly expressed, that placed him under surveillance by the Department of Justice). He yearned for the type of "face-to-face, primary social groups" that could only be found in "village communities."[30]

On his way to Mexico to chase his dream, Collier received a letter from Mabel Dodge inviting him to Taos, where he had the transformative experience of his life. Already predisposed from his wilderness sojourns to intense spiritual visions, he discovered in Taos a "Red Atlantis," an ancient civilization harboring secrets of a communal, cooperative way of life that were desperately needed by modern Western society. There he found an inspirational model for American redemption, "a new direction in life—a new, even wildly new, hope for the Race of Man." Writing about his experience, Collier exulted: "Here, at Taos, a whole race of men, before my eyes, passed into ecstasy through a willed discipline, splendid and fierce" that he imagined was "near to the first day of creation." In Pueblo ritual, he found "tranquil, yet earth-shaking intensity," which persuaded him that these Indians possessed "the fundamental secret of human life." Remaining in Taos for five months, he discovered the communal structure that he had tried to build as a social worker in New York. Here was the "human perfection" he had been seeking, "matured outside of our modern civilization."[31]

Collier was enraptured with Taos. "At twilight when the men come riding through the fields, they are singing. They are irresistible creatures." There was "no harshness or quarreling anywhere . . . the adolescent boys and girls are the most earnest and most sweet. . . . None so young . . . and none so aged . . . that he has not a communal function." Among Indians, whose cause Collier passionately espoused for the next quarter-century, he found answers to all the social problems he had confronted as a social reformer: "the uprooting of populations, the disintegration of neighborhoods, the end of home and handicrafts, the supremacy of the machine over man." The "communal spirit" of the Pueblo Indians, he wrote, "made them living exemplars of all that was lacking in modern society."[32]

Although Collier returned to California to teach at San Francisco State Teachers College, he was inexorably drawn back to the Pueblo Indian cause. Charles F. Lummis introduced him to local Indian rights advocates, and Collier worked with them to oppose federal government efforts to seize pueblo land. His "*greatest* hope," he wrote in 1922, was "to keep alive the

Pueblo civilization with its cultural elements and its romantic point of view. To make possible for these archaic communities to live on, and to modernize themselves economically (on a cooperative, communal basis) while yet going forward with their spiritual life." A year later, he founded the American Indian Defense Organization and became its active lobbyist in Washington. Eventually, his work catapulted him to an appointment as Franklin D. Roosevelt's Commissioner of Indian Affairs, where he presided over a "new deal" of tribal autonomy and rights for Native American peoples. Remaining at his post throughout the Roosevelt presidency, Collier never lost his belief, sparked by his first visit to Taos, that "it is the ancient tribal, village, communal organization which must conquer the modern world."[33]

Collier's biting critique of the fragmentation of modern society set him on the trail to the pueblos blazed before him by Cushing and Lummis. For each of these men, Pueblo Indians offered an escape from "the materialism, the secularism, and the fragmentation of modern white life under industrialism"—and from the private torments of their own lives. In his later years, Collier still excoriated the United States for "its hostility to human diversity, its fanatical devotion to downgrading standardization, its exploitative myopia," and its "all-haunting insecurity and the consequent lust for personal advantage."[34]

The pueblos, by contrast, exemplified an alternative social vision: "the relationship of humans with one another, with the supernatural, and with land and nature." Here was everything that utopian communitarians yearned for. "Only the Indians," Collier wrote in his memoir, possessed "the secret of building great personality through the instrumentality of social institutions."[35]

Yet Collier, much like Mabel Dodge who opened his eyes to the new possibilities of Taos, distorted the pueblos virtually beyond recognition in his desperation to find an alternative to modernity. Their "romantic inflation of pueblo culture," as historian Richard H. Frost suggests, concealed the underlying theocratic rigidity, social conservatism, and internal conflict that was rampant within the pueblos. Their dreamy images of Pueblo Indians revealed less about the natives than about their own despair with American culture. Collier, as his son observed, was "vehemently opposed to civilized modernity . . . He saw modernity as a disaster that was defeating man's perfectibility. He saw the Indian as the last remnant of natural perfection, a model that must be preserved for human rejuvenation." Collier's "zeal" to preserve Indian culture became the dominant impulse of his postwar professional career. His salvation efforts, like Curtis's photographs and Cushing's fieldwork, were a desperate effort to save the ever-dying native peoples of North America. Among them, Collier discovered possibilities for national and personal redemption.[36]

Collier never lost his pessimism about American culture. Speaking in 1934, he declared that "We—I mean our white world in this century—are a shattered race—psychically, religiously, socially, esthetically shattered, dismembered, directionless." He believed that Indian communities, by contrast, expressed "a great age of integrated, inwardly-seeking life and art" that might yet inspire American society. But it was a forlorn hope. Indeed, Collier's utopian fantasies about the Pueblo Indians struck D. H. Lawrence as deeply harmful to the very people whose cause he so passionately espoused. "He will destroy them," Lawrence told Mabel Dodge. "It is his Saviour's will to set the claws of his own white egoistic *benevolent* volition into them."[37] It was a harsh verdict, from a skeptic with little patience for Collier's reforming zeal. Yet Collier, virtually alone among all the disaffected artists and intellectuals who were summoned to Taos by Mabel Dodge to save the world, kept the faith, fighting for Indian rights until the end of his life.

~

Mabel Dodge and John Collier were hardly alone in their flight to the pueblos to escape public discontents and private torments. In their postwar struggle to become New Women, Elsie Clews Parsons proclaimed, avant-garde feminists found in the Southwest a "land of women's rights." ("Only through my association with Pueblo Indians," Parsons wrote, "has it occurred to me to be a feminist.") Pueblos, once places of female degradation that required the efforts of "white civilized womanhood" to uplift their inhabitants, were recast as a feminist utopia based on gender equality and, in the imaginings of some, female supremacy.[38]

This reinvention of Pueblo culture expressed the embrace of primitivism that suffused American intellectual circles after World War I demolished faith in Western civilization. In Vachel Lindsay's poetry, Margaret Mead's anthropology, and Harlem jazz, primitive purity was exalted over the tawdry corruption of modernity. As women—privileged women especially—waged their own struggle for freedom from the constraints of domesticity and gender inequality, they rejected the sexist society that stifled them. Often they projected their yearning for empowerment upon Pueblo Indian women—or, at least, Pueblo women as they imagined them. Mabel Dodge was not the only modern woman yearning to be free who embraced "a people that were not implicated in the disaster of war and a place unmarred by the industrialization that blighted the Northeast"—and to discover a feminist utopia there.[39]

While Mabel Dodge was forging her flamboyant synthesis of culture, politics, and self, Elsie Clews Parsons was living out her own rebellion against the confining gender constraints of her Victorian girlhood. With her scripted future as a debutante and society matron looming, she had broken with family conventions to enter Barnard College as a sixteen-year-old in 1892. She remained at Columbia to earn a Ph.D. in sociology, a new discipline that offered valuable intellectual weapons in her struggle for personal freedom. A member of the Barnard College faculty, she married Herbert Parsons, a prominent New York lawyer and Republican politician with impressive patrician credentials of his own.[40]

As a professional woman, wife, and, in time, mother (of five children), Elsie Clews Parsons was eminently qualified to experience the gendered tensions and contradictions inherent in the complex life she had chosen for herself. In a photograph taken just after the turn of the century, with her baby daughter seated on her lap, she appears elegantly maternal, already matronly in her mid-twenties (fig. 14). With her hair fashionably coiffed, her dress trimmed with lace, her collar high, and her choker necklace snug, she was the very model of a refined young Victorian mother. But Herbert's election to Congress in 1905, which assured long and frequent absences in Washington, gave them both a new measure of freedom, which they eagerly seized. While Herbert busied himself as a legislator and, in his spare time, as a womanizer, Elsie combined teaching with work for the College Settlements Association, comprising young social workers eager to apply their professional expertise to the amelioration of urban problems. With her pioneering studies of the tribal attributes of tenement families, Parsons rapidly gained a reputation as an ethnographer with a strong social conscience.[41]

With publication of *The Family* in 1906, Parsons left her distinctive imprint on Progressive feminism. Already active in Margaret Sanger's birth-control movement, and strongly committed to women's suffrage, she now offered sweeping radical suggestions for women—such as sexual freedom and professional careers—that sharply challenged gendered conventions. Her most radical proposal, trial marriage, immediately became a public scandal. Advocating "toleration of freedom of sexual intercourse on the part of the unmarried of both sexes before marriage," she was publicly excoriated by

FIG. 14. "Elsie Clews Parsons and Lissa, 1902."
American Philosophical Society, with permission of Fanny P. Culleton.

prominent ministers for her "abominable suggestion," which was dismissed as a "disgusting theory" that would appeal primarily to "seditious communists and the murderous Anarchist."[42]

In 1910, Elsie and Herbert confronted a crisis in their work and marriage. After several terms in Congress, he was defeated for reelection, abruptly ending his political career. Within a year, she lost a newborn infant and then had a pregnancy terminated. With their marriage floundering, they traveled to the Southwest in search of rejuvenation. While he visited the Grand Canyon, she went to New Mexico, where, on horseback, she discovered ancient ruins near San Ildefonso Pueblo. "As I examined the wall niches and hearths, the lintels and passages I tried to reconstruct the past. . . . Presently I was beset by that infantile impulse to dig which sublimated a bit . . . turns people into archeologists."[43]

Exhilarated by her visit, Parsons began to study the Southwest more seriously, using Herbert's extensive contacts to gain access to Indian experts at the American Bureau of Ethnology and to museum collections in Washington, New York, and Chicago. Returning to New Mexico two years later, she arrived with a packet of introductions from Pliny Earle Goddard, one of the "Indian men" at the American Museum of Natural History. Traveling more than two hundred miles on horseback to observe Apache dances, she was delighted by her encounters with Pueblo Indians "with pottery and fruit to peddle." With her interest in the pueblos perked, she visited Acoma in 1913 and Zuni two years later. She lived in the governor's house (as Cushing had done before her), the welcoming center for an increasing number of aspiring fieldworkers. "In Zuni," she wrote to Herbert with eager anticipation, "I shall have a great opportunity for brief periods of fieldwork, the thing I've been hankering for years."[44]

While cultivating her new interests in the Southwest, Parsons enjoyed national stature as a feminist critic. As a member of Heterodoxy, comprising several dozen radical women who gathered for bimonthly lunches in Greenwich Village, she mixed with other avant-garde feminist luminaries— Charlotte Perkins Gilman, Elizabeth Gurley Flynn, and Crystal Eastman among them—who rejected the inhibitions they had inherited from their Victorian mothers. A participant in Mabel Dodge's salon, she was a prolific author, contributing widely to radical and liberal publications and to an array of scholarly journals.

Parsons's biting critique of constraints on women broadened into an indictment of social systems, whether primitive or modern, that sustained gender hierarchies. With a staff of housekeepers and nurses to attend to her children (and assure her freedom), she carved out her new life as an outspoken feminist within the very gendered constraints and social contradictions that her writing explored. *The Old-Fashioned Woman*, published in 1913, which by her own assessment was "propaganda by the ethnographic method," condemned an array of cross-cultural taboos on women. Her alertness to the power of culture to mold individuals pervaded her work, which included five books published within three years that explored the controls imposed on women by family, marriage, social etiquette, and religion.[45]

For Parsons (as for Collier), settlement-house work and Lower East Side tenement culture ultimately proved too constricting, even as her experiences there sharpened her radical critique of American society. Determined to pursue tolerance, diversity, and equality to their furthest limits, she increasingly relied upon feminism as the vehicle of her escape from "the prison house of categorization" to become "a truly new woman who was . . . unclassifiable." And, as she had discovered on her first trip to the Southwest, anthropological fieldwork offered women unrivaled possibilities for intellectual freedom, cultural criticism, and personal autonomy.

Yet paradoxically, Parsons (much like Mabel Dodge) found it necessary to depend upon men to encourage and sustain her own liberation. She developed a lifelong friendship with Professor Franz Boas of Columbia, whose experiences as a Jew in Germany, and then as an immigrant in the United States, had refined his own sensibilities as an intellectual outsider and cultural relativist. Boas's attentive mentoring of her work, and her generous financial support of his graduate program, solidified their working partnership. The creative collaboration of a rebellious American patrician and a German Jewish immigrant transformed anthropology into the academic discipline that would exceed all others in its welcoming receptivity to women.[46]

Parsons also turned to Pliny Earle Goddard of the Museum of Natural History, who actively supported her fieldwork in the Southwest and introduced her to Alfred Kroeber, whose Zuni research became a major source of inspiration. Her relations with Goddard and Kroeber were close and complex. Their correspondence, at times, was exceedingly intimate. In Herbert's absence, she welcomed them to her summer home in the Berkshires, where they avidly competed for her attention and favor. In 1917, to Goddard's intense displeasure, she and Kroeber went off to Zuni together.[47]

Kroeber was an especially important intellectual influence on Parsons and, by extension, the young women she sent to study with Boas. Based on his fieldwork in Zuni, Kroeber had concluded that "the foundation of Zuni society is the family. . . . Life centers around the house." And the house, he learned, "belongs to the woman born of the family." Generations came and went, he wrote, with "the slow stream of mothers and daughters forming a current that carried with it husbands, sons, and grandsons." Home owner-ship determined "the Zuni woman's position in the world." Her "obvious preeminence" was exemplified when she "receives her husband into her and her mother's home," which, along with her sisters and female ancestors, she owned. This, for Kroeber, defined the Zuni "matriarchate"—even though, as he also discovered, women had absolutely "no voice" in Zuni governance, nor could they serve as priests and thereby participate in the religious ceremo-nial life that profoundly molded Zuni culture. The social fabric of Zuni life, he concluded, was "thoroughly un-American"—and, therefore, irresistibly appealing to critics of American society.[48]

More than anyone, however, it was Boas who attracted Parsons to the discipline of anthropology, supported her work, and encouraged her nurtur-ing of his female students. Parsons was drawn to Boas and to the academic discipline of anthropology that was so formatively molded by his scholar-ship and cultural criticism. As her marriage continued to deteriorate, she drew increasing intellectual—and emotional—sustenance from their rela-tionship. In turn, she generously provided his Columbia graduate students with home-cooked meals, box seats at the opera, and the financial support they desperately needed. If her work as a sociologist had made her attentive to conventional American family patterns, Parsons created an alternative ver-sion of family life in her deepening relationships with Boas and his students. "Together," writes one of her biographers, Parsons and Boas formed "a pow-erful blend of intellect, dedication, and energy." Through him, she gained entrée to the social and intellectual circle of elite male scholars who would sustain her newly independent life as a professional woman.[49]

Like other disillusioned intellectuals of the postwar era, Parsons despaired over the possibilities of social reform. When her militant pacifism adversely affected her relationships with editors at *The New Republic*, she re-channeled her energy to the New School of Social Research, which she helped to estab-lish as a refuge for intellectual criticism and scholarly dissent. After teaching there for a year, she decided to leave contemporary America, including the women's movement, behind. "The world would not change," observes biographer Rosemary Levy Zumwalt, "so she turned her back on it and followed her own paths." From the "sociological feminism" of her prewar years, she moved toward the "more private feminism" that anthropology encouraged. As Parsons wrote, "It may seem a queer taste, but Negroes and Indians for me. The rest of the world grows duller and duller."[50]

Parsons was prepared to abandon her life in New York, she told her husband, for cultures that rejected the pervasive xenophobia, racism, sexism, and anti-Semitism of postwar America. The Southwest offered an escape from "the Americanizing hysteria" unleashed by war, stoked by the Bolshevik revolution, and reinforced by postwar repression and conformity. Accompanying Boas to Laguna, Cochiti, and Jemez, she plunged eagerly into fieldwork, enthusiastically embracing Pueblo culture as a lost, but recoverable, paradise.[51]

Not only did the pueblos offer Parsons an inspiring matriarchal model; they also represented a blending of cultures that she found especially appealing. She described mainstream American society as "encroaching," highly "intolerant of social dissimilarity." Pueblo culture, she realized, was molded by Spanish, Mexican, and Native traditions. Its "tangle and fusion of cultures" intrigued her. By absorbing foreign mores, and integrating Catholicism into their own religious heritage, Zunis demonstrated to Parsons that "the Pueblo Indian is unsurpassable as a pourer of new wine into old bottles!" She overlooked the harsher historical reality: the repressive Spanish conquest had afforded Pueblo Indians little choice but to accommodate their religious tradition to the demands of their powerful new rulers. Under Spanish rule, native religious ritual had been pushed underground into the kivas, where it flourished under strict male control, and was publicly expressed in the male ceremonial dances that attracted tourists—and anthropologists—in droves.[52]

"A new scene," Parsons acknowledged, "is an incredible help in distress of the spirit." Her work in the pueblos offered an antidote to her postwar political despair. She embraced the Southwest when her marriage was disintegrating, and she recommended it to others (including Boas, after the death of his wife) as solace for their personal suffering. As the channels of political reform and social action narrowed in mainstream society, the pueblos offered an escape from disillusionment and helplessness. Yet Parsons's attachment to the Pueblo Indians was based upon contradictions that she understood but could never untangle. She had become dedicated, after all, to uncompromisingly traditional native peoples, whose lives were deeply grooved by seasonal rhythms and religious ritual, which—along with rigid gender divisions—had endured, largely unchanged, for centuries. As Parsons candidly acknowledged, "she could accept among the Pueblo Indians what she could not accept in her own society."[53]

As a newcomer and outsider, Parsons—like Matilda Stevenson before her—stumbled obliviously over local customs, generating conflict among the very people whose harmonious relations she found so appealing. Her studies in Jemez and Taos caused problems for tribal members who were accused of providing her with privileged information. As much as she might wish not "to hurt their feelings or disturb them in any way," her reliance upon informants stoked mistrust that generated internal conflict and made the pueblos less hospitable to outsiders. As an independently wealthy Anglo woman, Parsons, like Mabel Dodge, easily afforded comforts that local people could hardly imagine. Greenwich Village renegades, they lived luxuriously in their self-chosen Southwestern exile. For several seasons of fieldwork, Parsons located herself on a dude ranch near San Juan Pueblo, before buying her own ranch near Santa Clara. By the end of the postwar decade, tiring of the Southwest, she turned her attention south to Mexico, which had gained favor among disaffected intellectuals as the newest model "for integrating indigenous populations without destroying their cultures."[54]

At a time when marital unhappiness and political frustration converged, Parsons—again like Luhan—reinvented herself in the Southwest as a liberated woman. Her prodigious Southwestern scholarship, especially noteworthy for someone without professional training, continues to inspire a new generation of feminist scholars. She wrote nearly one hundred articles, and her two-volume *Pueblo Indian Religion*, published in 1939 shortly before her death, was greeted with professional enthusiasm and respect. That it was also a transparent critique of American society for its stifling conformity was hardly surprising. Parsons had long been a vigorous, outspoken critic of the American cultural mainstream; her work in the Southwest, like Luhan's, whose multi-volume memoir retains its inspirational appeal to contemporary feminists, was driven by her animus against the very society that privileged her.[55]

Precisely that contradiction targeted Parsons, like Luhan, for sharp barbs from (male) critics. The acerbic Edmund Wilson, visiting Santa Fe and Taos a few years after Lawrence offered his own biting observations, discovered an "extraordinary population of rich people, writers and artists who pose as Indians, cowboys, prospectors, desperadoes, Mexicans, and other extinct species." Dressing "native," as it had been for Cushing nearly half a century earlier, was a costume change that proclaimed freedom by replacing one set of conventions with another.[56]

Yet the Southwest offered opportunities for a rising generation of female anthropologists that could not be found in any other academic discipline. Parsons came too late to the discipline to be more than a talented amateur, but she nonetheless became the recognized and respected female mentor to Boas's young protégés, the first generational cohort of women trained as professional anthropologists. For all of them, anthropological work was inseparable from their new freedom as women. By working openly in the field

FIG. 15. "Elsie Clews Parsons in the Southwest, c. 1915."
With permission of Fanny P. Culleton.

with Boas and Kroeber, Parsons assertively challenged conventional stereo-types of gendered propriety. Inadvertently, however, she may also have rein-forced them. Pliny Goddard's attachment to Gladys Reichard, another Boas student, and Ruth Benedict's deepening intimate relationship with Margaret Mead, triggered Kroeber's observation that travel grants to aspiring female anthropologists were "helping to liberate" the young women who belonged to Boas's "little harem."[57]

Parsons experienced a burst of personal freedom in the pueblos. There the once prim and proper Victorian mother became a liberated woman. Photographed in 1915, she stood alone on a rock, silhouetted against the harsh New Mexican landscape, wearing a flowing dress and shawl; her hair was long and loose, tied with a bandanna; her saddle shoes were fashionable among the young (fig. 15). Rejecting her Victorian past, she felt free to become a new woman. Here was the way, Desley Deacon writes, for her "to 'kill' nineteenth-century ideas of classification and hierarchy, and to establish new twenti-eth-century standards of sexual plasticity and cultural tolerance." Yet even as she forged anthropology into "a weapon," the better, historian Rosalind Rosenberg suggests, "to retaliate against the society that had tried to tie her down," she still depended upon her established male elders for professional opportunities.[58]

Parsons's "feminist sensibility" has inspired a new wave of academic women to celebrate her as "a forerunner" of contemporary feminism, who "fearlessly rejected all conventions that constrained the free development of personality." Like the younger anthropologists she mentored, Parsons has been praised for displaying "a preoccupation with other cultures, other differ-ences and inequalities, and an advocacy of cultural relativism"—all of which, to be sure, simultaneously served the feminist cause. Yet Parsons, paradoxi-cally, discovered freedom within a culture that demanded even more con-formity to gender norms than the one she fled. Quite correctly insisting that female anthropologists would enjoy unrivaled opportunity in the pueblos to observe what men could not, she directed them to the most traditionally female subject of all, the lives of women and children. Parsons searched for a way out of the gendered dilemmas of modernity in the pueblos. Images of the Garden of Eden might yield to visions of a feminist paradise, but the old contradictions inherent in the flight from modernity remained, for women no less than for men.[59]

CHAPTER FIVE

Papa Franz's Family

F or Franz Boas, cultural relativism became a scholarly truth that assuaged his discomfort as a Jew. Born in 1858, Boas was the child of lapsed Orthodox parents who, he subsequently wrote, "had broken through the shackles of dogma." Although his father, Boas recalled, "retained an emotional affection for the ceremonial of his parental home," he had not permitted it "to influence his intellectual freedom." This proved to be a blessing to Franz, who appreciated being "spared the struggle against religious dogma that besets the lives of so many young people." Yet nothing had greater impact upon his work as an anthropologist than his struggle with the consequences of his Jewish identity. His egalitarian commitments, manifested as cultural relativism, expressed his deepest yearning as an assimilated German Jew.[1]

Even for enlightened Jews at the end of the nineteenth century, opportunities in German universities were tightly restricted. Academic life was infested with anti-Semitism, and Boas felt its sting. Indeed, his father advised him not even to try to "improve the position of the Jews through your personal intervention." As a young man, Boas yearned to be free from Jewish constraints, even as he struggled to belong somewhere. Leaving Europe for the first time in 1882, he participated in a geographical survey expedition to Alaska. There he encountered a "primitive" people who taught him how civilized the "savages" really were. "The more I see of their customs," he concluded, the more evident it was "that we have no right to look down upon them." Indeed, he enthusiastically exclaimed, "I am now a true

Eskimo." From his Alaska encounters, Boas emerged with abiding tolerance for human diversity.[2]

Amid the national chauvinism of the Bismarck era, Germany seemed ever more menacing to Boas. Discouraged over his academic prospects, he immigrated to the United States just before his thirtieth birthday to accept an editorial position with a scientific journal. He would, he wrote, "give up traditions and follow the path to truth." As an immigrant Jew, however, Boas never entirely left behind his formative years in Germany, or the painful anti-Semitism that he experienced there. They remained as much a part of him, if less vividly displayed, as the dueling scars on his face. His pursuit of truth invariably returned him to the enlightened precepts of nineteenth-century European liberalism that were forged in the revolutionary struggles of 1848: liberty, reason, and tolerance. They guided his passionate commitment to individual freedom, multiracial democracy, and cultural relativism, and his "identification with all humanity and devotion to its progress."[3]

Yet his intellectual commitments may have been less the product of dis-interested scientific inquiry, as Boas preferred to claim, than a deeply per-sonal conviction forged in his encounters with anti-Semitism. His passionate embrace of Enlightenment ideals was attributable to, and inseparable from, his experiences as a German Jew. With rejection of Judaism the most con-spicuous component of his Jewish identity, cultural relativism—the rejec-tion of evolutionary determinism—became his most salient intellectual trait. His critique of racism and race theory, like his unwavering emphasis on the common humanity of all people, was an implicit rebuke to the torments of anti-Semitism that he had endured as a young man.

In his adopted country, Boas was alerted to the "vanishing" Indian tribes that had been decimated by Westward expansion. "It is only a question of a few years," he wrote, "when everything reminding us of America as it was at the time of its discovery will have perished." Only by intensive study of these tribes, he insisted, could future generations satisfy their "urgent desire to know the beginnings of the history of our country." It had not taken long for the United States to become "our country," nor for Boas, for whom tra-dition was otherwise highly suspect, to revere American national origins in the pre-history of its native peoples.[4]

After brief stints at Clark University, the Field Museum of Natural History in Chicago, and the American Museum of Natural History, Boas received an appointment at Columbia, where he became professor of anthropology in

1899. Throughout his long and distinguished career, he would find justification for the academic discipline of anthropology in his own experience as a German Jewish immigrant. To escape the ghetto walls of tradition, culture must be variable and identity contingent. With cultural malleability as his theoretical alternative to racial determinism, Boas set anthropology on a new disciplinary course. "My whole outlook," he conceded in 1938, near the end of his life, "is determined by the question: how can we recognize the shackles that tradition has laid upon us." With his abiding appreciation for "the contingent position of Western civilization and values," relativism became his preferred "methodological tool to foster scientific objectivity."[5]

By the turn of the century, anthropology and Native Americans were inextricably intertwined. Boas's appointment at Columbia initiated graduate training in anthropology in the United States and signified a profound disciplinary shift. Now, for the first time, university departments of anthropology would claim the disciplinary primacy that until then had been monopolized by the Bureau of American Ethnology in Washington and museums in Cambridge, Chicago, and New York. With this transition, the older evolutionary approach that justified the elevation of Americans (and, implicitly, white Anglo-Saxon Protestant Americans) to the top rung of the evolutionary ladder yielded to the precepts of university-trained cultural relativists. Led by Boas, they demanded democratic access and meritocratic progress—thereby justifying their own professional ascendancy. Speaking at the Louisiana Purchase Exposition in 1904, Boas insisted upon "the relative value of all forms of culture" and invited "the teachings of other cultures." In *The Mind of Primitive Man*, published a decade later, he emphasized difference, not inferiority, undercutting the evolutionary props that sustained racism and replacing them with a plea for variety and tolerance. As always, his cosmopolitan relativism was inextricably linked to the sources and consequences of his Jewish marginality.[6]

Once Boas blended his own personal, professional, and intellectual attributes into academic theory, his "egalitarian critique" of racism was sweeping. His theory not only demanded tolerance for cultural differences; it implicitly justified new opportunities for professional outsiders (Jews and women conspicuous among them). As the sons of immigrants and daughters of privilege were drawn to anthropology, to Columbia, and to Boas, they refined the tools of intellectual analysis that encouraged appreciation of "savage" peoples for their cultural distinctiveness. Dogma gave way to contingency and indeterminacy—until, in time, the dogma of relativism became as deeply entrenched in the professional culture as the dogma of hierarchy had been before Boas and his disciples undermined it.[7]

In 1917, after a long fallow period in his research, Boas was newly energized by his trip to Zuni with Elsie Clews Parsons (accompanied by Esther Schiff, his secretary and a future student). He gratefully told Parsons that the experience "has made me younger & reborn a good deal of my energy and enterprise, and for that I have to thank you." For Parsons, soon to become known as the "Department Angel" for funding the work of Boas and his students, the experience was equally reinvigorating. She drew strength from "his ardor in combating the scientific fallacies which bolster up social injustice." The time Boas spent in the pueblos reinforced his conviction—soon to be widely popularized by his student Margaret Mead based upon her fieldwork in Samoa—that "fundamental individual reactions depend upon cultural setting more than upon hereditary or innate characteristics." Cultural relativism was the defining article of faith that Boas transmitted to his disciples. Not only did it challenge venerable scientific certitudes about evolutionary superiority; it implicitly undermined such exclusionary policies as anti-Semitism and sexism.[8]

The emergence of "Papa Franz" and his "daughters" into a family of anthropologists, with Parsons as their benevolent maternal patron, represented the convergence of personal aspirations with broader social and intellectual trends. Before World War I, Boas had mentored only one female graduate student (among an array of men—including Alexander Goldenwieser, Robert Lowie, Alfred Kroeber, and Edward Sapir—who comprised the emerging professional elite). But as men became scarce in academic programs during the war years, the number of female students increased. Boas's academic theory inspired a cohort of intellectually gifted young women, whose coming of age after World War I marked a formative moment in their lives, in the evolution of modern feminism, and in the historical development of anthropology. By 1920, Boas observed, "All my best students are women."[9]

The war had a powerful impact on Boas, both personally and professionally. Like other German-Americans who were caught between their countries of origin and adoption, he resolved his acute loyalty dilemma by becoming a pacifist. In retaliation, Columbia president Nicholas Murray Butler dispatched him across Broadway into academic exile at Barnard. There he discovered a coterie of intellectually gifted young women who became his devoted students. As women, they were professional outsiders who confronted severely restricted academic opportunities. But anthropology proved to be the exception, gaining a well-deserved reputation as a liberating and welcoming discipline. Boas—although formal, aloof, and rigorous—was an inspirational mentor. Like a stern but doting Victorian father, he insistently dispatched his female students to the Southwest because he feared for their safety elsewhere. In the pueblos, they could discover intellectual and gendered freedom.

Boas and Parsons were ideal mentors who functioned, simultaneously, as surrogate parents. His female students appreciated Boas for his genuine respect for them as women, his affirmation of their intellectual abilities, and his patronage in a tightly restricted academic market. As Ruth Bunzel said, Boas "never felt women have to do only women's things." Even his "ambiguous benevolence"—he encouraged the entry of single women into the profession but favored men and was inclined to bypass married women—was more than they could hope to find elsewhere. It was hardly coincidental that several of Boas's academic "daughters" (and most of his outstanding prewar "sons") were Jews. Like their mentor they, too, had left the constraints of Judaism behind for personal freedom, cultural assimilation, and professional opportunity.[10]

Parsons offered a different kind of inspiration and nurturing: financial generosity aside, she was an avowed feminist whose inner freedom, and strong will, empowered her to break down gender taboos. She could hardly have been a better role model for the young female students who entered the Columbia anthropology program. Once she and Boas traveled to the Southwest together to do fieldwork, the boundaries of possibility for women—for personal fulfillment no less than professional achievement—significantly expanded. This new freedom was sufficiently conspicuous to prompt Kroeber's testy complaint to Parsons that if anthropology became "a feminine science," he would change academic fields.

Boas's mentoring coincided with ratification of the nineteenth Amendment, which empowered women whose right to vote culminated nearly a century of struggle. His hostility to "the irrational authority of tradition" implicitly supported their broader struggle for freedom from gendered constraints. It is hardly surprising that aspiring female anthropologists would discover in Southwestern Pueblo culture a uniquely benevolent environment for their own personal liberation. For "father" and "daughters" alike, personal aspirations could be sublimated in professional and scholarly quests.

As anthropologist George W. Stocking Jr. has astutely observed, Boas's scientific work "was not only self-justifying, but to a very great degree self-centered." That was no less true for the female students who belonged to his professional "family." Boasian anthropology, with its emphasis on cultural construction, offered a vital intellectual source of self-validation as female graduate students matured into professional women.[11]

Among them, the most idiosyncratic, tormented, self-revealing, yet ultimately influential scholar surely was Ruth Fulton Benedict, whose *Patterns of Culture*, published in 1934, became one of the seminal anthropological texts of the twentieth century. "The story of my life," she wrote soon after its publication, "begins when I was twenty-one months old, at the time my father died [1888]." Her mother, "in an hysteria of weeping," insisted that the young girl view her father's body, while she "implored me to remember" the moment forever. With only that memory to sustain—and torment—her for the remainder of her life, "I identified him with everything calm and beautiful that came my way." Her childhood, she recalled, was scarred by the virtual absence of "warm human relationships." Nobody "really got past my physical and emotional aloofness." With the added burden of a hearing impairment, she lived in an enclosed world of her own, "inhabited by alien people." Viewing herself as "isolated and odd," she was virtually friendless until, as a student at St. Margaret's School in Buffalo, she met Mabel Ganson, "the first person I ever saw who, I knew, belonged somewhere else than in the world I stood so aloof from."[12]

Ruth Fulton attended Vassar, her mother's alma mater, as a scholarship student. After graduation and a year of travel abroad, she returned to Buffalo to do volunteer charity work before moving to California to live with her married sister and teach in a girl's school in Pasadena. It was an especially unhappy time in her life. "So much of the trouble," she wrote in her diary, "is because I am a woman. To me it seems a very terrible thing to be a woman. There is one crown which perhaps is worth it all—a great love, a quiet home, and children." In her mid-twenties, she agonized over her gendered fate: "It is all so cruelly wasteful. There are so few ways in which we can compete with men. . . . If we are not to have the chance to fulfill our one potentiality—the power of loving—why were we not born men?"[13]

Two years later, she was deeply in love with Stanley Benedict, the older brother of a Vassar classmate and, like her own father, a research doctor. But rather than resolve her gendered torment, their marriage seemed only to exacerbate it. While he was preoccupied with his biochemistry research at the Cornell Medical School, she was left to confront her female "destiny." Longing for the emotional closeness that Stanley could not provide, she conceded: "against his harshness I was powerless." Wanting children, she remained childless. Determined to find solace, and inspiration, in "the lives of restless and highly enslaved women of past generations," she began to write a biography of Mary Wollstonecraft, the pioneering women's rights activist who was "forever testing, probing." Benedict "wanted so desperately to know how other women had saved their souls alive." Just when she felt most spurned by her husband, a publisher rejected her book proposal. Depressed and despairing, she was driven to wonder, "Why must we go on hurting each other so cruelly?" She realized that "the more I control myself to [Stanley's] requirements, the greater violence I shall do to my own—kill them in the end."[14]

Struggling to break free, she enrolled in a course on "Women and the Social Order," taught by Parsons at the New School. Benedict found her to be "a kindred spirit and a courageous role model." In Parsons's class, she first learned about the matrilineal structure of society that Kroeber had explored in the pueblos. She was excited by anthropology, which offered an "outsider's view of life" that was compatible with her own sense of isolation, and a critique of social norms that she found appealing. Recommended by Parsons for graduate study with Boas, Benedict, in her mid-thirties, entered Columbia in 1921. Inspired by Boas, whose mix of scientific rigor and fervent idealism strongly evoked her father's memory, Benedict completed her doctorate in two years.[15]

Benedict's Columbia experience was formative, both intellectually and emotionally. Her continuing search for a benevolent male replacement for her devastating childhood loss found expression in her complex relationship with Boas, who became her nurturing yet authoritarian "father." Her deepening friendship with Margaret Mead, a Barnard student in her section of Boas's course, culminated in the most intimate relationship of her life. Mead, fourteen years younger than Benedict, became a favorite student, then a special friend, a surrogate daughter, and, finally, a source of love to compensate for Benedict's barren marriage. No longer was it necessary for her to find "our whole world in the love of a man."[16]

Under Boas's tutelage and with Parsons's financial beneficence, the presence of Benedict and Mead, and an expanding cohort of intellectually gifted female graduate students, gave the Columbia anthropology department its distinctive academic—and gendered—identity. In its "tiny, cramped quarters" in the Journalism building, a nuclear academic family emerged. Boas, "harried, shy, and abrupt," was unfailingly "chivalrous," if also—according to Mead—"uncompromisingly strict." He "brooked no opposition" from anyone, even as he charted the personal and professional lives of his female students. Uneasily sending them off to do fieldwork in remote places that might prove unsafe for unattached women, he worried incessantly about "their health, safety, and vulnerability"; whenever possible, he steered them to the Southwest, enticingly exotic but nonetheless securely within the continental United States.

Boas assumed that women could gain access to intimate tribal family information that was inaccessible to men; women, he believed, had interpersonal skills that men lacked. He admonished Mead, who conspicuously disregarded his advice to go to the Southwest, to be sure to protect her health and to return home from Samoa if the climate proved inhospitable. He forwarded an explicit research agenda for her to follow: study "the excessive bashfulness of girls in primitive society" and "how the young girls react to the restraints of custom." And, he added, she must scrutinize "crushes among girls." The proper sphere of study for aspiring female anthropologists, in Samoa as in the Southwest, was native women and children. Under Boas's guidance and encouragement, his female students had a new field to make their own.[17]

Within the department, Benedict, an older married woman presumably "neither needing his help nor expecting him to take responsibility for her," functioned as a respected conciliator. Her "gentle, faraway accessibility" provided a measure of stability that kept discordant personalities from disruptive clashes. A hierarchy of professional advancement emerged, with successive Barnard graduates Esther Schiff Goldfrank and Ruth Bunzel serving as department secretary while they were in training to become Boas's graduate students. Boas, Goldfrank, and Bunzel shared a "German Jewish ethos," Mead recalled, that enabled "the remote, frightening Herr Professor" to become, in Goldfrank's affectionate characterization, "'Papa Franz' to all of us." For Benedict, from the American "hinterland" (as she described Buffalo), the unfamiliar presence of so many Jews contributed to her enduring sense of being an outsider wherever she was.[18]

The tangled personal and professional relationship between Boas and Benedict expressed his paternalistic convictions and her frustrated aspirations. In an era when few women held academic positions, Boas concentrated his job-placement efforts on young, single women who could benefit from his mentoring to become self-supporting. ("If he thought we could manage," Mead wrote, "he turned with a sigh to those who needed help, guidance, and direction.") This all but excluded Benedict; Boas saw her as "a wife, amply supported and with the obligations of a wife"—although Stanley Benedict was "repelled" by the idea of a working spouse. Boas preferred to offer teaching positions at Barnard to unmarried young women, so Benedict was assigned work as Parsons's research assistant and provided with a stipend, which was insufficient to assuage her grievances. Infuriated by the "driblets of research" that came her way (Boas had suggested that she study Southwestern mythology), Benedict "wept with vexation" (she wrote in her diary) over her plight. Maintaining two residences, a rented room near Columbia and her Bedford Hills home with Stanley, she lived a divided life, torn between her thwarted maternal and marital longings and her realization, as she poignantly expressed it, that "I haven't the strength of mind not to need a career."[19]

Benedict, accompanied by graduate student Ruth Bunzel, made her first visit to Zuni in 1924. Her experiences there initiated a decade of astonishing personal growth and achievement, during which her marriage ended, her relationship with Mead deepened into intimacy, she finally received her much coveted academic appointment as assistant professor at Barnard, and *Patterns of Culture* became an instant classic of anthropological literature. With her book, Zuni Pueblo was forever enshrined as the "placid and harmonious" utopia that Benedict had pursued ever since childhood. It was the "consensus-oriented, anti-individualistic, harmony-loving alternative" to the incurable conflicts and contradictions endemic in modern Western society. Like Boas, if from thwarted female yearnings rather than Jewish exclusion, Benedict forged anthropology into "a weapon for culturally criticizing modern civilization."[20]

Benedict's independence would not have been possible without Boas. Not only did he offer extraordinary support for the professional ambitions of aspiring young Jewish women such as Goldfrank and Bunzel; women of impeccable social lineage, such as Benedict and Mead, also waged their "social, professional and personal struggle for independence" under his attentive mentoring. They each had their own intensely personal reasons for their attachment to him: Benedict was seeking to escape from marital misery and intellectual frustrations; Bunzel, as she wryly recalled, could choose between "fleeing to Paris, selling the *Daily Worker* on street corners," or becoming an anthropologist; the orphaned Goldfrank found emotional solace as a member of the Boas "family." They were drawn to Boas, embracing his rebellion against "the shackles that tradition has laid upon us" as their own. Benedict strongly urged her younger female colleagues to make use of their own backgrounds and identity dilemmas in their anthropological work, especially by focusing on marriage and the family, the social institution that had tormented her ever since childhood.[21]

Benedict faithfully followed her own prescription. Yearning for personal freedom, she grew ever more determined to reject "the values and beliefs that make up the framework of a culture"—especially her own culture. Thwarted and frustrated, still without career security, she finally "rejected the validity of Victorian claims upon her as a woman: the inflexible expectations, the narrowness of the allowed female roles, the parched sexuality." In her work as an anthropologist, no less than in the intensity of her relationship with Mead, Benedict struggled to escape the repressive confines of her culture. She yearned to find "a really important undiscovered country" to study, which in important respects turned out to be her own interior self.

Benedict's quest for autonomy brought her to Zuni, which, by the 1920s, hardly was undiscovered. (Indeed, it was said that a typical Zuni family included the father, mother, two children, and an anthropologist.) But it inspired her nonetheless. She "discovered in myself a great fondness for this place—it came over me with a rush." Driven "almost to madness" by her years of suffering, she internalized the tranquility that she discovered in the Southwest and made it the foundation of her academic career.[22]

Amid her isolation and solitude in Zuni, Benedict discovered the joy of work. She depended (as had Matilda Stevenson forty years earlier) almost entirely upon information provided by an informant who was a renegade in Zuni. (Branded as a witch by Zuni priests, he took revenge by revealing tribal secrets to this female stranger.) Removed from the domestic "culture" that had constricted her, Benedict found freedom in her academic work to ask painful questions—about gender, deviance, sexuality, and identity—that were grounded in her own personal quest for fulfillment as a woman. "Three years ago," she wrote to Mead, "it would have been enough to fill me with terror. I was always afraid of depressions getting too much for me.... But that's ancient history now." The appeal of the "welcoming" discipline of anthropology lay in its rejection of "biological fundamentalism" for cultural relativism. It offered "a haven for the individual who did not fit." Whether in the

Southwest or Samoa, aspiring anthropologists—young women conspicuous among them—could escape from their own cultural alienation and professional marginalization.[23]

Benedict's loneliness and isolation fed her yearning to become an academic insider. But a frustrating succession of one-year appointments between 1923–30 left her at the academic margins. While she remained married, Boas—encountering administrative resistance to adding another woman to the faculty—was unable to secure a regular academic appointment for her. She found herself trapped within limitations imposed by her mentor and her husband. Mead described her dependent relationship with Boas as "a kind of second self," in which she functioned as his assistant, confidant, editor, classroom substitute, and procurer for departmental funding. Yet "hard as she worked, devoted as she was, she still seemed to him . . . essentially a visitor from afar who might go away." Only after her separation from Stanley in 1931 was Boas finally able to offer her an assistant professorship at Columbia. She was forty-four years old. It is hardly surprising that Benedict came to value the "deviants" among her students, who, like her, were willing "to transgress the patterns set by American society."[24]

Three years later, *Patterns of Culture* was published. It culminated a long and arduous struggle for Benedict, whose focus had shifted from her earlier interest in Pueblo mythology (which, she was advised, "doesn't excite people any more than Athabaskan verbs would") to the idea of culture as "personality writ large." While working in Arizona with the Pima tribe, she discovered contrasts with Zuni that had deep personal resonance. Each tribe, she observed, displayed its own distinctive pattern of culture: in their commitment to moderation, Pueblo Indians were "Apollonian"; but the surrounding tribes, in their lives of excess, were "Dionysian." That distinction, the central polarity of her book (and her life), formed the core of her cultural analysis.[25]

There was "nothing wild" about the Zunis, Benedict wrote; their "love of moderation" shaped the harmonious cooperation within their human relationships just as it guided the elaborately formal style of their ceremonial dances. "The ideal man in Zuni," she wrote, "is a person of dignity and affability who has never tried to lead, and who has never called forth comment from his neighbors." Zuni children were not disciplined, for authority—Benedict erroneously believed—was irrelevant to Zuni life. Like so many Anglo visitors, she was attracted to the "long homogeneous history" of the Zunis, who still lived distinctively "after the old native fashion," apart from American culture. In Zuni, "the life-history of the individual is first and foremost an accommodation of the patterns and standards traditionally handed down in his community." For Benedict, the lesson of Zuni was "the relativity of our cultural habits" and "the immensely important role of culturally conditioned behavior." Much like Parsons, Benedict appreciated traditional values in Zuni as she never did in American society.[26]

Benedict discovered—or imagined—a matrilineal culture that provided a range of female choices and opportunities. In Zuni, where houses belonged to women, she learned that divorce occurred whenever the husband's possessions were placed "on the doorsill"; marital jealousy was "soft-pedalled"; sex was but "an incident in a happy life"; homosexuality was an "honourable estate"; "guilt complexes" were unknown; and menstruation made "no difference in a woman's life." Among Zuni children, who were rarely disciplined, there was no "possibility of the child's suffering from an Oedipus complex." An "unparalleled lack of vehemence" characterized Zuni life, where a culture "of measure and of sobriety" fulfilled her Apollonian ideal. The extent of sexual freedom in Zuni understandably appealed to Benedict, whose tortured identity struggle and sexual frustration had taken her from an oppressive marriage to an older man into a lesbian relationship with a younger woman. In its subtext, at least, *Patterns of Culture* bore vivid witness to Benedict's lengthy and painful struggle to define the terms for her fulfillment as a woman.[27]

Yet Zuni confronted Benedict, as a cultural relativist, with contradictions that she could not resolve and barely acknowledged. It was, after all, a tightly structured tribal culture, where "neither in religion nor in economics is the individual autonomous." It was constrained by the very shackles of tradition that Boas and his disciples vigorously condemned everywhere else in American society. Indeed, as Benedict conceded, it was "a theocracy," rigidly focused on ceremony and ritual under the unchallenged direction of its exclusively male priesthood. Yet, "fed by tradition," Zuni had become "an organic whole." According to Zuni ideals, she wrote, "a man sinks his activities in those of the group and claims no personal authority." In Zuni, there could be "no courting of excess in any form, no tolerance of violence, no indulgence in the exercise of authority, or delight in any situation in which the individual stands alone." (Her deviant informer might have believed otherwise.) Zuni, ironically, was precisely the kind of culture from which any self-respecting and rebellious American individualist—repelled by unyielding traditional values and intrusive authoritarian supervision—would instantly flee.[28]

What, then, accounted for Zuni's unrivaled appeal, especially to the procession of female anthropologists who went to study its culture—and to learn about themselves? "All of us," Benedict wrote to Mead in 1925, are "wrestling with the problem of the individual and culture." Manners and morals "are not racial, nor the necessary consequence of human nature, but have grown up historically in the life history of the community." Early on, she had been struck by the "highly ritualized, highly formalized" lives of Zuni Indians, and by their lack of concern "with personal prestige or exploit." This suggested a "fundamental psychological set among the Pueblo peoples" that led to Benedict's distinction between Apollonian and Dionysian, between moderation and excess, between Zuni and neighboring tribes—and, ultimately, between Zuni and the United States.

In *Patterns of Culture*, these polarities framed Benedict's sharp indictment of American society and history. She compared the "arrogant and unbridled egoists" of her era to the "abnormal" Puritan ministers of seventeenth-century New England, who displayed "intolerable aberrations" in their exercise of "psychopathic" dictatorial power. (Benedict surely would have been shocked to learn of the high praise heaped upon seventeenth-century Salem residents for extirpating witches by a Zuni member of Cushing's delegation.) "In our own generation," she observed, "extreme forms of ego-gratification are culturally supported in a similar fashion," in family life as in business. The men "who display these traits are entrusted with positions of great influence and importance and are as a rule fathers of families." But "they are not described in our manuals of psychiatry because they are supported by every tenet of our civilization." Pleading for "the recognition of cultural relativity," she urged tolerance for "coexisting and equally valid patterns of life," where the collective welfare of the community was elevated above individualism; sexual deviance was tolerated; and human interactions remained unregulated by coercive authority. Measured by the Dionysian excesses of American culture, Zuni was an Apollonian utopia, and Benedict unabashedly embraced it.[29]

In her idealization of Zuni culture, Benedict discerned the outlines of a female alternative to the aggressive dominance of American masculinity. Like other female anthropologists, she was struck by the matrilineal family structure that formed "the most strongly institutionalized social bond" in Zuni. With home ownership and inheritance passing through the maternal line, and divorce uncomplicated (as it certainly had not been for Benedict), gender seemed malleable and the empowerment of women was possible. Benedict discovered "pleasant relations between the sexes" that contrasted sharply with her own experience. Without any conception of sin, the Zunis "do not suffer from guilt complexes." The Zuni way of life was the truly Apollonian "way of measure and of sobriety."[30]

Benedict's starkly binary perception of culture may have emerged from the excruciating trauma of her childhood. To a very young girl, her father's peaceful tranquility in death had seemed "beautiful," while her mother's "confusion and explosive weeping which I repudiated" was deeply unsettling. She internalized the contrast and retreated into solitude, insulated from turbulent emotions that were too frightening to confront. Her memories of her father's calm and her mother's hysteria were woven into her mistrust of Dionysian excesses and the allure of Apollonian tranquility. For Benedict, Zuni offered the cultural extension—and, perhaps, the resolution—of her most painfully formative childhood experience.[31]

Pueblo culture, Benedict observed, "presents probably the most abrupt cultural break that we know in America." Her work in Zuni led her to conclude that "normality . . . is culturally defined"; therefore, abnormality is what "that particular civilization does not use." As she wrote in *Patterns of Culture*, "It is not possible to understand Pueblo attitudes toward life without some knowledge of the culture from which they have detached themselves: that of the rest of North America." She instinctively understood, and greatly valued, such cultural detachment; it paralleled and affirmed her own lifelong insulation from the turbulence that swirled around, and inside, her.[32]

It was hardly coincidental that *Patterns of Culture* was written by a woman. With her book, Benedict issued a plea "for cultural relativism and tolerance by toppling images of male dominance in our own society." Zuni culture had such powerful appeal to her precisely because it served as a model for her critique of American society and the patriarchy that it nurtured and sustained. Zuni, she insisted, was different. As Benedict once wrote euphorically: "When I'm God I'm going to build my city there." In her heavenly city, women would be as empowered as men in American society. "Who better," Barbara Babcock asks, "to describe the constraints of custom and the power of patriarchal institutions" than a woman?[33]

But the earthly Zuni was far more complex, turbulent, and fractious than Benedict—or most anthropologists who followed Cushing there—ever acknowledged. She wrote nothing about alcoholism or violence, the draconian punishment of deviance, or the tension and factionalism that often shattered her imagined Apollonian tranquility. Beneath Benedict the anthropologist, Babcock accurately perceived "the feminist Benedict," writing a book that was laced with a "feminist subtext" assaulting "images of male dominance" in American society. As critic Richard Chase wrote in his review of an anthology of her writings, Benedict "was passionately committed to the Party of Woman." In her search to discover her own identity, Mead observed, Benedict "had persistently wondered whether she would have fitted better into another period or another culture than she fitted into contemporary America." She found her answer and her escape in Zuni, the feminist utopia of her imagination.[34]

Among Boas's "daughters," Esther Schiff Goldfrank and Ruth Bunzel exemplified the appeal of cultural relativism to aspiring anthropologists who confronted the double barrier of gender and Jewish identity. Barnard College classmates, they graduated just before World War I ended. Schiff, funded by Parsons, became Boas's secretary in 1921. At the time, Boas comprised the entire anthropology department; for twenty-five dollars weekly, Schiff became the staff. After a year in the office, she asked permission to accompany him to the Southwest. Boas, conspicuously culture-bound in his hesitation, was "somewhat disconcerted at the idea of taking a young, untrained, and unmarried woman" with him to do fieldwork, even for a study as comfortably domesticated as Pueblo cooking recipes. But Schiff, duly forewarned by her relatives of potential dangers from Boas and Indians alike, persevered, and he finally relented. That summer, Schiff subsequently wrote, Boas "shed his role of employer to become, in effect, my 'father-protector.'"

Schiff began to attend Boas's graduate courses, returning with him to the Southwest the following summer. Somewhat adrift without an assigned informant, she wandered through Cochiti Pueblo until she spotted a "comely" young woman, drawing water at the pump, who greeted her with a welcoming smile. Schiff already knew that "women the world over were—and are—notorious for their small talk," and she needed to establish contact with someone who was "well informed regarding 'secret' matters (men's business)." Her hostess-informant took Schiff into her home and facilitated her "adoption" ceremony into a Pueblo clan, which welcomed her with the new name of "Abalone Shell."

Not long afterward, Schiff married Walter S. Goldfrank, a widower with three children; their daughter was born two years later. Domestic demands, she conceded, "brought my anthropological studies to a complete stop," but her new life was "so full and fulfilling" that she had "no regrets." Boas, still enough of a traditionalist to believe that "marriage and a family came first in a woman's life," accepted her decision. Parsons, however, advised her to "leave behind a good nurse" and, with her husband's support, she decided to "mix marriage and anthropology." She managed to publish her monograph on Cochiti in 1927, but the double burden of domestic and professional responsibilities overwhelmed her and she all but abandoned anthropology for nearly a decade.

After her husband's death in 1935, she returned to Columbia, where Boas was nearing retirement. For Goldfrank, whose father had died when she was nine and whose husband had died prematurely, Boas remained a comforting older male presence. And, to the aging *paterfamilias*, Goldfrank was "still a beloved daughter." At Benedict's suggestion, she worked on a project about adolescent adjustment (while her daughter was a teenager). But she wrote little and never taught; her career remained circumscribed "by her own vision of her role as a mother and wife." In her memoir, *Notes on an Undirected Life*, she showed no signs of regret.[35]

Ruth Bunzel, who succeeded Schiff as Boas's secretary in 1922, followed her to the Southwest, joining Benedict in Zuni. (Schiff, slightly more qualified for her own secretarial appointment, had already taken one course with Boas.) "My plan," Bunzel conceded, "was not too ambitious—I was a good stenographer and I would take down folk tales and interviews in shorthand, and do all our typing." Boas urged her to develop her own project, but Bunzel, untrained in anthropology, was hesitant. "You're interested in art," Boas told her. "They make pottery there. Go do a project on the relationship of the artist to her work." In the pueblos, pottery—like cooking—was "women's work"; it was, therefore, an especially appropriate subject for an aspiring female student. Obediently, Bunzel did as she was instructed.[36]

Bunzel was struck by the "great lack of knowledge" among anthropologists "about people's lives—particularly about women. . . . So being a woman, that was the obvious place to start." In Zuni, she learned about Pueblo pottery by actually becoming a potter and working alongside Pueblo women. It was not an easy experience. "I was really alone in a big sea and I had to swim," she recalled. She correctly assumed that "Zuni artists were not going to be any more articulate about what they were trying to do than the poets and painters I had met in Greenwich Village." Not only were artists "notoriously inarticulate" about their work; she also encountered "the general pueblo attitude of intense hostility to all white people." Persisting, Bunzel came to perceive

Zuni as "a woman's society," where women have "a great deal of power and influence," even though they could not participate in the religious and ceremonial life of the pueblo.

Like Schiff before her, Bunzel found a welcoming family to nurture and protect her within a tribal culture that looked askance at single women living on their own. During five summers and some winter months between 1924 and 1929, Bunzel was formally adopted by a Zuni family, and renamed "Blue Bird." Living "as intimately as possible within the orbit of their lives," she learned their language and culture as a participant observer, precisely as Cushing had done forty years earlier. Alone among Boas's students, she preferred to live and work with the Zunis rather than question informants "with notebook in hand." By doing what Zuni potters did, she came to understand many of the human and artistic complexities of Zuni society.

Bunzel's landmark study, *The Pueblo Potter*, was published in 1929 to enthusiastic acclaim as the first work of anthropology to examine art through psychological scrutiny of the artist. Making a determined effort "to enter fully into the mind of primitive artists," she recognized that in Zuni "the great source of decorative ideas is, of course, tradition." But Bunzel also detected attributes of modern Western individualism among Zuni potters, which appeared as "a mirror image of the self" in their work. Although Pueblo pottery spoke in "a universal language," it was "non-intellectual and non-analytical," and most likely to be guided by "sense and intuition." Detecting a mixture of aboriginal and modern styles, Bunzel embraced the contradiction. Like every Zuni girl, she even learned to walk with a pot balanced on her head. Only in Zuni could an American Jewish woman be reborn as the biblical Rebecca.[37]

Bunzel eventually left the Southwest to study culture in Latin America, Spain, and China. But she never lost her affectionate attachment to the time in her life when she was "young and energetic and bright," and the Southwest revealed a wondrous new world to her. In the twenties (which were also her twenties), she recalled: "Some of us fled to the freer air of Paris. . . . Some of us joined radical movements . . . and some of us went into anthropology, hoping that there we might find some answers to the ambiguities and contradictions of our age." Even as an elderly woman, she still fondly recalled her time in Zuni, "sleeping on the pueblo roof on summer nights, far from New York, and being awestruck at the spaciousness and beauty and intricacy of nature." For Bunzel, Zuni—despite its gendered boundaries—offered professional satisfaction and personal fulfillment that earned her lifelong gratitude.[38]

For the female anthropologists under Boas's tutelage, professional training raised complex issues of gendered autonomy. For Bunzel and Schiff, as for Mead and Benedict (significantly older than the others, but beginning her career later in life), anthropology offered professional opportunities—once they earned Boas's approval—that were unavailable to women in other academic disciplines. They were all "the daughters of distinguished men who enabled them either intellectually or financially." Coming from financially comfortable, even privileged, families (Benedict was the significant exception), educational expectations were high, even for daughters. At a time when very few women attended college, they all earned doctorates. They broke sharply with "the drawing-room domesticity" that controlled the upbringing of Mabel Ganson Dodge and Elsie Clews Parsons, who were a half-generation older. For the younger women, anthropology offered the freedom to escape, to explore, and, in the process of studying another people, to redefine themselves as modern women.[39]

It may not have been coincidental that Benedict, Schiff, and Bunzel, all of whom lost their fathers during childhood, were strongly drawn into the Boas orbit. The younger women, perhaps less conflicted over their own independence, responded to Boas respectfully but affectionately. Benedict, tortured by family issues from childhood through marriage, never became one of Boas's "daughters" in the way that Schiff and Bunzel did. Nor, however, could she escape her dependence on "Papa Franz," for freedom from her husband seemed to depend upon Boas's ability to find an academic position for her that would assure her independence.

The complexities of gender identity were conspicuous in the tangled "familial" relationships that developed between Boas and his "daughters." Among them, George W. Stocking Jr. discerns "obvious analogies to the psychodynamics of a large late-Victorian family," featuring Oedipal rebellions, fierce sibling rivalries, and, "most notably, in the softening of the patriarch toward the younger generation of daughters." But Boas never relinquished his patriarchal prerogatives. He spoke with the voice of authority; and he presided over the anthropology department with a firm hand, demanding and receiving deference from his students. Mead, virtually alone, disregarded the advice he gave to all his female students that they conduct their fieldwork in the safety of the Southwest, within the protected confines of Pueblo family life. Yet even remote Samoa was a frequently visited American protectorate.[40]

For Schiff and Bunzel especially, Boas was their teacher, mentor, and surrogate father ever since their undergraduate years. (In her book, Bunzel profusely thanked her "beloved teacher" for his "zeal and encouragement.") For these assimilated Jewish women, struggling to escape their own parochial cultural constraints, Boas, whose Jewish identity had been formed in Jewish self-denial, must have been an especially appealing surrogate father. They gained their freedom, paradoxically, through their dependence upon him. Yet as welcoming to women as Boas surely was, he nonetheless channeled them into research topics that were "appropriate" to their gender: family, cooking, pottery. And as liberated as Benedict, Goldfrank, and Bunzel were by the gendered standards of their time, their focus on "women's work" in the pueblos was conventionally "female." Dutiful daughters under his stern mentoring, they served their apprenticeships in Zuni and matured intellectually to become distinguished professional women.

Their idealization of Pueblo culture, expressive of their rebellion against American conventions, sharply distinguished this cohort of female anthropologists from the genteel women who had preceded them to the Southwest. Many of the earlier liberal reformers, who taught in pueblo missionary schools, had little good to say about Pueblo women. For Boas's students, however, Pueblo women were "powerful women whose traditions embodied ideal gender relations." Arriving "as strangers, they left as kin." Adopted by families, and receiving new names, they experienced "a new sense of self and purpose" as women. In the Southwest, the New Woman of the Twenties rejected the postwar culture of "capitalism, industrialism, Puritanism, and rural morality." In the pueblos, finally, she could find "a place to be free."[41]

Captivated by the "indescribable romance" of the Southwest, women discovered new gender possibilities there. As one anthropologist explained, "These Pueblo women are given an equality that is then passed on to the rest of us when we come into the picture." Frustrated with "a culture suspicious of intellectual ambition in women," and inspired by Pueblo women, they tried to emulate them, even as their fieldwork channeled them back into traditional domestic spheres. Goldfrank studied recipes and Bunzel became a potter, just as Mabel Dodge Luhan, eccentric as always, found her new freedom in Taos by scrubbing floors, baking bread, and knitting. If anthropology became, as it did for Parsons, a "weapon" in the struggle of women against social constraints and separate spheres, it could also return them to the very arena of domesticity—home, family, and women's work—that they were struggling so fiercely to escape.[42]

These pioneering female anthropologists, Ruth Behar suggests, "wanted to figure out the origins of sexual inequality in order to see what it would take to change men and thus raise the status of women." Yet their reliance upon Pueblo culture as a source of inspiration was riddled with inconsistency. Not only did their rejection of Victorian conventions lead them directly to their embrace of pueblo domesticity; they projected their own fantasies of freedom upon the Pueblo women they encountered. It is little wonder, therefore, that Margaret D. Jacobs, a sympathetic feminist historian, would question whether Anglo women who were drawn to the pueblos were not "hopelessly befuddled, a mass of contradictions."[43]

The adventurous cohort of female anthropologists who went to the pueblos saw themselves and their work with Native peoples as evidence of their "tolerance, curiosity, and openness in the face of cultural differences." As Boas students, they displayed a "basically liberal and ethical stance" at a time when most American men were not inclined to respond to Indians (or, for that matter, women) as their equals. Yet, Deborah Gordon suggests, there was also a patronizing superiority in these encounters, as female anthropologists "came to know Native American women as the embodiments of their desires." Searching for ways to recast the sexist contours of their own society, they wanted to make Native American women into "models of femininity" who were deserving of emulation. But even as they looked to Pueblo women "for the reconstruction of themselves," their own "female paternalism" intruded. "The desire for both authority and equality in their relationships with Native Americans," Gordon perceptively observes, placed Anglo women on the horns of a painful, unresolved dilemma.[44]

Nor is this surprising. The female anthropologists who went to the Southwest comprised a privileged cohort of women. By birth or marriage, or both, they occupied the upper economic and social strata of American society. They came, for the most part, from economically advantaged and educated families whose daughters were encouraged to attend excellent (often women's) colleges such as Vassar and Barnard at a time when few young women enjoyed such opportunities. As much as they might be excluded, as women, from male centers of privilege and power in mainstream American society, in the Southwest, Gordon indicates, they formed "part of white governance and management of Native Americans." Their strong identification with Pueblo women could not conceal their own positions of power and authority. They were privileged outsiders (and, to be sure, uninvited intruders), to whom Pueblo women were expected to defer. The result, Gordon concludes, was a mixture of "genuine concern and friendship," combined with "underlying arrogance and delusion." Liberated from male domination, women wielded the authority that accompanied their own newly acquired professional status.[45]

"Matronization," Gordon's apt term for this role transformation, suggests the inherently unbalanced relationship between anthropologists and pueblo dwellers. It was a relationship, she observes, "shot through with desires marked by race, class, and gender." Female anthropologists "both created and were caught within a historical problem of trying to change inequality but preserve difference." But "like mother and child," Gordon observes, they participated in a relationship of "interdependency in which white women tried to relinquish certain privileges and powers on the condition that Native American women love and care about them." Pueblo women were expected to cooperate with their visitors "so that white women could produce knowledge about them to educate the white public."[46]

The exemplar of such "matronly" intrusion and domination in its most blatant forms had been Matilda Stevenson, the first female ethnographer to investigate Pueblo culture. Brushing aside Zuni objections to her note-taking, photography, and presence at kiva ceremonies, she took refuge in her claim of responsibility to record information about their lives before there was nothing left to document. In the process, she demonstrated her "overriding sense of knowing what was good for the Zuni." Rebuffed, Gordon observes, she behaved like a "hurt mother." No matter how sensitive to local mores Boas's students might be by contrast, these women (no less than their male counterparts) "maintained relations of authority" with Pueblo Indians who were, indisputably, their "political unequals."[47]

Ruth Benedict was sharply reminded by a Pueblo friend that her efforts to obtain the services of informants were not only personally hurtful, but "just that sort of thing that kills the Indians. . . . That's what you anthropologists with your infernal curiosity and your thirst for scientific data bring about." Why did Benedict want to know such things, he asked, admonishing her: "You must not rob them. You must not sneak into their house." In a revealing reminder where power ultimately resided in the pueblos, he warned Benedict that if she continued to engage in "ferreting out secrets," he would "immediately denounce her and her informants to the old men."[48]

Female anthropologists might prefer to see themselves as the "fictive daughters" of native women, "who have aided and befriended and shared their homes and their lives with us." But the distance between anthropologists and Pueblo Indians turned on class and cultural differences that even shared gender identity could not overcome. The discipline of anthropology has been criticized for being "deeply rooted in the narrative of the male quest," but female anthropologists were hardly immune from questing or from the conflicts and contradictions that accompanied it. Women may "know what it is like to be othered," as Ruth Behar writes, but assumptions of cultural superiority can exist independent of gender.[49]

Women who were drawn to the Southwest after World War I projected their own feminist agenda upon Pueblo culture. In return, they received affirmation as professional women. But just as they suppressed the reality of intra-pueblo conflict (which, as with Benedict, their own use of informants encouraged), their exaggeration of Pueblo matrilineality distorted realities of gender division and hierarchy. Using the pueblos to frame their conceptions of gendered correctness, they conscripted Native women for their own feminist cause. Evidence of male authority that contradicted their feminist assumptions—and fantasies—was largely ignored.

Boas's female students insisted that the gendered division of labor, normally taken as a measure of male domination, "enhanced, rather than diminished, women's status" in the pueblos. At the very least, there were "different but equal and complementary" power realms. Indisputably, pueblo houses were owned and inherited by women, who could divorce their husbands merely by placing their belongings outside the front door. But political power in the pueblos was the exclusive prerogative of male elders, who monopolized the secret religious societies and ceremonial rituals. In their eagerness to find inspirational models for their own struggle against sexism, female anthropologists viewed Pueblo gender patterns through the lenses of their own personal aspirations. In the process, Pueblo women, "degraded by their men and by tradition, suddenly became elevated . . . to the status of powerful women whose traditions embodied ideal gender relations."[50]

The "new woman," Elsie Clews Parsons bluntly proclaimed, wanted "to be not only a masterless woman, one no longer classified as daughter or wife, she wants a share in the mastery men arrogate." Yet Boas's female students became collectively identified as "Papa Franz's daughters," an affectionate label that revealed their dependence upon Boas no less than their respect for him. To gain "mastery," they discovered in Pueblo culture what they needed to find there to satisfy their own gendered aspirations. Unselfconsciously, they followed the trail to an Edenic—if now feminist—utopia once blazed by intrepid (male) explorers.[51]

In the end, anthropologists—male and female alike—contributed to undermining the very culture they so admired and idealized. Like the hordes of tourists who flocked to the Southwest once the Santa Fe Railroad extended its line through New Mexico early in the 1880s, anthropologists, by their very presence, diluted the isolated "purity" of the native peoples whose ostensible insulation from modernity was so appealing to them. Margaret Jacobs describes it as a "relationship of cultural appropriation." Hilary Lapsley, in her study of the Mead-Benedict relationship as a paradigm of the kinship of women, precisely captures the irony: "in their search for the untouched, the timeless, and the whole, escapees from the soulless life of modern America themselves contributed to the dismemberment of traditional native American cultures." Rejecting biological imperatives for cultural relativism, the better to liberate themselves as women, they abetted the Anglo penetration of Pueblo culture, diligently "harvesting intellectual rather than material spoils" to serve their burgeoning professional careers.[52]

The flight from Greenwich Village to the pueblos after World War I was driven by the lure of primitive simplicity, authenticity, and redemption. It was a rebellion against Progressive reform turned sour, Red Scare repression, the corrupt excesses of a business civilization, and restrictive gender boundaries. The idea of the primitive, Marianna Torgovnick writes, is always "conditioned by a sense of disgust or frustration with Western values." Its attraction is a measure of "the condition of exile or cultural estrangement" of those who pursue it. The embrace of the primitive reveals a yearning for "physical, psychological, and social integrity." In the end, Torgovnick observes, themes of primitivism invariably intersect with issues of gender, and "those familiar tropes for primitives become the tropes conventionally used for women."[53]

Once the Victorian consensus fractured, the Southwest became a place of new gendered possibilities for women. Mabel Dodge Luhan and Elsie Clews Parsons, venturesome pioneers on the gender frontier, assaulted the repressive moral edifice of female purity and piety. They responded to Pueblo culture as a source of feminist inspiration and empowerment, not a pitiable symbol of female degradation. Unlike Matilda Stevenson, who had castigated Pueblo Indians for their primitive deficiencies, Luhan, Parsons, and the younger women who followed them to the Southwest discovered "psychological as well as geographical space, an otherness that intrigued and renewed." No longer were Pueblo Indians a helpless, backward people requiring an infusion of Christianity and American civilization for their salvation, as missionaries had so often insisted. In a remarkably swift transformation, the pueblos became a vital source of cultural inspiration for American society, especially for the New Woman of the postwar era.[54]

Once the Southwest became a "paradisiacal, primitive island," Margaret Jacobs writes, Anglo women found "Our Ancients" in the pueblos. Not only was it a lost world of antiquity, stability, and innocence; it exemplified the matriarchal supremacy that these women desperately yearned for, but could not experience, in their own lives. To the privileged, educated women who struggled during the postwar decade "to articulate a new womanhood and a new sexuality," pueblos emerged as the shining symbols of gendered freedom where women might find "the utopian antithesis of modern American culture."[55]

At a time when American intellectuals fled to Paris, Samoa, and Mexico, the pueblos offered women a genuinely American culture, whether in reality or fantasy, of gendered alternatives and new possibilities. In Zuni, Ruth Benedict could imagine that she had "stepped off the earth onto a timeless platform outside today," where her nagging, often debilitating, conflicts over identity and sexuality might finally be resolved. Learning about Zuni, she insisted, Americans would be better equipped "to pass judgment upon the dominant traits of our own civilization." Like Mead's Samoa, Benedict's Zuni expressed a longing for primitive virtue as a corrective to the stifling frustrations of modernity. Both women, struggling to define their sexuality, their intimate relationship, and themselves, used primitive culture to identify new possibilities. Such "cultural criticism, moral questioning, and sexual experimentation," as George W. Stocking Jr. has dryly observed, were stimulated wherever "handsome brown-skinned natives led untroubled lives."[56]

The Southwest gained a well-deserved reputation for the welcome it extended to independent, trailblazing women. There, wrote Elizabeth Sargeant, who belonged to a cohort of Bryn Mawr graduates living in Santa Fe, women could elude entrenched gender patterns and "reinvent their identities." Educated and ambitious, they discovered enticing possibilities for success and fulfillment in the pueblos. In the emerging field of native folk art, they gained an important foothold where men had not yet established themselves. Immersing themselves in traditional cultures, they succeeded in transcending the traditional boundaries of their own culture. Submerging themselves in the lives of Pueblo women, they expanded their own possibilities. Long reputed to be "no place for a lady," the Southwest became the place where Anglo women "created new identities for themselves." Yet Parsons and Luhan, like the first generation of female philanthropists in the Southwest (including Mary Hemenway, Mary Wheelwright, and Millicent Rogers), were independent in curiously dependant ways. They all tapped substantial family financial resources to fund expeditions, research, publications, the collection of native crafts, and the struggle for Indian rights—nurturing their own careers in the hospitable cultural environment of the Southwest. It was, as Georgia O'Keeffe had said after visiting Taos, "a new world . . . and I thought this was my world."[57]

At a pivotal historical moment in the quest of American women for personal freedom and self-expression, Franz Boas's students constructed the "pueblo" of their fantasies as a feminist paradise. As academic outsiders, his "daughters" followed his advice and went to the Southwest. There they experienced self-transformation, writing themselves into their books and eventually leaving their welcoming Pueblo "family" behind as they launched their own professional careers. With pueblos recast as a feminist alternative to patriarchal America, they could even liberate themselves from "Papa Franz" to become independent professional women. More than Boas or his students ever acknowledged, cultural relativism was itself a malleable cultural construct that served their own needs and ambitions.

CHAPTER SIX

Feminist Utopia

L ong after Franz Boas's students left the Southwest, a new generation of feminist scholars rediscovered Pueblo Indians, exploring the lives of the female anthropologists who had studied them, and deconstructing the romantic imagery of Pueblo culture that the Fred Harvey Company and the Santa Fe Railroad had once popularized. Feminist anthropologists, literary critics, and historians have found inspirational role models among their female predecessors, and grist for their gendered critique of American society. In their retelling, the artistic and literary "construction" of the Southwest as an American paradise was interlaced with sexism, exploitation, domination, and, worst of all, "Orientalism"—among postmodern academic critics the ultimate term of scholarly denigration and contempt.

Within the past two decades, Pueblo culture has become a virtual cottage industry of feminist scholarship. Searching for the sources of their own feminist heritage, scholars have turned for inspiration to the lives of the "restless and rebellious" women who forged their professional reputations in the pueblos after World War I. "In our quest," writes anthropologist Nancy Parezo candidly, "we are searching for our legendary heroines." Grounded in contemporary feminist criticism, their scholarship seeks to reclaim a neglected feminist past.[1]

It is, simultaneously, a scathing indictment of American corporate capitalism for packaging, marketing, and selling (therefore, exploiting) Pueblo Indians to Americans who were yearning to recapture a lost age of innocence and virtue. Accordingly, the partnership between the Santa Fe Railroad and the Fred Harvey Company in the development of the Southwest as a major tourist attraction becomes "a way of incorporating yet containing the other . . . [that was] central to the rhetoric of empire." It produced a pattern of "ahistorical representations" of pueblo life, whose "imaging was part of the continuing campaign to make 'hostile' natives manageable and safe for tourists." With profitable commissions awaiting them, painters and photographers became collaborators who "aestheticized the colonialist gaze while enhancing the railroad's business." Their "feminization of the other," which elevated Pueblo women and their pots to iconic status among nostalgic (yet rapacious) Americans, exemplified a process of Western (patriarchal) cultural conquest that demeaned women in the guise of romanticizing their lives. To Americans frightened by the pace of social change, what better alternative to "masculine" industrialization at the turn of the last century "than red earth shaped into 'pleasing shapes' by the 'warm hands' of Pueblo women"?[2]

Embedded in this gendered critique is a question posed by anthropologist Barbara Tedlock, who has lived among the Zuni Indians for long stretches since 1968. In *The Beautiful and the Dangerous*, her dialogues with Zunis, she reveals how "I fell in love with the beauty of the high desert and the native peoples of the American Southwest." Those feelings prompted her to inquire: "Why cannot [female] ethnographers make the professional personal?" Why should not ethnographic writing become "the product of a multivocal postmodern feminist discipline" in which "the precise nature of the interaction between Self and Other" is directly confronted? In her call for a feminist ethnography, Tedlock imagines "an explicitly feminine environment for the ethnographic encounter." Instead of an "outdoor male adventurer," like Cushing, "pitching his tent among the natives," why not adopt the Benedict model, with "two women seated at a kitchen table chatting"?[3]

With the kitchen table, a venerable symbol of female domesticity, elevated as an honored feminist shrine, Parezo wonders why the work of female anthropologists (other than Benedict and Mead) has so rarely been cited by (male) scholars. "Was it because they were women?" she asks. Despite the reputation of anthropology as a "welcoming" discipline for women, she describes the female scholars who preceded her as "a marginalized group without a recognized voice," trapped in a scientific discipline that was "phallocentric in intent and outcome." And yet, she observes, "the more one learns to read between the lines of official discourse and accepted history, the more one discovers how much women have contributed to our understanding of anthropology." There was "something about the Southwest as a place, as an idea, and as a locale for anthropological research," she insists, that made it attractive to women—and still does. Was it, she wondered, "a place where [women] could thrive and create new identities for themselves"? The question, which all but answers itself, goes a long way toward explaining why a new generation of feminist scholars has reaffirmed the Southwest as a gendered paradise.[4]

Barbara A. Babcock, sharply critical of popular representations of Pueblo Indians in her prolific scholarship, has made explicit her emotional debt to her feminist predecessors in the Southwest. She recalls her encounter with Elsie Clews Parsons's work on Pueblo mothers and children just when her own mother was dying and she learned that she could not have children. Babcock "came to terms with her losses," she writes, by immersing herself in Parsons's trailblazing feminist anthropology. She was riveted by Parsons's focus on "the cultural construction of gender and sexuality," the core principle of modern feminist criticism. Babcock applauded Parsons's pioneering application of anthropology "as a feminist cultural critique," lauding her predecessor's determination to locate women at the center of scholarly inquiry. It was Parsons, Babcock wrote, who "challenged the . . . essentializing which is the basis of racist and sexist ideologies."[5]

Babcock, in turn, has condemned the incessant representations of pueblo life in which "both bread and pottery are shaped by a 'traditional' process handed down from mother to daughter in an unbroken matriline." She notes the repetitive images of Pueblo women with pots, whether in their hands or on their heads, as the artistic signature of pueblo life. This exemplifies the "representational violence" that "keeps Pueblo women imprisoned in 'timeless indigeny.'" Indeed, she suggests, Pueblo culture has long been symbolically reproduced "in the bodies of women and clay vessels." Such images offer "a narrative of more than a century of oppression, appropriation, and commodification."[6]

Why, Babcock wonders, have Anglo-Americans lavished so much attention, for so long, on the "New Mexican Rebecca," the alluring Pueblo maiden with her aesthetically pleasing pot? The answer, she concludes, is to be found in the "refusal to see Pueblo women in their 'psychological, social, and cultural complexity.'" Rebecca imagery was so captivating, she suggests, precisely because it simultaneously romanticized Pueblo Indians as exotic while reinforcing their confinement to domestic roles. Ultimately, the Pueblo woman, like her pot, became "a vessel of desire," exploited by Anglo (male) outsiders for their own pecuniary benefit and voyeuristic pleasure.[7]

To Babcock, the special attention given to Pueblo potters, especially in Fred Harvey Company literature, raises "disturbing questions about the aesthetic appropriation of non-Western others—issues of race, gender, and power." Why, she asks, "has a traditionally dressed woman shaping or carrying an *olla*, a water jar, become *the* classic metonymic misrepresentation of the Pueblo, and why has Anglo America invested so much in this image for more than a century?" The fascination, she suggests, expresses "a form of colonial domination—a gaze which fixes and objectifies, which masters." This "glorification of the exotic" exemplified "the cult of domesticity" that imprisoned Pueblo women—and, by implication, all women—within masculine gender categories. Company image-makers provided a vision of "subjugated beauty" that confirmed the cultural inferiority of the Southwest—even as its natural wonders were exalted.[8]

The representation of Pueblo culture "in the bodies of women and clay vessels," according to Babcock, demonstrates the insidious consequences of imperial nostalgia. Pueblo girls, invariably depicted as olla maidens with pots, provided a "spectacle of reproduction and fetishization of fertility." In her reading, the Harvey postcard showing women selling pottery at the train stop outside Laguna Pueblo (see fig. 8)—a classic depiction of the tourist encounter with Native people—can best be understood as a transaction in which Pueblo women were compelled to sell themselves to Anglo men. Wondering why Pueblo women "have been imprisoned for over a century within our ethnocentric vision of domesticity and motherhood," Babcock finds the answer embedded within "patriarchal and capitalist arrangements." The Pueblo women whose enviable autonomy inspired modern feminists are now perceived, ironically, as passive and helpless victims of Anglo patriarchal domination.[9]

By now, the Fred Harvey Company lives in historical memory, if at all, for its unrelenting exploitation of Pueblo Indians, especially their women. For its imaginative "construction" of "the great Southwest" as the American paradise, it has been summoned to the dock of historical judgment and convicted of an array of transgressions against feminist sensibilities. Its "corporate appropriation" of people and objects, Weigle and Babcock declare, was guided by "the language of science, progress, imperialism, and commerce."[10]

The Santa Fe Railroad may have promoted itself as the protector of a vanishing culture but it, too, helped to undermine that culture by freezing it forever "in a primitive time, tying [pueblo] authenticity to the age and crudeness of their traditions." The emphasis in its corporate images on the "picturesque beauty" of Pueblo culture was demeaning, ultimately even dehumanizing, especially to women and children. Pueblo Indians were commonly romanticized "as people doomed to vanish or as living relics of the past, as performers of colorful ceremonies, and as makers of pots, baskets, blankets, and jewelry."

These images, Leah Dilworth suggests, assumed that "things were more whole, more harmonious at some time 'before.'" While urban industrial America displayed all the pathologies of anomic, violent modernity, the Southwest was romantically depicted as pure and unsullied, "a place of the unique, the handmade, the rural, and the authentic." The buying, selling, promotion, and collection of native crafts, Dilworth writes, exemplified "imperial conquest" combined with "nostalgia for what imperialism had destroyed." Pots, baskets, and photographs all were "trophies of the hunt," captured by Anglo men from native culture. In the end, however, the creation of a fantasy past, with the pueblos as its surviving remnants, was but "a thin veil for imperialism." [11]

Native peoples had little choice but to accept these impositions and indignities. As tourism to New Mexico increased, "exotic but docile Indians proved profitable." The convergence of craft with commerce, and the unbalanced partnership of native artisans and Anglo merchants, prepared the way for the popular and lucrative Indian arts and crafts markets that proliferated in the Southwest throughout the twentieth century. The predatory capitalistic activities of the Fred Harvey Company and the Santa Fe Railroad, working in tandem, swept Indian crafts "into [their] imagery and ideological values: as 'otherness,' old-fashioned, charming, exotic, natural, primitive, universal." Such airbrushed images of pueblo life masked corporate domination of a culturally subjugated people. [12]

This feminist critique locates the Fred Harvey Company and the Santa Fe Railroad within the "hegemonic assertion of ruling-class authority" by predatory business corporations at the end of the nineteenth century. To be sure, the indictment of Gilded Age corporate capitalism is at least as old as Henry Demarest Lloyd's *Wealth Against Commonwealth* (1894), reinforced by Progressive muckrakers such as Ida Tarbell and embellished by Matthew Josephson's Depression-inspired critique of the Robber Barons. Updated by feminist scholars, it calls attention to "a colonialist gaze [that] entails domination and mastery, representation and hierarchy." The "fetishizing of others' maternity," Babcock writes, is a common way of "domesticating and feminizing the exotic," the easier to tame it in the service of Western imperial and colonial interests. Indeed, she concludes, the Southwest long ago became "America's Orient."[13]

For postmodern academic critics, no term of opprobrium cuts deeper than "Orientalism," defined as an insidious strategy "for dominating, restructuring, and having authority" over non-Western peoples. In his trendsetting polemic by that title, published in 1978, Edward Said described how "the West"—where he made his comfortable home in exile and carved out his stellar academic career as its critic—had asserted its domination over the Middle Eastern Arab culture that defined his idyllic boyhood world in Cairo. The imperial West, with its nineteenth-century assumptions about the biological basis of racial inferiority, imposed "backwardness, degeneracy, and inequality" upon "Oriental" peoples. The proliferation of Western images, Said suggested, assured that "the one thing the Orient could not do was to represent itself." Indeed, "every European in what he could say about the Orient, was consequently a racist, an imperialist, and almost totally ethnocentric."[14]

At its core (Said wrote in the afterword to a revised edition of his book), Orientalism was a "discourse of power." It "approaches a heterogeneous, dynamic, and complex human reality from an uncritically essentialist standpoint," in which real or imagined individual attributes are assigned to an entire people. In his indictment, the West, armed with formidable weapons of analysis and interpretation, proclaimed itself to be "rational, developed, humane, superior," when compared to the "aberrant, underdeveloped, inferior" Orient. It followed that non-Western cultures were "either to be feared ... or to be controlled."[15]

Yet Said's scathing critique of Orientalist essentialism can easily be redirected to Said himself—and to his academic disciples. It reduces a complex process of cultural interaction, exchange, and response to his own essentialist assumptions about "the West," which, like any culture, is—and was—far less monolithic than his analysis suggests. The feminist scholars of the Southwest, who borrow heavily from Said in their own critique of corporate domination and cultural exploitation in the Southwest, follow their leader by simplifying and distorting a more complex, and less invidious, process of historical encounter and exchange.

To be sure, "Oriental" was a common descriptive term at the end of the nineteenth century. Applied to the pueblos by men and women alike, it evoked images of "Palestinian villages," where Indian women with water jars were "Maids of Palestine" or "Rebecca at the Well" (while men were "keen-eyed Bedouins"). Charles F. Lummis, writing in 1893, described Pueblo costumes as "strikingly picturesque, and even handsome. That of the women in particular is Oriental, characteristic, and modest." George A. Dorsey, curator of anthropology at the Field Museum in Chicago who served as liaison with the Fred Harvey Company, wrote a popular introduction to the pueblos in which the "beautiful and graceful form" of Acoma pottery, Oriental in its aesthetic design, received conspicuous attention. (Dorsey, Babcock observes, was only "one of many seduced by the 'graceful form' of Acoma pottery and women, and prone to confusing the two.") In the 1920s, Erna Fergusson's Indian Detours advised tourists that they were about to encounter "a foreign people, with foreign speech and foreign ways, offer[ing] them spectacles which can be equaled in very few Oriental lands."[16]

Even where the language was less explicit, Oriental imagery was commonplace. Captain Bourke, one of the early visitors to the Southwest, identified Pueblo culture with the Middle East: Pueblo girls with "black, flashing eyes, long lashes, aquiline noses, and olive complexions recalled to mind the physiognomies of the women of Judea." So, too, a Fred Harvey Company ethnographer assured the passenger traffic manager for the Santa Fe Railroad that the "splendid railroad . . . should make possible the exploiting and scientific study of the quaint peoples through whose ancient land it runs." The exploitation of "quaint peoples" is a phrase that understandably grates on modern academic sensibilities. It helps to explain why the Southwest has become a scholarly arena where issues of culture and gender in American society are now vigorously contested.[17]

This "trope of orientalism," Babcock asserts, "both exoticizes and appropriates" Pueblo culture for Western entertainment and pleasure. Most egregiously, women in "America's Orient" became "receptacles and products of desire." Such "orientalized" representation of Pueblo Indians, Dilworth writes, "was part of the rhetoric of empire building and colonialism. . . . It remained the burden of American civilization to take command of these primitives in the name of progress." Even feminist writers who represent the pueblos "as ancient and unchanging," Margaret Jacobs suggests, have "tended to associate Pueblo culture with 'Oriental' culture." It was a repetitive trope in late nineteenth-century travel writing, highlighting with wonder and appreciation—if also superiority—what was perceived to be foreign and exotic about the Southwest. In our time, however, it has become conclusive evidence of the cultural oppression of Pueblo Indians.[18]

Whether "Orientalism" retains value even as a critique of Western imperialism—which historians Bernard Lewis and David Cannadine, among others, have sharply challenged—its application to the Southwest is problematic. Gender relations, in particular, provide sharp and revealing contrasts between European imperial contact in Africa and Anglo penetration of the American Southwest. In her analysis of imperialist travel writing, Mary Louise Pratt documents European travelers in Africa who commonly demeaned local women with observations about their indolence, idleness, savagery, and sensuality. Yet American visitors to the pueblos, by contrast, not only admired women for their "exotic" appearance, but consistently complimented them for their artisanship and creativity. Pratt cites examples of rampant sexual exploitation in Africa, where European men—in their role as dominant and intrusive outsiders—frequently purchased local women for domestic and sexual service. In the Southwest, however, Anglo women used Native men for their own purposes. Matilda Coxe Stevenson "captured" We'wha and brought him to Washington to showcase her ethnographic achievements. Mabel Dodge Stern, driven by her quest for self-transcendence, lured Tony Luhan from his wife and family in Taos Pueblo. And Ruth Benedict jeopardized the status of her male informants with her reliance upon them. Pratt suggests that Europeans imagined African natives as "incomplete beings suffering from the inability to become what Europeans already are." By contrast, Anglo explorers in the Southwest endlessly celebrated Pueblo Indians for their exemplary cultural achievements, which all Americans were urged to emulate.[19]

There was, however, one revealing similarity. Female travelers in Africa, Pratt notes, repeatedly discovered "idealized worlds of female autonomy, empowerment, and pleasure." In these remote "feministopias," as she aptly labels them, Western women imagined freedom and power that were unknown to them back home. So it also was in the Southwest, where the idealization of Pueblo women by their Anglo counterparts was commonplace. From Boas's female students in the 1920s to contemporary feminist scholars, modern women have found in the Southwest a promised land of unrivaled possibilities, not only for gender equality but even for female supremacy. In modern

American history, no "feministopia" (except, perhaps, women's colleges) has exerted a stronger pull than the pueblos.[20]

"The symbolic duality of the Orient and the West," Thierry Hentsch suggests, first appeared in recognizably modern form in the mid-nineteenth century, when urban industrialism triggered a nostalgic longing for the imagined past. Wherever it appeared, Orientalist nostalgia flourished as an "antitoxin" to the evils of modern industrial society. The Orient has been described as a "construct" of the Western imagination: "elusive, omnipresent yet evanescent. . . . The Orient is in our minds." Yet "Orientalism," too, is a construct of the Western imagination, existing largely in the minds of postmodern critics. Indeed, Said himself discerned "no deeply invested tradition of Orientalism" in the United States until after World War II, with the waning of British and French colonial rule, long after the commercial development, or "exploitation," of the Southwest had crested and subsided. Its application to the nineteenth-century Southwest is an anachronism embedded in the ahistorical premises of contemporary scholarly analysis.[21]

Unlike nineteenth-century Europeans, Americans were far more preoccupied with expanding their own frontiers than exploring the Middle East, either in reality or fantasy. To be sure, references to the "Oriental" attributes of Pueblo Indians were commonplace, and some recognizably "Orientalist" images surfaced in frontier painting. Western heroes were occasionally depicted as sheiks; and Charles M. Russell incorporated the Odalisque in his portrait of the Indian woman Keeoma (with his wife posing languorously as his model). But the enticing Southwest, not the degraded Orient that Mark Twain so vividly described, had more than sufficient exotic allure of its own. Wrenched from historical context, attributions of Orientalism to the Southwest divert attention from its deepest appeal, not as a decadent Ottoman Shangri-La filled with quaint but inferior people, but as an identifiably American Eden with undiminished inspirational value. Indeed, the endlessly nostalgic tropes for Pueblo Indians sounded variations on a theme as old as the American experience itself: the imagined state of perfection that once existed, in a vanished past, before corporate predators introduced their evil machines into the garden of American innocence.[22]

The pueblos certainly were "aestheticized"—if that means romanticized for their architecture, ritual, clothing, and crafts. But this was hardly to pacify "hostile" natives, for the Pueblo Indians were anything but hostile to visitors—one important reason why, unlike the Plains Indians, they received so many of them. Indeed, they seemed to possess limitless patience for the intrusions of Anglo outsiders; and, as Cushing's experience demonstrated, they were at least as adept at using visitors for their own purposes as their visitors were in using them. Boas's female students, discovering their own feminist utopia in Zuni (around the kitchen table, no less), were as beguiled by pueblo domesticity as their male predecessors. Indeed, the attention that contemporary feminist scholars have lavished on the pueblos suggests that they, too, have been captivated by the enticingly female space that they find there. All those "ahistorical representations" of pueblo life that so irritate Babcock not only testify to the sustained power of the pueblos to evoke nostalgia for a vanished past, but also their equivalent power to evoke yearning in disillusioned Americans for a better future.

Anglo-American nostalgia was hardly "misplaced" in the Southwest, as feminist critics allege. It unerringly focused on precisely those Native Americans who most vividly, and poignantly, evoked what urban industrialism was widely believed to have destroyed: a lost world of communal integrity and harmony. Unlike European Orientalism, so furiously condemned because it demeaned foreign peoples as primitive savages, the remarkably prolonged infatuation with Pueblo Indians elevated their culture as a veritable model for American society to emulate. At the historical moment when feminists were discovering utopia in the Southwest after World War I, disparaging remarks from Americans about inferior peoples were much likelier to target the benighted inhabitants of Babbitt's Zenith or the Lynds' Middletown, whose cultural shallowness demonstrated the vacuity, not the superiority, of modern America.

To be sure, the promotional activities of the Fred Harvey Company and the Santa Fe Railroad profoundly impacted upon the economic relations and culture of the pueblos, but not necessarily, or unremittingly, for the worse. As Pueblo Indians were "captured, framed, and tamed within the tourist spectacle," they became recognizable, even iconic, figures in the popular culture of the time, much like professional athletes or movie stars, who were also idealized for audiences of avid consumers (and well compensated for their celebrity). Perhaps the most popular Pueblo artisans (like Babe Ruth or Jack Dempsey) even became "a commodity to be consumed." Certainly talented potters and weavers, beginning with Nampeyo and Ellie of Ganado, and extending by now through the branches of family trees into the fourth generation and beyond, inexorably became producers of arts and crafts for a cash economy. As Indian pottery was drawn into a new world of crafts shows and an expanding web of relationships with dealers, museums, and galleries, potters became increasingly dependent (as did other American producers) on popular taste and the vicissitudes of the marketplace. They also became respected independent artisans, whose work was—and, more than ever, remains—greatly admired and avidly purchased.

These changes exacted costs from some while providing benefits to others. Money was valued, recalled an Indian from Santa Clara Pueblo, but "we were made to feel totally devalued." A Zuni Indian observed, "We've gone from ritual to retail." As Edwin L. Wade describes it, Pueblo Indians, "grasping for cultural legitimacy and survival in the industrialized West," ultimately had no choice but to accept "the economic option of converting culture into commodity." Yet even Babcock concedes "the profitability of primitivism" for native artisans. Pueblo women may have been stereotyped by the aesthetic judgments of the Fred Harvey Company and the Santa Fe Railroad, but they were also liberated from their traditional roles by "money, mobility, and mediating with the outside world." Indeed, the expanding Pueblo crafts market brought power and prestige (traditionally male prerogatives) to Native women, who, ever since the end of the nineteenth century, have been recognized and remunerated for their artistic skill.[23]

The gradual inclusion of Pueblo artisans within the boundaries of American economic opportunity was by no means the unmitigated tragedy of malevolent capitalist exploitation, imperial domination, patriarchal power, or Orientalist condescension that feminist critics so insistently allege. It may be that "the ideological reduction of native cultures to their malleable artistic products" symbolized a form of Anglo "conquest" of the Pueblo peoples. The talented weaver Ellie of Ganado, it has been claimed, "would not languish in prison like Geronimo, but she was captured many times—on film." Yet photographs of Ellie presenting her splendid weaving of American patriotic symbols to President Theodore Roosevelt suggest that she was respected and rewarded for her talent. In the end, the much-maligned commercialization of Pueblo culture seems to have enhanced, rather than diminished, the stature of Pueblo women as independent and talented artisans. The Southwest may have been "artificially constructed" by Anglo image makers eager to profit from its romantic appeal, but economic opportunities undeniably expanded for the Pueblo artisans whose "vanishing" civilization had become a major tourist attraction by the turn of the twentieth century.

Anglo cultural penetration, to be sure, was intrusive. When a Taos Indian was asked "What did you call this country before the Europeans came?" he curtly replied "Ours." But the historic resilience of the pueblos should not be underestimated. Pueblo culture never was as isolated as Anglo visitors imagined it had been on the day before the Santa Fe Railroad track first reached Gallup. Centuries of cross-cultural contact with Spanish and Mexican rulers, long before the Anglo explorers arrived in the wake of Cushing's popularization of Zuni, suggest that Indian culture was not so fragile as to be shattered by its newest visitors. A Native people whose traditional religious life flourished in underground kivas, even as they worshipped in Catholic churches to satisfy their Spanish conquerors, knew something about strategies of cultural survival amid the intrusions of foreigners.[24]

Far from exploiting women, the Fred Harvey Company remains noteworthy for its creation of new opportunities for Native and Anglo women alike. As the popularity of Pueblo crafts increased, the economic prospects for women in the Southwest improved. Skilled Native artisans were brought to Harvey tourist centers to work and display their talents. Mary Colter was retained to design and decorate Harvey hotels, while Minnie H. Huckel was given responsibility for building the company art collection. Erna Fergusson's innovative automobile touring business was brought under the Fred Harvey Company corporate umbrella. The growing prominence of museum and art communities in Santa Fe and Taos opened new possibilities for college-educated women in an emerging, popular, and increasingly lucrative sector of the national art market.

Indeed, ever since Harvey first provided an escape for his "girls" from the desolation of rural life, he had re-gendered work opportunities for ambitious women—Anglo and Native alike—in ways that few corporate executives of his era could match. An immigrant boy who quickly learned American ways, Harvey had a shrewd understanding of the role that Pueblo Indians could play in the marketplace of nostalgia that urban industrialism encouraged. He was hardly alone in profiting from it. To be sure, Harvey and the Santa Fe Railroad dispensed romantic representations of Pueblo Indians in their postcards, playing cards, calendars, and brochures. But Pueblo Indians had a long history of representing themselves through their distinctive architecture, religious rituals, and highly stylized pottery—and they would continue to do so long after the Fred Harvey Company had come and gone.

As gender boundaries began to shift around the turn of the twentieth century, women joined men in pursuing their personal dreams in the Southwest. With Matilda Coxe Stevenson as the pioneering exemplar, a steady stream of educated and ambitious women discovered new gendered possibilities among the Pueblo Indians. They rapturously described the vast and beautiful desert landscape (its "austere virginity," according to Mary Austin) as necessary space for their own interior struggles to define themselves as modern women. Here, Austin wrote dreamily after World War I, was "the only society in the world in which culture exists as an expression of the whole, unaffected by schisms of class and caste, incapable of being rated in terms of power or property." The Apollonian community discovered by Ruth Benedict in Zuni "attracted the feminine eye" with its harmony, spirituality, and matrilineal attributes. For these independent women, the appeal of a vibrantly feminist community, whether real or imagined, was irresistible. Along the way, they demonstrated that they were no less disposed than the male explorers who had preceded them to redefine and idealize gender identity in the pueblos of their imagination.[25]

Anglo women who went to the Southwest, Nancy Parezo writes, were "fleeing private demons, seeking private dreams, or searching for personal physical or psychic health." They found "a place for individuals who felt alienated from their own society yet wanted to return to simpler times to save civilization from the effects of industrialization." Using Pueblo culture as their standard and Pueblo women as their models, they confronted issues at the core of their dilemma as intelligent, independent women for whom there was as yet no fulfilling place in mainstream American society. "I have been treated badly by men," Austin complained, "as have most gifted women." Women needed "ways of expressing their greatness which will prove more expressive than the ways they have adopted from men." It was in the Southwest, Austin wanted to believe, "not in the cafés of Prague or the cellars of Leningrad," where "the fair new shape of society is molded."

For Anglo women, the Southwest not only was an escape, or even "an active political statement," it was also where they could experience the welcoming hospitality of Pueblo Indians that might heal wounds inflicted by their own shattered families. Adopted for the duration of their visit, often renamed according to Pueblo custom, Boas's students were treated as the "fictive daughters" of their hosts. In the emotional warmth of these encounters, they discovered "a new sense of self and purpose." Mentored by "Papa

Franz," then embraced by a Pueblo family, these rites of passage moved them from female dependence toward independent professional adulthood.[26]

Despite the efforts of feminist critics to reduce complex cultural encounters to a simple narrative of male domination, exploitation, and conquest, the pueblos have proven to be endlessly malleable in the American imagination. Back in 1880, a time of heightened anxiety about patterns of female behavior in modern society, *Harper's Weekly* had reassured its readers that "handling dear old mother earth does not leave much time for hysteria." At the end of the nineteenth century, the arts and crafts impulse to restore premodern artisanship to a place of honor in the American industrial economy was expressed in a growing fascination with Pueblo crafts. After World War I, Ruth Bunzel learned to make pots for the unique access it offered her to the inner lives of Pueblo women. For Erna Fergusson, leading tours to the pueblos, a woman with a pot merely symbolized "a primitive life away from the world's hurly-burly." Over time, Pueblo pots were receptacles for many meanings, which women and men alike scripted from their own needs and yearnings.[27]

For contemporary feminist scholars, identification with the female anthropologists who did their fieldwork in the pueblos in the 1920s and 1930s, and with the Pueblo women they studied, has become a self-validating political statement. It affirms the values of cultural relativism and diversity, in service to the cause of gender equality, that Franz Boas championed and his students exemplified. In her conclusion to *Hidden Scholars*, an illuminating collection of essays about her female predecessors in the Southwest, Nancy Parezo candidly acknowledges that "the quest, or the political agenda, of this book has been to overcome sexism." In this way, Pueblo culture continues to inspire professional women, who imagine gendered virtues there that are lacking elsewhere in American society.[28]

How ironic, therefore, that feminist scholars would reduce Pueblo women, such exemplary models of female autonomy and power, to passive victims of predatory capitalism and patriarchal exploitation. No one, after all, forced Pueblo artisans to display their pots and baskets, or sell them, at Harvey Houses along the Santa Fe line. Once they did, to be sure, they were expected to comply with company aesthetic standards regarding color and size to maximize their appeal to the tourist market. But it is more than a little patronizing to imply that Pueblo women remained docile and subservient until feminist scholars came along to rescue them from the capitalist clutches of predatory corporate executives. Using Pueblo Indians to sharpen their criticism of corporate malfeasance and male power in American society, feminist scholars have appropriated them for their own personal, political, and polemical purposes.

In the end, the feminist critique is seriously weakened by its failure to perceive the historical function that "Eden," "Israel," and "Palestine" had served for Americans ever since the earliest Puritan settlements in New England. By indiscriminately applying Orientalist categories to Anglo encounters with Pueblo Indians, the better to criticize American capitalist culture, feminist critics have overlooked the centuries-old, deeply ingrained yearning of Americans to imagine themselves as a new Israel, enjoying the inherited mantle of divine promise and protection that their New England forebears had claimed for themselves and their progeny.

The explorers, men and women alike, who went to the pueblos between 1880 and 1940, romantically embellished the Southwest with biblical imagery that simultaneously expressed their own painful estrangement from modernity and their anguish over the diminished promise of American life. Unlike the Spanish conquistadores, and the missionaries who had followed in their wake to save the souls of the native savages, Anglo explorers in the Southwestern Eden were fired by fantasies of personal redemption and visions of national salvation. From the moment that Cushing gazed in transfixed wonder in Zuni and imagined "the Pools of Palestine," Pueblo Indians inspired their deepest longings for harmony and community. It took a new generation of feminist critics, projecting on the past the gender struggles and cultural politics of our own time, to reduce Pueblo Indians to hapless victims of sexist domination and rapacious capitalist exploitation.

Conclusion

During the 1930s, the romantic appeal of the pueblos was severely depleted by the devastation of the Depression. Fewer Americans could afford the luxury of travel; and newer heroic victims of capitalist failure, such as the "Okies" who were memorialized by John Steinbeck, attracted public sympathy. Walker Evans, Dorothea Lange, and other talented photographers focused their cameras on newly dispossessed Americans: sharecroppers, coal miners, unemployed factory workers. Anthropologists, only recently drawn to the pueblos in droves, drifted away to do their fieldwork elsewhere. By the time Ruth Benedict's *Patterns of Culture* was published in 1934, Zuni seemed to have lost much of its Apollonian magic.

Among the last relics of pueblo romanticism was Laura Gilpin's "camera chronicle," as she called it, of its native Indians. Gilpin had been fascinated by photography—and by indigenous peoples—ever since she had taken pictures of the Philippine Igorots at the Louisiana Purchase Expedition with her Brownie camera as a twelve-year-old girl. Her encounters with Pueblo Indians reinforced her sense of a lost golden age, whose timeless verities still endured. She intended her photographs as a tribute to "this ancient American civilization," with "a history 'old as Egypt.'" Linking Pueblo Indians to the cliff dwellers of Mesa Verde and Canyon de Chelly, whose ancient ruins she had enthusiastically explored, Gilpin posed one comely young (Navajo) woman, her shoulder alluringly bare, staring dreamily from the window of

FIG. 16. "House of the Cliff Dweller." Acc No.: P1979.125.28
Laura Gilpin, platinum print, 1925 c. 1979, Amon Carter Museum, Fort Worth, Texas.

a cliff dwelling, a pot strategically located in the foreground (fig. 16). In a companion photo, the same Indian maiden stands reverently absorbed in contemplation of sacred ritual, starkly framed by the contrasting light and shadows within the ancient ruins. More frequently, however, Gilpin represented Pueblo women in their most traditional domestic roles: mothering children, kneading clay for pots, grinding corn.[1]

A striking photograph of two women at "The Water Hole, Acoma," facing the title page of her book, might have been posed by Edward S. Curtis so precisely did it evoke his own compelling sequence of Acoma photographs. Gilpin, too, was captivated by "a procession of graceful women with beautiful waterfilled ollas balanced on their heads winding up the trail from the cistern to their homes." There was, she wrote, "something infinitely appealing in this land which contains our oldest history." It lingers in memory "with a haunting tenacity." Even as she stereotypically described Pueblo Indians as "a simple and childlike people," she honored them because "they have endured." Her book, *The Pueblos: A Camera Chronicle*, was published on the eve of World War II. It might have served as an epitaph to the prominence of Pueblo Indians in the American artistic imagination.[2]

The Depression of the 1930s brought Southwestern tourism to a virtual halt—at least until the postwar years revived American prosperity. The already hardscrabble existence of Native peoples deteriorated even further. The Fred Harvey Company slid into financial hard times from which it never recovered. Although New Mexico remained "a fairyland of high mountains, swift streams, broad mesas, and brilliant sky," the fantasies of Cushing and Lummis, Parsons and Luhan, Collier and Benedict, like so many others, had finally yielded to a less romantic reality. The pueblos no longer offered an Edenic mirage of paradise, even if the Southwest would, in time, be revived as a flourishing tourist attraction and, during and after the Sixties, a counterculture haven. By the time the WPA Guide to New Mexico was published in 1940, it noted that "to the beat of the Indian tom-tom" had been added "the roar of the air transport and the sweep of the transcontinental streamlined train." Pueblo Indians could now be described as ordinary people, "courteous and reserved," selling pottery and welcoming tourists at ceremonial dances, where their "remarkable adherence to old rules" provided visitors with glimpses of rituals "that had their origin in an early primitive culture."

Despite these vestiges of the past, the guide noted, pueblo life had been gradually transformed under the impact of modernity, which increased its exposure to mainstream American society. The pueblos still remained "remote from those elements of American civilization that tend to make cities so inhospitable to creative work," but their struggle to "preserve the ancient ways and modes of thought . . . amidst modernism and change" seemed doomed. The golden age of Southwestern myth-making had finally ended. Only the "radiance of symbolism," in John Collier's elegiac tribute to the Edenic visions that the pueblos once had inspired, endured.[3]

The WPA Guide barely noticed two other New Mexico communities, which had not yet captured public attention: Los Alamos, site of a ranch school, and Alamogordo, a minor trading and recreational center. There, just five years later, not very far from the pueblos that for so long had captivated Americans as a utopian paradise, the Atomic Age began. Eden all but disappeared beneath a mushroom cloud over New Mexico.

Even in Edenic Zuni, Frank Hamilton Cushing had experienced forebodings of doom that were activated by the imminent arrival of the Santa Fe Railroad. Ever since, Americans have journeyed to the Southwest, lured to the pueblos in search of the past, the future, and above all, themselves. By their very presence, however—to say nothing of the attention they attracted to the pueblos with their cascade of letters, postcards, articles, books, photographs, and paintings—they stripped away the shield of isolation that might otherwise have protected Pueblo Indians from modernity for just a little longer.

After the 1880s, Pueblo Indians were catapulted with astonishing speed into the very world that their admiring visitors flocked to the pueblos to escape. Once the railroad traversed New Mexico, the transformation of the Southwest into a modern tourist attraction was a foregone conclusion. But the serpent in the garden was less the Santa Fe Railroad or the Fred Harvey Company than the irrepressible fascination of American men and women with their own expansive dreams of self-transformation. In the pueblos, among Indians they barely understood, they discovered ancient wisdom, imagining harmony and cohesion that modernity had stifled. There they found the elixir for their discontent with the modern world they yearned so desperately to escape.

The source of American "geopiety" toward the Holy Land, and the veneration of Pueblo Indians that expressed it, is not to be found in capitalism, paternalism, or Orientalism. It is comfortably enfolded within the long and rich biblical imagery that located our history as a newly chosen people in the divinely promised American homeland. It was less an expression of imperialism or colonialism than an integral part of how Americans, even as British colonists ruled by an imperial power, began to define their own unique identity as far back as the seventeenth century, when America was first envisioned as another Eden, the new land of Canaan. It was not lust for conquest or domination, but the transforming experiences of the exodus from England, filtered through Puritan piety, that inspired Americans to appropriate biblical imagery for their own errand into the wilderness and their unfolding adventure in nation-building.

Biblical images lingered and were repeatedly reactivated. Edward Robinson, who discovered the Holy Land of myth and faith during his Connecticut boyhood before the Civil War, was fascinated by his childhood encounters with biblical stories. "As in the case of most of my country men, especially in New England, the scenes of the Bible had made a deep impression upon my mind." Robinson grew up to lead pioneering explorations in Palestine that helped to rekindle the biblical imagination of nineteenth-century Americans. By exploring Palestine, he understood with uncommon insight, he could explore his own identity as an American.[4]

The enduring popularity and astonishing profusion of "Rebecca" images is more appropriately located within this historical context than in modern gender politics. Zuni maidens at the well reminded Cushing of "the Pools of Palestine." Bourke saw "the women of Judea." Anthropologist John G. Owens recalled "pictures of Palestine." Susan Wallace described "maidens of Palestine." Kodak bestowed a prize, taken by an amateur photographer with its popular new camera, for the photograph of a Pueblo "Rebecca." From Curtis to Gilpin, photographers offered evocative glimpses of biblical maidens, with their pots gracefully balanced. They all reaffirmed America's atrophied, yet still compelling, allure as a promised land. They expressed, with remarkably similar visual images, the enduring promise of American life as it once had beckoned, despite the rapid and wrenching changes that threatened to annihilate it.

In a time of doubt and uncertainty about the consequences of modernity, biblical metaphors reiterated the oldest sources and deepest virtues of our national experience. Americans, Cushing believed, were captivated by Pueblo Indians who embraced their own religious traditions "in a way that passes our comprehension, for we are weaned from love of our traditions." Their "reverence for these traditions," he insisted, must be respected. Pueblo Indians, wrapped in biblical metaphors, offered powerful symbols of reassurance to Americans about their own historical origins at a time when, for many, faith in religious truths had been tested by scientific inquiry and found wanting. In the Southwest, Americans were reminded of what they had lost; there they discovered an enduring, evocative definition of national purpose. Riveted by evidence of its continued vitality, their faith in the American promise could be renewed.[5]

Biblical imagery and Middle Eastern reality might overlap rhetorically, but they diverged sharply, and often painfully, for American tourists. For the trickle of nineteenth-century visitors to the actual Holy Land, a neglected and barren outpost of the Ottoman Empire, Palestine often proved ugly and unappealing. Mark Twain famously described it as "a country of disappointments." A "hopeless, dreary heartbroken piece of territory out of Arizona," it seemed to him "a howling wilderness instead of a garden." Twain expressed his irritation with Arabs who "sat in silence, . . . with that vile, uncomplaining impoliteness which is so truly Indian."

Other Americans affirmed Twain's degrading identification of local Arabs with Indians (who, revealingly, had long been associated in American fantasies with the Lost Tribes of ancient Israel). The Bedouin, wrote William F. Lynch in his expedition report, "continually reminded us of our Indians." George William Curtis, recounting his Nile journey, wondered, "For what more are these orientals than sumptuous savages?" Joseph Taylor concluded that Arab women represented only "slight improvement" over Indian squaws. For John Franklin Swift, even the presence of "twenty Rebeccas" at a fountain near Ramleh was insufficient to mitigate the pervasive bleakness he encountered in Palestine. The biblical "Garden," after all, had long since been relocated in the American imagination to the United States, the newly promised Eden of innocent yearning.[6]

As the longing for a premodern paradise intensified toward the end of the nineteenth century, the dyspeptic Henry Adams yearned for the Christian majesty exemplified by Chartres cathedral, while Edward Bellamy wrote *Looking Backward* to express his visionary dream of a socialist utopia. But if the real Palestine no longer was quite as inspirational to American visitors as it once had been in their Holy Land fantasies, the discovery of the Southwest and first encounters with Pueblo Indians inspired exciting new imaginings of a restored American paradise. For a time, Holy Land and Southwestern images converged as complementary "emblems of the exotic." Cigar-store sultans competed in popularity with cigar-store Indians. At the St. Louis World's Fair of 1904, Arabs in "tattered, yet picturesque, garments" and "Bedouins from the desert" were placed on display adjacent to the Pueblo potter Nampeyo as compatible exotic primitives. Although Zion in the wilderness, "the great American foundation myth," seemed ever more incongruous with modern American realities, the dream of an American Eden, brought back to life in the Southwest, still flickered with promise.[7]

The Southwest attracted adventurers who needed a place of escape from civilization where they could become "real" men or, later, liberated women. For Cushing, Lummis, Baxter, and others, quite beyond the appeal of unspoiled nature and undiluted tradition, the Southwest offered the possibility for rediscovering the meaning of true manhood. Whether or not, as one historian suggests, men had suffered "in a society with severely distorted gender relations" and "deep gender deformities," they certainly found in the Southwest the freedom to pursue new adventures and realize thwarted ambitions, redefining their own conceptions of manliness along the way. Far from Washington and Boston, in Zuni and Isleta, Cushing and Lummis could become "free, self-directed" men. Using evocative biblical metaphors to describe the region and its Native peoples, and to express exuberance with their own experiences of freedom, they regained the masculine paradise of their dreams. Once again, as they had done as young boys, Cushing and Lummis could roam the countryside at will, released from the restrictions of civilization. The pueblos offered safe space, stripped of domestic ("female") constraints—at least until Cushing's wife arrived with her refined decorator's taste and Lummis decided to relocate his fantasies to the opulent comforts of his Los Angeles mansion.[8]

Biblical imagery had faded by the 1920s, when the feminization of the pueblos suddenly accelerated. For college-educated young women in pursuit of scientific truth and personal freedom, other metaphors more evocatively defined their quest. Esther Schiff Goldfrank enthusiastically declared that anthropology in the Southwest was "a woman's party." The Southwest, Nancy Parezo has written, was a place of "gendered romance," where (Anglo) women could imagine their escape from gender constraints and, while engaging in fieldwork, live their dreams of freedom and creativity. To Barbara Tedlock, it is "an explicitly feminine environment for the ethnographic encounter." And to Barbara Babcock, it was a place to find solace for private grief where she could challenge the patriarchy with her critique of "the way that Anglo

America has been imagining, describing, and fetishizing the Pueblo Southwest for over a century."[9]

First perceived as an uninhabited wasteland, then imagined as the biblical promised land, the pueblos evolved from a testing ground for manhood into a feminist utopia. Infinitely malleable in the minds of its explorers, they have been appropriated by a succession of Americans, men and women alike, with dreams of escape and self-transformation. So many "very good minds," writes Eliza McFeely in her perceptive study of the allure of Zuni in the American imagination, have focused on Pueblo culture, "looking for a way to make sense of larger things."[10]

Along the way, the pueblos became a point of reference for taking the measure of American society—and, invariably, finding it wanting. Ruth Benedict was inspired by the Zuni pattern of culture, which displayed new possibilities for Apollonian harmony in human relations. Aldous Huxley used Zuni to frame his critique of the West in *Brave New World*. In Robert Heinlein's science fiction, Martians convey a message of cooperation and harmony that seems to come directly from Zuni. For Will Roscoe, analyzing We'Wha the berdache, Zuni represented a new frontier of trans-gendered possibilities. In the end, however, it may be as McFeely wisely suggests that "our fascination with Zuni is still a fascination with ourselves."[11]

In Zuni—as in Acoma, Isleta, Laguna, Walpi, Taos, and the other pueblos—Americans were inspired to yearn for a past they never experienced, a past that existed only in their dreams of future possibility. Pueblo Indians revived the most durable and resonant trope of our historical experience, the renewal of biblical promise to the American people. Returning us to the pristine garden of our imagination, the pueblos were much less an exotic or exploited "Orient" than our own rediscovered "Eden."

Epilogue

Just moments into our first morning in Santa Fe, as we wandered through a maze of adobe buildings under a blazing summer sun, Susan turned to me and asked, "Doesn't this remind you of Jerusalem?" Her observation precisely expressed my own inchoate feeling that we had stepped outside the boundaries of the United States, beyond "American" culture as we knew it, into a strangely familiar foreign land, with deep historical and personal resonance.

Certain places become embedded in our imaginations, nurturing fantasies of escape, self-discovery, and transformation. Twenty-five years earlier, Jerusalem had become that place for me. In that ancient holy city, King David's city, then in Hebron, the burial place of the patriarchs and matriarchs of the Jewish people, and finally in the Sinai desert and the Judean wilderness, I was reconnected to the enduring power of the biblical narrative. During a prolonged twenty-year odyssey, as I moved between the United States and Israel in a restless quest to locate "home," Jerusalem became my city of refuge. Could there possibly be another "Jerusalem?"

Our shared epiphany was curiously affirmed a few days later, in a Santa Fe store filled with Indian pottery, katsina dolls, and silver jewelry, easily recognizable as native crafts produced for the tourist market. But in the rear of the store, in a large double-room gallery, I discovered a treasure trove of old photographs of Pueblo Indians, offering glimpses of a lost world of indigenous Native people, still virtually untouched by Western modernity. One photograph riveted my gaze. Two women emerged from the shadows of a sylvan setting of tall, leafy trees. The older woman stared impassively at the camera. The younger, probably her daughter, modestly remained half-hidden behind her. Each woman balanced an *olla*, a large clay pot, on her head. Identified as "Taos Water Girls," they were returning to their pueblo with water drawn from a well fed by its source high up in the mountains, dimly visible in the background (fig. 10).

Photographed by Edward S. Curtis during his life-consuming mission to preserve a pictorial record of every vanishing tribe of American Indians, the younger woman could have stepped directly from the biblical narrative: "And the girl was very fair to look upon . . . and she went down to the well, and filled her pitcher, and came up" (Gen. 24:16). Here, indeed, was the biblical Rebecca, relocated to New Mexico from ancient Haran, where Abraham's faithful servant had journeyed to find a suitable wife for Isaac. Rebecca with her water pitcher is as familiar a biblical icon as Noah and his ark or Moses with the stone tablets. Curtis had recast her as the archetypal Pueblo maiden. Confronting the Curtis photograph, and then so many other variations on biblical themes in Anglo encounters with the pueblos, piqued my interest. As a historian, I could understand their appeal. The turbulent new realities of urbanization, industrialization, and immigration, which defined "modernity" for Curtis and his contemporaries, threatened cherished American verities that had been formed in earlier centuries. Curtis was hardly alone in his fondness for biblical motifs that emphatically reasserted the original promise of the American experience, and its enduring—if attenuated—inspirational power. I wanted to learn who the others were, why they instantaneously associated Pueblo Indians with the Biblical narrative, and what it meant historically.

Whenever I glance at that photograph of the Taos water girls, now adorning our living-room wall, I am reminded of the visual jolt of cross-cultural appropriation that I experienced that morning in the Santa Fe gallery. Even before I realized it, the inquiry that ultimately became this book had been ignited. My encounter with Curtis led me to other photographers, who were as impelled as he was to preserve visual images of the newly discovered, but already "vanishing," Pueblo Indians. It quickly became evident that by the end of the nineteenth century, pueblo photography had become for Americans what Holy Land photography already was for Europeans: the tangible expression of a romantic yearning to return, at least spiritually and visually, to the promised land of antiquity—and, for Americans, to relocate it to United States. For a long historical moment from the 1880s through the 1930s, as I would discover, a palpable yearning for the lost innocence of American life transformed Pueblo Indians into the last best hope for American redemption.

"You can't repeat the past," Nick Carraway tells Jay Gatsby in F. Scott Fitzgerald's haunting elegy to the romantic imagination in America. "Why of course you can," Gatsby responds—the "colossal vitality of his illusion," Fitzgerald writes, undiminished by reality. At the end of *The Great Gatsby*, Fitzgerald returns us to the magical moment when Dutch sailors first encountered that "fresh, green breast of a new world," a garden of infinite possibilities in America. For many Americans at the end of the nineteenth century, and after, Southwestern Pueblo culture came to symbolize the continuing vitality of that dream. It was their American Eden, the garden of their dreams, where the innocence, purity, and harmony of an imagined past might yet heal the debilitating afflictions of modernity.

That first day in Santa Fe, without yet realizing it, I had already begun to follow in their footsteps. My own identification of Santa Fe with Jerusalem, and then my encounter with Curtis's "Rebecca" photograph, had revealed the powerful resonance of the Southwest, especially the pueblos, within a familiar biblical paradigm. Unknowingly, I had made an association that many other visitors to the Southwest, beginning more than a century earlier, had made before me. At the time, I had not the faintest clue that my historical predecessors, of whom I was completely unaware, would emerge as my subjects and companions, in a shared quest to encounter Pueblo Indians—and, ultimately, to learn something about America and ourselves in the process.

As I began to explore a vast array of diaries, letters, memoirs, photographs, paintings, postcards, advertisements, anthropological field studies, and scholarly monographs, I tapped into a powerful, enduring, and richly revealing American fascination with Pueblo culture. Learning to identify Curtis photographs and Fred Harvey postcards, to distinguish Acoma from Hopi pottery, and to separate fantasy from fact amid a cascade of fanciful impressions and reminiscences about Pueblo Indians, I began my own journey of discovery.

Along the way—while experiencing the rewards and rigors of travel, research, and writing—I accumulated many debts to institutions, archivists, students, friends, and family members. My appreciation extends to all of them, but they should not be implicated in the consequences of their generosity. Wellesley College awarded a research grant that made possible visits to archives in

New Mexico and Arizona and helped me to meet other expenses of publication. Once there, I was expertly assisted by Arthur L. Olivas, Photographic Archivist at the Museum of New Mexico Photo Archives (Santa Fe); Ann M. Massmann, Librarian at the Center for Southwest Research at the University of New Mexico (Albuquerque); and LaRee Bates, Archivist at the Heard Museum (Phoenix). Kim Walters, archivist at the Braun Research Library of the Southwest Museum (Los Angeles), was exceedingly helpful during several pleasurable visits to the Library and Museum. At the Smithsonian Institution, Ruth Selig graciously secured and guided my access to important collections. Librarians at the Zimmerman Library of the University of New Mexico and the Beinecke Library and Manuscripts and Archives at Yale University were also helpful. At Wellesley College, Heather Woods did speedy and efficient scanning of visual materials. At the National Anthropological Archives, Daisy Njoku went out of her way to help me locate elusive images, as did Barbara Moore and Margaret Kieckhaefer at the Library of Congress. The staff of the Huntington Library extended a warm welcome during each of my visits; my only regret is that my tenure as Mayers Fellow was more abbreviated than planned. I have never worked in a more beautiful, indeed Edenic, setting.

Wellesley College students who bravely enrolled in my first seminar on the Southwest, especially Emily Coddington ('02) and Lili Schwan-Rosenwald ('02), asked good questions while their enthusiastic encounters with Pueblo Indians helped to convince me that my subject was worth pursuing. Rachel Hart ('02) was a splendid research assistant, gathering biographical information about female anthropologists and exploring College Archives to locate Lucia Grieve's letter about Cushing's visit. Jessica Linker ('03) guided me through the thicket of nineteenth-century gender historiography. Ashley Baker ('04) wrote an excellent senior honors thesis, filled with important insights into Mabel Dodge Luhan and the social functions of the salon.

Several scholars generously scrutinized portions of my manuscript in its various incarnations. I am grateful to Professor Emeritus Richard W. Etulain of the University of New Mexico, who appreciated the work of a novice in a field where he excels. Professor Nan Rothschild of Barnard College, Professor Stephen Whitfield of Brandeis University, and Professor Helen Lefkowitz Horowitz and Professor Daniel Horowitz of Smith College gave me the benefit of their close critical reading of various portions of a manuscript in progress. For nearly forty years, I have counted on Dan's friendship and wisdom.

At the University of New Mexico Press, Editor-in-Chief David Holtby understood what I was trying to do and guided my manuscript into the publication process. I consider myself very fortunate to have benefited from his wise counsel. I am grateful to everyone at the Press who worked with me to prepare the manuscript for publication. Sonia Dickey patiently prodded me to complete the task, while responding to all my questions. Linda Kay Quintana was an attentive and helpful copyeditor who also prepared the index. Melissa Tandysh tastefully designed the book and dust jacket while remaining responsive to my concerns. Maya Allen-Gallegos expertly supervised the journey into print.

Within my family, Pammy, with her abundant legal talents, reminded me why I had chosen to become a historian. Cole and Jonah were engaging playmates during my research visits to Washington. During moments of desperation, Shira generously helped to program and prepare my footnotes and Rebecca diligently searched for elusive sources in obscure places. Jeff gave my manuscript an exceedingly careful, critical, and constructive read, with questions and challenges that were enormously helpful. His hospitality, warmly shared by Nancy and enhanced by the delights of Dalia, to say nothing of his willingness to brave the Los Angeles freeways to get me to my chosen libraries, greatly enhanced the pleasure of my visits to Southern California. Susan, my fellow explorer in discovering the Southwest, patiently tolerated the profusion of Pueblo artifacts that accumulated with each visit, and rescued me from organizational disarray near the end. Most important by far, as my partner in life her love has been sustaining.

J.S.A.

Manuscript and Photographic Collections

Autry National Center, Southwest Museum of the American Indian, Los Angeles
    Frank Hamilton Cushing Papers
    Frederick W. Hodge Papers
    George Wharton James Papers
    Charles F. Lummis Papers

Center for Southwest Research, University of New Mexico, Albuquerque
    Mary Austin Papers
    Erna Fergusson Papers

Heard Museum, Phoenix
    Fred Harvey Company Records

Huntington Library, San Marino
    Mary Austin Papers
    George Wharton James Papers
    Horatio Nelson Rust Papers
    Pueblo Diaries of A.C. Vroman and Charles F. Saunders
    Frederick Monsen Ethnographic Indian Photographs
    Grace Nicholson Photographic Albums
    A. C. Vroman Annotated Photographs

Museum of New Mexico Photographic Archives

National Anthropological Archives
    Matilda Coxe Stevenson Papers
    Records of Bureau of American Ethnology

Smithsonian Institution Archives
    Frank Hamilton Cushing-Spencer Baird Correspondence

University Microfilms, Ann Arbor
    John Collier Papers

Yale Collection of American Literature, Beinecke Rare Book and
Manuscript Library
    Mabel Dodge Luhan Papers
    Elizabeth Shepley Sergeant Papers

Zimmerman Library, University of New Mexico
    Erna Fergusson Papers
    Mabel Dodge Luhan Papers

Notes

Introduction

1. Mason I. Lowance Jr., *The Language of Canaan* (Cambridge, 1980), vii–viii, 28–32; Richard Slotkin, *Regeneration Through Violence: The Mythology of the American Frontier, 1600–1860* (Middletown, CT, 1973), 361; John Davis, *The Landscape of Belief: Encountering the Holy Land in Nineteenth-Century American Art and Culture* (Princeton, 1996), 3, 13–14. See also Conrad Cherry, ed., *God's New Israel* (Englewood Cliffs, NJ, 1971), 41–43; Moshe Davis, *With Eyes Toward Zion* (New York, 1977), 4–7; Sacvan Bercovitch, *The Puritan Origins of the American Self* (New Haven, 1975), 61–62, 121–22.

2. These quotes, with citations, can be found in an argument more elaborately developed in Jerold S. Auerbach, *Rabbis and Lawyers: The Journey from Torah to Constitution* (Bloomington, 1990), 8–10, 210. For the power of the Holy Land idea on American Protestant thought around the turn of the twentieth century, see Burke O. Long, *Imagining the Holy Land: Maps, Models, and Fantasy Travels* (Bloomington, 2002).

3. Davis, *Landscape of Belief,* 20–23; Michael Walzer, *Exodus and Revolution* (New York, 1985).

4. Nitza Rosovsky, "Palestine and the Nineteenth Century," in *Revealing the Holy Land: The Photographic Exploration of Palestine,* ed. Kathleen Stewart Howe (Santa Barbara, 1977), 10–14; Julie Aker, *Sight-Seeing: Photography of the Middle East and Its Audiences, 1840–1940,* Harvard University Art Museum Gallery Series 30 (Cambridge, 2000), 2–5, 11–12; Nissan N. Perez, *Focus East: Early Photography in the Near East* (New York, 1988), 49–50, 57, 59, 62; Herbert Hovenkamp, *Science and Religion in America, 1800–1860* (Philadelphia, 1978), 147–48; Yeshayahu Nir, *The Bible and the Image: The History of Photography in the Holy Land, 1839–1899* (Philadelphia, 1985), 19; Long, *Imagining the Holy Land,* 4. Palestine Park in upstate New York and the Jerusalem exhibit at the St. Louis World's Fair (1904) were among the most popular of these reconstructions. For more on Mark Twain in the Holy Land, see Franklin Walker, *Irreverent Pilgrims* (Seattle, 1974), chaps. 7–8.

5. Nir, *Bible and the Image*, 143; Perez, *Focus East*, 53, 103, 219; Long, *Imagining the Holy Land*, 140.

6. Frank H. Cushing, *My Adventures in Zuni*, with an introduction by Oakah L. Jones Jr. (Palmer Lake, CO, 1967), 4, 6–7.

7. Sylvester Baxter, "The Father of the Pueblos," *Harper's New Monthly Magazine* 65 (June 1882): 81–82.

8. Cushing to Spencer C. Baird, 29 October 1879, Record Unit 7002, Box 18, Frank Hamilton Cushing-Spencer Baird Correspondence, Smithsonian Institution Archives.

9. William H. Truettner, "Science and Sentiment," in *Art in New Mexico, 1900–1945: Paths to Taos and Santa Fe*, by Charles C. Eldredge, Julie Schimmel, and William H. Truettner (New York, 1989), 28–29, 179; Philip J. Deloria, *Indians in Unexpected Places* (Lawrence, KS, 2004), 166.

10. Eliza McFeely, *Zuni and the American Imagination* (New York, 2001), 155–56.

11. T. J. Jackson Lears, *No Place of Grace* (Chicago, 1983), xi, xv–xvi, 5.

12. Ibid., 60–61, 142, 225. Lears omits Pueblo Indians, who exemplify his thesis, from his analysis.

13. Susan E. Wallace, *The Land of the Pueblos* (New York, 1888), 8, 16, 34, 43, 51–52.

14. Lee Clark Mitchell, *Witnesses to a Vanishing America* (Princeton, 1981), 3–4.

15. Truettner, "Science and Sentiment," 67.

16. Charles C. Eldredge, "The Faraway Nearby," in Eldredge, Schimmel, and Truettner, *Art in New Mexico*, 179; Eric R. Wolf, foreword to *In Search of the Primitive: A Critique of Civilization*, by Stanley Diamond (New Brunswick, 1974), xiii.

17. Fred Harvey Company "Photostint" postcard #79009, in the author's possession. Steven Conn suggests that by 1900, with the closing of the frontier and the end of the Indian wars, Native Americans had all but disappeared from American consciousness. *History's Shadow: Native Americans and Historical Consciousness in the Nineteenth Century* (Chicago, 2004), 1–2. If so, the "explorers" of this study clearly were the exception. But the growing popularity of the pueblos among tourists by the end of the nineteenth century suggests otherwise.

18. Charles Francis Saunders, *The Indians of the Terraced Houses* (1912; repr., Glorietta, NM, 1973), vi, 99–101, 142, 146.

19. Christopher Lyman, *The Vanishing Race and Other Illusions* (Washington, DC, 1982), 28; Paula Richardson Fleming and Judith Lynn Luskey, *Grand Endeavors of American Indian Photography* (Washington, DC, 1993), 82.

20. Kathleen L. Howard and Diana F. Pardue, *Inventing the Southwest: The Fred Harvey Company and Native American Art* (Flagstaff, 1996), ix–xiii, 4, 7, 89, 93, 95; Marta Weigle and Barbara Babcock, eds., *The Great Southwest of the Fred Harvey Company and the Santa Fe Railway* (Phoenix, 1996), 157; T. C. McLuhan, *Dream Tracks: The Railroad and the American Indian, 1890–1930* (New York, 1985), 33–34.

21. Edwin L. Wade, "The Ethnic Art Market in the American Southwest, 1880–1980," in *Objects and Others: Essays on Museums and Material Culture*, ed. George W. Stocking Jr. (Madison, 1985), 167, 169, 171, 174; Sandra D'Emilio and Suzan Campbell, *Visions and Visionaries: The Art and Artists of the Santa Fe Railway* (Salt Lake City, 1991), 5–28.

22. Rosemary Levy Zumwalt, *Wealth and Rebellion: Elsie Clews Parsons, Anthropologist and Folklorist* (Urbana, 1992), 137; Desley Deacon, *Elsie Clews Parsons: Inventing Modern Life* (Chicago, 1997), xiii. See Nancy J. Parezo, ed., *Hidden Scholars: Women Anthropologists and the Native American Southwest* (Albuquerque, 1993).

23. Mabel Dodge Luhan, *Edge of Taos Desert.* Introduction by Lois Palken Rudnick (Albuquerque, 1997), xii–xiv, xvi–xvii, 199; Mabel Dodge Luhan, *Winter in Taos* (New York, 1935), 155; Lois Palken Rudnick, *Mabel Dodge Luhan: New Woman, New Worlds* (Albuquerque, 1984), 149.

24. Parezo, *Hidden Scholars*, xii, 359.

25. For the extent and consequences of Spanish penetration in the Southwest, centuries earlier, see David J. Weber, *The Spanish Frontier in North America* (New Haven, 1992). For a highly critical history of the impact of Spanish colonialism and racism on the pueblos, see Ramón A. Gutiérrez, *When Jesus Came, the Corn Mothers Went Away* (Stanford, 1991).

Chapter One

1. J. W. Powell, *The Hopi Villages* ([1875]; Palmer Lake, CO, 1972), 1, 18, 20, 26, 33–34; J. W. Powell, introduction to Frank Hamilton Cushing, *Zuni Folk Tales* (New York, 1901), xvii.

2. J. W. Powell to James Stevenson, 4 August 1879 and 8 September 1880, Matilda Stevenson Papers, MS 4689, Box 2, Smithsonian Institution Archives; Katherine Spencer Halpern, "Women in Applied Anthropology in the Southwest: The Early Years," in Parezo, *Hidden Scholars*, 189.

3. Jesse Green, ed., *Cushing at Zuni: The Correspondence and Journals of Frank Hamilton Cushing, 1879-1884* (Albuquerque, 1990), 5–6; Frederick W. Hodge to Charles F. Lummis, 4 May 1900, 2085B, Charles F. Lummis Papers, Autry National Center, Southwest Museum of the American Indian; Curtis Hinsley, "Ethnographic Charisma and Scientific Routine," in *Observers Observed: Essays on Ethnographic Fieldwork*, ed. George W. Stocking Jr. (Madison, 1983), 56; Sylvia Gronewold, "Did Frank Hamilton Cushing Go Native?" in *Crossing Cultural Boundaries: The Anthropological Experience*, eds. Solon T. Kimball and James B. Watson (San Francisco, 1972), 34–36.

4. Frank H. Cushing, "My Adventures in Zuni," *Century Illustrated Monthly Magazine* 25 (December 1882): 191.

5. Green, *Cushing at Zuni*, 3.

6. Ibid., 34.

7. Cushing, *My Adventures in Zuni*, 8; Green, *Cushing at Zuni*, 2–4, 6, 39.

8. Green, *Cushing at Zuni*, 2–4, 6, 39–40, 351n1; Gronewold, "Did Cushing Go Native?" 38–40. Cushing was not the only Anglo in Zuni; Dr. Taylor F. Ealy, a missionary, teacher, and doctor in the Presbyterian Mission School, lived there between 1878 and 1880. Unlike Cushing, Ealy's objectives were "Christianization and Americanization." Ealy believed that Cushing's identification with the Zunis was "a form of regressive conduct." The men had little to do with each other. See Norman J. Bender, *Missionaries, Outlaws, and Indians: Taylor F. Ealy at Lincoln and Zuni, 1878–1881* (Albuquerque, 1984), xiii–xv, 97, 123.

9. Curtis Hinsley, "Zunis and Brahmins: Cultural Ambivalence in the Gilded Age," in *Romantic Motives: Essays on Anthropological Sensibility*, ed. George W. Stocking Jr. (Madison, 1989), 177; McFeely, *Zuni*, 76–78, 103; Philip J. Deloria, *Playing Indian* (New Haven, 1998), 7, 106, 119, 129, 156.

10. Deloria, *Playing Indian*, 40–41.

11. Cushing to Spencer C. Baird, 1 October and 29 October 1879, MS.6.Zuni.1.2; Cushing to Baird, 29 October 1879, RU 7002, Box 18, Cushing-Baird Correspondence, Smithsonian Institution Archives.

12. Cushing, *My Adventures in Zuni*, 27, 39.

13. Ibid., 9, 14.

14. Ibid., 16–17.

15. John L. Kessell, *Spain in the Southwest* (Norman, OK, 2002), 37–39.

16. Cushing, *My Adventures in Zuni*, 20–21; Cushing to Baird, [1879], Record Unit 28, Reel 12, Secretary, (1879–82), Cushing-Baird Correspondence, Smithsonian Institution Archives.

17. Cushing, *My Adventures in Zuni*, 27–29.

18. Green, *Cushing at Zuni*, 8, offers an insightful analysis of this process.

19. Ibid., 59–60. To Col. Stevenson, his expedition leader, Cushing added: "The advantages accruing from this course seem to me very great. Their confidence and closer acquaintance are thereby secured."

20. Ibid., 82–85. An eighteen-year-old guard concurred, recalling that Cushing, after living among the Zunis, had become "almost one of them" (81–82).

21. Cushing to Baird and Powell, 18 February 1880, quoted in Green, *Cushing at Zuni*, 94–97; Jesse Green, ed., *Zuni: Selected Writings of Frank Hamilton Cushing* (Lincoln, 1979), 17.

22. Green, *Cushing at Zuni*, 94; Green, *Zuni*, 83.

23. Green, *Cushing at Zuni*, 91–92, 144; Cushing to Baird, 21 July 1880 (draft), MS 6 Zuni 1.3, Frank Hamilton Cushing Papers, Autry National Center, Southwest Museum of the American Indian.

24. Cushing to Baird, 18 July 1880, #10,488 (copy), MS 4677, National Anthropological Archives, Smithsonian Institution.

25. Cushing to Baird, 21 July 1880 (draft), MS 6 Zuni 1.3, Cushing MSS, Autry National Center, Southwest Museum of the American Indian; Green, *Cushing at Zuni*, 118, 136–37.

26. Green, *Cushing at Zuni*, 9, 12, 88, 91, 129, 182, 196; Cushing, *My Adventures in Zuni*, 31, 35, 44; Green, *Zuni*, 155–56, 418.

27. Curtis M. Hinsley and David R. Wilcox, eds., *The Southwest in the American Imagination: The Writings of Sylvester Baxter, 1881–1889* (Tucson, 1966), 21, 66–68.

28. Green, *Cushing at Zuni*, 154–56.

29. Baxter, "The Father of the Pueblos," *Harper's New Monthly Magazine* 65 (1882), reprinted in Hinsley and Wilcox, *The Southwest in the American Imagination*, 69, 74–76, 79–82.

30. Cushing to Baird, 12 March 1881, in Green, *Zuni*, 148; Cushing to Powell, 11 April 1881, Records of BAE, Box 56, National Anthropological Archives, Smithsonian Institution; Cushing to John G. Bourke, 13 August 1881 (draft), in Green, *Cushing at Zuni*, 177.

31. Hinsley, "Zunis and Brahmins," 176–77; Green, *Cushing at Zuni*, 12–14. Both Hinsley and Green offer perceptive readings of the complex factors that shaped Cushing's multifaceted role.

32. Green, *Cushing at Zuni*, 8–14, 158.

33. Cushing to James C. Pilling, 25 December 1881, Records of BAE, Box 56, National Anthropological Archives, Smithsonian Institution.

34. Ibid.

35. Green, *Cushing at Zuni*, 16–17; Cushing to Baird, 12 October 1881, Records of BAE, Box 56, National Anthropological Archives, Smithsonian Institution; Hinsley, "Zunis and Brahmins," 180–81.

36. Cushing to Baird, 12 October and 4 December 1881, in Green, *Cushing at Zuni*, 180, 201; Sylvester Baxter to Cushing, 23 January 1882, MS 6 Zuni 1.10, Cushing MSS, Autry National Center, Southwest Museum of the American Indian.

37. Green, *Cushing at Zuni*, 16–17; Hinsley, "Zunis and Brahmins," 193, 195, 198–202; Charles F. Lummis, "The White Indian," *Land of Sunshine* 12 (1900): 11, 15.

38. Hinsley, "Zunis and Brahmins," 185; Sylvester Baxter, "An Aboriginal Pilgrimage," *Century Illustrated Monthly Magazine* (May 1882): 531–34.

39. Lucia Grieve Illustrated Diary, 25 March 1882, Wellesley College Archives.

40. For an interpretive account that suggests some latent sexual content in the exchanges between Cushing and the Wellesley students, see Hinsley, "Zunis and Brahmins," 185–86.

41. Edmund Wilson, *Red, Black, Blond, and Olive; Studies in Four Civilizations: Zuni, Haiti, Soviet Russia, Israel* (New York, 1956), 18.

42. Green, *Cushing at Zuni*, 218, 237; Cushing to Emily Magill [1882?], MS 6 Zuni 1.38, Cushing MSS, Autry National Center, Southwest Museum of the American Indian.

43. Cushing Daily Journal (19 September 1882), in Green, *Cushing at Zuni*, 237, 240, 249; Sylvester Baxter, "Zuni Revisited," *The American Architect and Building News* 13 (March 17, 1883): 124–26.

44. Green, *Cushing at Zuni*, 281–82; Cushing to Baird, 18 May 1883, in ibid., 292.

45. Green, *Cushing at Zuni*, 18–20, 237; photo of Cushing with Stevenson inscription, MS 6 BAE 3.25, Cushing MSS, Autry National Center, Southwest Museum of the American Indian; Letter of John A. Logan to editor, *Chicago Tribune* (22 May 1883), in Green, *Cushing at Zuni*, 295.

46. Green, *Cushing at Zuni*, 238, 319; Hinsley, "Ethnographic Charisma," 56.

47. Cushing quoted in Raymond Stewart Brandes, "Frank Hamilton Cushing: Pioneer Americanist" (PhD diss., University of Arizona, 1965. Available on microfilm, Ann Arbor, MI: University Microfilms), 180–81; Cushing to Miss Cushing (Draft), 16 March 1884, in Green, *Cushing at Zuni*, 319.

48. Cushing to Miss Cushing (Draft), 16 March 1884, in Green, *Cushing at Zuni*, 319; ibid., 352–53n45.

49. Ibid., 6; Cushing to Miss Faurote, 14 February 1897, in ibid., 345.

50. Cushing was voicing his complaints about missionary-school teachers who had followed him to Zuni to "civilize" Indians. See Green, *Cushing at Zuni*, 345, 415–16n13.

51. Mary Austin, introduction to Frank H. Cushing, *Zuni Folk Tales* (New York, 1931), xxviii; Joan Mark, *Four Anthropologists: An American Science in its Early Years* (New York, 1980), 109, 121.

52. Curtis M. Hinsley, "Boston Meets the Southwest: The World of Frank Hamilton Cushing and Sylvester Baxter," in Hinsley and Wilcox, *The Southwest in the American Imagination*, 22, 26, 33.

53. William E. Curtis, *Children of the Sun* (Chicago, 1883), 27; Green, *Cushing at Zuni*, 2–3, 23–24.

54. John F. Kasson, *Houdini, Tarzan, and the Perfect Man* (New York, 2000), 10–11; E. Anthony Rotundo, *American Manhood: Transformations in Masculinity from the Revolution to the Modern Era* (New York, 1993), 228, 232, 246, 251–52; Gail Bederman, *Manliness and Civilization* (Chicago, 1995), 238–39; Michael Kimmel, *Manhood in America: A Cultural History* (New York, 1996), 78, 82–83. Kristin L. Hoganson explores the context for the "belligerent ideals of manhood" that were expressed in late nineteenth-century imperialism. Hoganson, *Fighting for American Manhood* (New Haven, 1998), 200–208.

55. Kimmel, *Manhood in America*, 135–36; McFeely, *Zuni*, 104–5, 108–9.

56. Cushing to Powell, 2 July 1880, #10,465 (copy), MS 4677, National Anthropological Archives, Smithsonian Institution.

57. Brandes, "Cushing," 123–26, 128, 141–53.

58. Mark, *Four Anthropologists*, 114–15; Hinsley, "Ethnographic Charisma," 61.

59. Hinsley, "Ethnographic Charisma," 66; McFeely, *Zuni*, 165–68; Leah Dilworth, *Imagining Indians in the Southwest* (Washington, 1996), 59; Hinsley, "Zunis and Brahmins," 169–70; Curtis M. Hinsley, "The Promise of the Southwest: A Humanized Landscape," in Hinsley and Wilcox, *The Southwest in the American Imagination*, 182, 197.

60. Hubert Howe Bancroft, *The Native Race of the Pacific States*, 5 vols. (New York, 1875), 1:472–73, 536, 555; Hinsley, "Zunis and Brahmins," 172–75.

61. Hinsley, "Promise of the Southwest," 198, 231n57.

62. Hinsley, "Zunis and Brahmins," 202–3.

Chapter Two

1. Nancy J. Parezo, "Matilda Coxe Stevenson: Pioneer Ethnologist," in Parezo, *Hidden Scholars*, 39–40, 53.

2. Parezo, "Stevenson," 40, 45; Nancy J. Parezo and Margaret A. Hardin, "In the Realm of the Muses," in Parezo, *Hidden Scholars*, 272.

3. Parezo, "Stevenson," 40, 53.

4. Ibid., 40–41; McFeely, *Zuni*, 54–55, 58.

5. Parezo, "Stevenson," 46, 48; McFeely, *Zuni*, 47.

6. Parezo, "Stevenson," 48–49; Matilda Coxe Stevenson, "The Zuni Indians," *Twenty-Third Annual Report of the Bureau of American Ethnology 1901–1902* (Washington, DC, 1904), 392–93, 399, 406.

7. Parezo, "Stevenson," 49–51; Will Roscoe, *The Zuni Man-Woman* (Albuquerque, 1991), xi–xiii. Matilda Stevenson's response exemplifies the mixture of repulsion and fascination often demonstrated by nineteenth-century Anglo-American observers of Pueblo religious rituals. The use of snakes, especially, was taken to

reveal the diabolical origins of Native religions. By the end of the century, however, a new tolerance toward Native, especially Pueblo, religion was evident. See Philip Jenkins, *Dream Catchers: How Mainstream America Discovered Native Spirituality* (New York, 2004), chaps. 2–3.

8. Roscoe, *The Zuni Man-Woman*, 18–19, 227n15.

9. McFeely, *Zuni*, 61, 67.

10. Ibid. 58, 62–63.

11. Green, *Cushing at Zuni*, 351n31; Matilda Coxe Stevenson, "The Zuni Indians," *Fifth Annual Report of the Bureau of American Ethnology, 1883–1884* (Washington, DC, 1887), 204; Frank Hamilton Cushing, "Zuni Fetishes," *Second Annual Report of the Bureau of Ethnology, 1880–1881* (Washington, DC, 1883), 11.

12. McFeely, *Zuni*, 62–63; Roscoe, *The Zuni Man-Woman*, 22, 28.

13. Other Anglo women in Zuni were less tolerant of We'Wha's deviance. To Mary Dissette, head of the mission school, berdaches were "unsexed mysterious creatures." Roscoe, *The Zuni Man-Woman*, 46, 48–49, 53, 55–56, 59, 122, 128, 145, 169.

14. Parezo, "Stevenson," 42–43, 54, 60n8.

15. Deborah Gordon, "Among Women: Gender and Ethnographic Authority of the Southwest, 1930–1980," in Parezo, *Hidden Scholars*, 132–34.

16. Mark Thompson, *American Character: The Curious Life of Charles Fletcher Lummis and his Rediscovery of the Southwest* (New York, 2001), 30–31.

17. Thomas H. Wilson and Chedri Falkenstein-Doyle, "Charles Fletcher Lummis and the Origins of the Southwest Museum," in *Collecting Native America, 1870–1960*, by Shepard Krech III and Barbara A. Hail (Washington, DC, 1999), 76–77; Charles Lummis, *Letters From the Southwest* (Tucson, 1989), xxvi–xxviii; Turbesé Lummis Fiske and Keith Lummis, *Charles F. Lummis: The Man and His West* (Norman, OK, 1975), 7, 15–16.

18. Fiske and Lummis, *Lummis*, 16; Wilson and Falkenstein-Doyle, "Lummis," 77; Lummis, *Letters*, 29; Robert E. Fleming, introduction to *A Tramp Across the Continent*, by Charles F. Lummis (New York, 1982), v, ix.

19. Lummis, *Letters*, 108, 116–17, 119, 122–23, 128; Fiske and Lummis, *Lummis*, 20–21; Martin Padget, *Indian Country: Travels in the American Southwest, 1840–1935* (Albuquerque, 2004), 119–20.

20. Lummis, *Tramp*, 93–94; Lummis, *Letters*, 186, 192, 199, 232.

21. James W. Byrkit, introduction to Lummis, *Letters*, xxiv–xxv, 195.

22. Thompson, *American Character*, 87–91, 107, 116; Fleming, introduction to Lummis, *Tramp*, xi. In *Some Strange Corners of Our Country* (New York, 1892), published the same year, Lummis lauded the Spanish people for providing the Southwest with "a heroic history which is quite without parallel" (165). With this book, Lummis became the best-known chronicler of "a romantic Spanish colonial past" in the American Southwest (Padget, *Indian Country*, 135). Lummis, profligate in his praise for the Southwest, also described it as an "Artist's Paradise," where "the ingenuity, the imagination, and the love of God are . . . visible at every turn." Charles F. Lummis, "The Artist's Paradise," *Out West* 29 (September 1908): 181.

23. Lummis, *Tramp*, 141–42, 222; Lummis, *Strange Corners* (New York, 1892), 141.

24. Charles F. Lummis, *The Land of Poco Tiempo* (New York, 1893), 3, 10, 76; Charles F. Lummis, "As I Remember," MSS copy, Lummis MSS, Autry National Center, Southwest Museum of the American Indian.

25. David M. Wrobel, *Promised Lands: Promotion, Memory, and the Creation of the American West* (Lawrence, KS, 2002), 159–60; Byrkit, introduction to Lummis, *Letters*, xvii; Wilson and Falkenstein-Doyle, "Lummis," 80–81, 83, 88–89.

26. Thompson, *American Character*, 307–8, 323–24.

27. Ibid. 336; Byrkit, introduction to Lummis, *Letters*, xlix. Padget praises Lummis as "arguably the most influential popular writer of travel-related literature on the Southwest," but he describes Lummis's work as "cultural incorporation," displaying "a colonizing gaze" that "exoticized" Pueblo Indians and "produced the Southwest" for the American public (*Indian Country*, 7, 117, 127).

28. L. G. Moses, *Wild West Shows and the Images of American Indians, 1883–1933* (Albuquerque, 1996), 1–3, 30, 132, 144, 148–49, 193, 222.

29. Earl Pomeroy, *In Search of the Golden West: The Tourist in Western America* (New York, 1957), 3, 7, 32–33, 37, 39, 159, 183.

30. McLuhan, *Dream Tracks*, 13, 15–17, 19, 23, 47, 49, 51.

31. Howard and Pardue, *Inventing the Southwest*, ix–xiii.

32. Lesley Poling-Kempes, *The Harvey Girls* (New York, 1989), 32–38, 42–44.

33. Ibid., xiv; Howard and Pardue, *Inventing the Southwest*, ix; Weigle and Babcock, *The Great Southwest*, 157; James Marshall, *Santa Fe: The Railroad That Built an Empire* (New York, 1945), 97–109.

34. Dilworth, *Imagining Indians*, 47–50, 58.

35. Fleming and Luskey, *Grand Endeavors*, 77–78, 80; Howard and Pardue, *Inventing the Southwest*, ix–xiii, 4, 7, 89, 93, 95; Dilworth, *Imagining Indians*, 78–81; Weigle and Babcock, *The Great Southwest*, 157; McLuhan, *Dream Tracks*, 33–34.

36. Kathleen L. Howard, "'A Most Remarkable Success': Herman Schweizer and the Fred Harvey Indian Department," in Weigle and Babcock, *The Great Southwest*, 88, 90, 92; Howard and Pardue, *Inventing the Southwest*, 13, 15, 26, 34–36, 42–44; Laura Jane Moore, "Ellie Meets the President: Weaving Navajo Culture and Commerce in the Southwestern Tourist Industry," *Frontiers: A Journal of Women's Studies* 22 (2001): 22–23, 27; Virginia L. Grattan, Mary Colter, *Builder Upon the Red Earth* (Flagstaff, 1980), 19.

37. Schweizer to Hearst, 4 April 190[?], 8 March 1911, RG 39 (1): 1.3, Fred Harvey Company Records, Heard Museum.

38. Howard and Pardue, *Inventing the Southwest*, 13, 15, 26, 34–36; Weigle and Babcock, *The Great Southwest*, 88–92, 95, 157; James David Henderson, "Meals by Fred Harvey," Harvey MSS.

39. Dilworth, *Imagining Indians*, 107, 109, 126, 147–48.

40. Ibid., 98, 145; Leah Dilworth, "Discovering Indians in Fred Harvey's Southwest," in Weigle and Babcock, *The Great Southwest*, 161.

41. George A. Dorsey, *Indians of the Southwest* (Chicago, 1903), 5, 19, 23–24, 95, 101, 119.

42. J. F. Huckel, ed., *American Indians: First Families of the Southwest* (Kansas City, 1913), Foreword.

43. Thomas J. Schlereth, *Victorian America: Transformations in Everyday Life, 1876–1915* (New York, 1991), 181.

44. Mark Neumann, "The Commercial Canyon," in *Discovered Country: Tourism and Survival in the American West*, ed. Scott Norris (Albuquerque, 1994), 200, 204; Lummis, "The Artist's Paradise," 191.

45. Jacob A. Riis, *How the Other Half Lives* (New York, 1971), 47, 77, 86; Zena Pearlstone, "Native American Images in Advertising," *American Indian Art* 20 (Summer 1995): 37, 42.

46. Dilworth, *Imagining Indians*, 174, 193–94; Weigle and Babcock, *The Great Southwest*, 1–3.

Chapter Three

1. Barbara Tedlock, *The Beautiful and the Dangerous: Dialogues with the Zuni Indians* (New York, 1992), xi.

2. Brian W. Dippie, "Representing the Other: The North American Indian," in *Anthropology and Photography, 1860–1920*, ed. Elizabeth Edwards (New Haven, 1992), 132–34; Fleming and Luskey, *Grand Endeavors*, 11–12; Alan Trachtenberg, *Reading American Photographs* (New York, 1989), 33; Martha A. Sandweiss, *Print the Legend: Photography and the American West* (New Haven, 2002), 11, 203–4, 219, 260–61.

3. Martha A. Sandweiss, "Undecisive Moments: The Narrative Tradition in Western Photography" in *Photography in Nineteenth-Century America*, ed. Martha A. Sandweiss (New York, 1991), 123–24; Van Deren Coke, *Photography in New Mexico* (Albuquerque, 1979), 13.

4. Patrick T. Houlihan and Betsy E. Houlihan, *Lummis in the Pueblos* (Flagstaff, 1986), 3–4, 17, 22, 24, 31, 36, 37 54, 60, 91.

5. Ruth I. Mahood, ed., *Photographer of the Southwest Adam Clark Vroman, 1856–1916* (New York, 1961), 12, 17; William Webb and Robert A. Weinstein, *Dwellers at the Source: Southwestern Indian Photographs of A. C. Vroman, 1895–1904* (Albuquerque, 1973), 13, 17, 20–21; A. C. Vroman, "On the Way to Moqui Snake Dance," photCL 86(106–11), No. 5–10 [1897?], A. C. Vroman Annotated Photographs, The Huntington Library, San Marino, CA. This item is reproduced by permission of The Huntington Library, San Marino, CA.

6. Webb and Weinstein, *Dwellers at the Source*, "A Belated Dedication," 8–9; Mahood, *Photographer of the Southwest*, 13–14.

7. Fleming and Luskey, *Grand Endeavors*, 36–39; Scrapbook of Clippings and Letters, Box 1; George Wharton James, "Chicago's Dark Places or How the Other Half Lives," Box 4 (10), George Wharton James Papers, The Huntington Library, San Marino, CA. This item is reproduced by permission of The Huntington Library, San Marino, CA.

8. Fleming and Luskey, *Grand Endeavors*, 38.

9. Sherry L. Smith, *Reimagining Indians: Native Americans Through Anglo Eyes, 1880–1940* (New York, 2000), 149–52; George Wharton James, *The Indians of the Painted Desert Region* (Boston, 1905), xvii, 1–2; Fleming and Luskey, *Grand Endeavors*, 62–66; George Wharton James, "The Wonderland of Arizona," [c.1911?], Box 5(4), James MSS. This item is reproduced by permission of The Huntington Library, San Marino, CA.

10. Trachtenberg, *Reading American Photographs*, 164–65, 205.

11. Lyman, *Vanishing Race*, 37–39, 51, 59–60. See also Mick Gidley, *Edward S. Curtis and the North American Indians, Incorporated* (Cambridge, 1998) for critical scrutiny of Curtis's production and distribution of his multi-volume work, "identifiable with that of the hegemonic consensus in white society" (37).

12. William H. Goetzmann and William N. Goetzmann, *The West of the Imagination* (New York, 1986), 231, 233–34; Lyman, *Vanishing Race*, 79; Gerald Hausman and Bob Kapoun, eds., *Edward S. Curtis: Prayer to the Great Mystery* (New York, 1995), xviii–xix.

13. Edward S. Curtis, *The North American Indian: The Complete Portfolios* (Cologne, 1997), 596.

14. Ibid., 601–5, 610, 620–22. In Curtis's pueblo photographs, Gidley writes, "Both woman and pottery are commodified" (Gidley, *Curtis*, 268). For examples of Curtis's "Orientalism," see ibid., 179.

15. Lyman, *Vanishing Race*, 65–78, 137, 147, 149; Hans Christian Adam, "Edward S. Curtis and the North American Indian," in Curtis, *North American Indian*, 26–27; Conn, *History's Shadow*, 75.

16. Vine Deloria Jr., introduction to Lyman, *Vanishing Race*, 11–13, 78, 147; Fleming and Luskey, *Grand Endeavors*, 117. See Mick Gidley, "Edward S. Curtis' Indian Photographs: A National Enterprise," in *Representing Others: White Views of Indigenous Peoples*, ed. Gidley, (Exeter, England, 1992), citing the "prodigious organization, massive funding from the financier J. Pierpont Morgan, and considerable attention to publicity" that characterized The North American Indian, Inc., Curtis's corporate arm headquartered on Fifth Avenue in New York City (104, 116).

17. Susan Sontag, *On Photography* (New York, 1978), 64; Dilworth, *Imagining Indians*, 111, 115–17.

18. Lee Clark Mitchell, "The Photograph and the American Indian," in *The Photograph and the American Indian*, by Alfred L. Bush and Lee Clark Mitchell (Princeton, 1994), xi; Weigle and Babcock, *The Great Southwest*, 158–59.

19. Sandweiss, *Print the Legend*, 228, 230, 233–34, 270–71.

20. Mitchell, *Witnesses*, 243–44. For the importance of photography in preserving memory in one Pueblo family, see Leslie Marmon Silko, *Storyteller* (New York, 1981). "Photographs have always had special significance with the people of my family and the people at Laguna," Silko writes, recalling the tall Hopi basket that contained hundreds of photographs taken by her grandfather and father since the 1890s (1).

21. Mitchell, *Witnesses*, 36, 40, 98; Fleming and Luskey, *Grand Endeavors*, 20.

22. G. Edward White, *The Eastern Establishment and the Western Experience* (New Haven, 1968), 31, 33, 59; Mitchell, *Witnesses*, 84.

23. Goetzmann and Goetzmann, *The West of the Imagination*, 266; Ariell Morgan Gibson, *The Santa Fe and Taos Colonies: Age of the Muses, 1900–1942* (Norman, OK, 1983), xi, xiii, 4, 25.

24. Goetzmann and Goetzmann, *The West of the Imagination*, 354; Richard W. Etulain, *Re-Imagining the Modern American West: A Century of Fiction, History, and Art* (Tucson, 1996), 68.

25. Sherry Clayton Taggett and Ted Schwarz, *Paintbrushes and Pistols: How the Taos Artists Sold the West* (Santa Fe, 1990), 61–63, 66; Keith L. Bryant Jr., *Culture in*

the *American Southwest* (College Station, TX, 2001), 90; Eldredge, Schimmel, and Truettner, *Art in New Mexico*, 12–13, 15; Bert G. Phillips, "The Taos Art Colony" [c. 1911], Box 5, George W. James MSS. This item is reproduced by permission of The Huntington Library, San Marino, CA.

26. Goetzmann and Goetzmann, *The West of the Imagination*, 357; Taggett and Schwarz, *Paintbrushes and Pistols*, 125–27, 132–33; Phillips, "Taos Art Colony," Box 5, James MSS. This item is reproduced by permission of The Huntington Library, San Marino, CA.

27. Goetzmann and Goetzmann, *The West of the Imagination*, 358–59.

28. Taggett and Schwarz, *Paintbrushes and Pistols*, 119–20, 125, 132–33, 137–39, 169, 191; D'Emilio and Campbell, *Visions and Visionaries*, 2–33; Patricia Trenton and Patrick T. Houlihan, *Native Americans: Five Centuries of Changing Images* (New York, 1989), 81.

29. Phillips, "Taos Art Colony," Box 5, James MSS. This item is reproduced by permission of The Huntington Library, San Marino, CA; Taggett and Schwarz, *Paintbrushes and Pistols*, 195; McLuhan, *Dream Tracks*, 28; Rina Swentzell, "Anglo Artists and the Creation of Pueblo Worlds," in *The Culture of Tourism, The Tourism of Culture: Selling the Past to the Present in the American Southwest*, ed. Hal K. Rothman (Albuquerque, 2003), 67. In the same volume, Chris Wilson, "Ethnic/Sexual Personas in Tricultural New Mexico," sees "the Anglo-American tendency to feminize images of Pueblo Indian cultures as a domestic antidote to rapid industrialization" (22).

30. Taggett and Schwarz, *Paintbrushes and Pistols*, 195, 222; William H. Truettner, "The Art of Pueblo Life," in Eldredge, Schimmel, and Truettner, *Art in New Mexico*, 60, 63–64; McLuhan, *Dream Tracks*, 31.

31. W. Jackson Rushing, *Native American Art and the New York Avant-Garde: A History of Cultural Pluralism* (Austin, 1995), 1–2, 39–40; Goetzmann and Goetzmann, *The West of the Imagination*, 355, 367; Nancy J. Parezo and Karl A. Hoerig, "Collecting to Educate," in Krech and Hail, *Collecting Native America*, 203–4.

32. Susan Brown McGreevy, "Daughters of Affluence: Wealth, Collecting and Southwestern Institutions," in Parezo, *Hidden Scholars*, 97–99; Rushing, *Native American Art*, 5, 13, 97.

Chapter Four

1. John G. Bourke, *The Snake-Dance of the Moquis of Arizona* (London, 1884), 233–34, 248.

2. Peggy Pascoe, *Relations of Rescue: The Search for Female Moral Authority in the American West, 1874–1939* (New York, 1991), 56–58; Bourke, *Snake-Dance of the Moquis*, 128; Margaret D. Jacobs, *Engendered Encounters: Feminism and Pueblo Cultures, 1879–1934* (Lincoln, 1999), 30, 35, 38.

3. Jacobs, *Engendered Encounters*, 60, 72–73, 180; Lois Rudnick, "Re-Naming the Land: Anglo Expatriate Women in the Southwest," in *The Desert Is No Lady*, eds. Vera Norwood and Janice Monk, (New Haven, 1987), 19. See also Sarah Deutsch, *No Separate Refuge: Culture, Class, and Gender on an Anglo-Hispanic Frontier in the American Southwest, 1880–1940* (New York, 1987); Joan M. Jensen, *One Foot on the Rockies: Women and Creativity in the Modern American West* (Albuquerque, 1995).

4. Howard and Pardue, *Inventing the Southwest*, 131–34; McLuhan, *Dream Tracks*, 41, 43.

5. Erna Fergusson, "An Autobiographical Sketch," MSS 45 (BC), Box 1, Folder 1, Erna Fergusson Papers, Center for Southwest Research, University Libraries, The University of New Mexico; Robert F. Gish, *Beautiful Swift Fox: Erna Fergusson and the Modern Southwest* (College Station, TX, 1996), 16, 18, 53, 55; Ethel Hickey and Erna Fergusson, eds., "The Koshare Book About New Mexico and Albuquerque: The Hub of the Indian Land" (n.d.), MSS 115 (BC), New Mexico Travel Literature Collection, Box 2, Folder 1, Fergusson MSS, Center for Southwest Research; Erna Fergusson, *Dancing Gods* (New York, 1931), xvi, xxvi.

6. Gish, *Beautiful Swift Fox*, 50–51, 59, 80; Molly H. Mullin, "Consuming the American Southwest: Culture, Art and Difference" (PhD diss., Duke University, 1995. Ann Arbor, MI), 105n35, 110; Marta Weigle, "Exposition and Mediation: Mary Colter, Erna Fergusson, and the Santa Fe/Harvey Popularization of the Native Southwest, 1902–1940," *Frontiers* 12 (1992): 130–31, 135, 137–38, 143. According to Martin Padget, Fergusson's Indian Tours "consolidated a long process of social, economic, and political incorporation" in which Southwestern peoples were "colonized" by the United States (*Indian Country*, 7). He echoes Hal K. Rothman, who describes Western tourism as "the most colonial of colonial economies." *Devil's Bargains: Tourism in the Twentieth-Century American West* (Lawrence, KS, 1998), 11.

7. Erna Fergusson, *Our Southwest* (New York, 1940), 18–19, 196, 287. For an interesting account of another pioneering woman, Grace Nicholson, who enabled upper middle-class women to become "virtual tourists" in the Southwest through their acquisition of Pueblo crafts for home decoration, see Erika Marie Bsumek, "Exchanging Places: Virtual Tourism, Vicarious Travel, and the Consumption of Southwestern Indian Artifacts," in Rothman, *Culture of Tourism*, 118–20, 135–36.

8. Fergusson, *Our Southwest*, 298.

9. Rudnick, *Luhan*, 6, 19–20, 23.

10. Ibid., 30–32, 42–43, 46.

11. Mabel Dodge Luhan, *European Experiences* (New York, 1935), 321–22; Rudnick, *Luhan*, 59–62; Christopher Lasch, *The New Radicalism in America* (New York, 1965), 60–62. For illuminating insights into parallels between the salons of Mabel Dodge and Gertrude Stein as social institutions, see Ashley Baker, "'We Are Part of the Spectacle and We Are Spectators, Too': Gertrude Stein, Mabel Dodge Luhan and the Expatriate Literary Salon as a Crucible for the Development of American Culture and Identity, 1900–1930," (Honors Thesis, Department of History, Wellesley College, 2004). For close scrutiny of Luhan and her circle in New York and New Mexico, see Flannery Burke, "Finding What They Came For: The Mabel Dodge Luhan Circle and the Making of a Modern Place, 1912–1930" (PhD diss., University of Wisconsin-Madison, 2002).

12. Christine Stansell, *American Moderns* (New York, 2000), 103–6, 316–17, 334. For the appeal of Indian art to the prewar avant-garde in New York, see Rushing, *Native American Art*, xi, 1–2, 5.

13. Mabel Dodge Luhan, *Movers and Shakers* (New York, 1936), 533–34; Luhan, *Edge of Taos Desert*, 6, 12, 25, 33, 45, 59, 62–63; Smith, *Reimagining*, 187, 191.

14. Luhan, *Edge of Taos Desert*, 6, 62–63; Rudnick, *Luhan*, 125–27, 141–42; Smith, *Reimagining*, 191; Luhan to Mary Austin, (Taos, n.d.), Mary Austin Papers, AU3572.

This item is reproduced by permission of The Huntington Library, San Marino, CA. Padget refers to Mabel Dodge Luhan's New Mexico home as "a Taos Eden" (*Indian Country*, 210). Taos was described as the place where Pueblo women ground corn "as in the days of the Old Testament." Agnes C. Laut, "Taos, An Ancient American Capitol," *The Santa Fe Magazine* 7 (September 1913): 28. But anthropologist Sylvia Rodriguez describes it as an "enclave of culturally disaffected spiritual refugees from urban, industrial America," belonging to "an alien, superordinate and colonizing society," who lived in New Mexico within "a social system of stringent ethnic-racial stratification and segregation." Sylvia Rodriguez, "Land, Water, and Ethnic Identity in Taos," in *Land, Water, and Culture: New Perspectives on Hispanic Land Grants*, eds. Charles L. Briggs and John R. Van Ness (Albuquerque, 1987), 344.

15. Rudnick, *Luhan*, 149; Rudnick, "Re-Naming," 20, 24; Jacobs, *Engendered Encounters*, 75; Luhan, *Edge of Taos Desert*, 18, 42, 45, 58, 64, 67, 77.

16. Lois Palken Rudnick, introduction to Luhan, *Edge of Taos Desert*, xiv; Luhan, *Winter in Taos*, 155.

17. Luhan, *Edge of Taos Desert*, 193, 197, 199, 221–22, 249, 301–2; Smith, *Reimagining*, 194.

18. Luhan, *Edge of Taos Desert*, 161, 177, 298, 301; Mabel Dodge Luhan, *Lorenzo in Taos* (New York, 1932), 193.

19. Rudnick, *Luhan*, xi, 149, 165–66; Luhan, *Edge of Taos Desert*, 66.

20. Bryant, *Culture*, 127, 131–40; Rushing, *Native American Art*, 13, 24–26, 29; Mabel Dodge Luhan, "A Bridge Between Cultures," *Theatre Arts Monthly* 9 (May 1925): 299–300; C. G. Jung, "The Pueblo Indians," in *The Spell of New Mexico*, ed. Tony Hillerman (Albuquerque, 1976), 30, 36, 39. Georgia O'Keeffe was a relative latecomer, arriving in New Mexico in 1929 at a time of difficulty in her marriage to Alfred Stieglitz. Mabel Dodge Luhan provided her with a guest cottage and studio in Taos, but O'Keeffe maintained her distance from "Mabeltown." She was captivated by the natural beauty of the Southwest, the primary subject of her paintings, not by the pueblos. See Laurie Lisle, *Portrait of an Artist: A Biography of Georgia O'Keeffe* (Albuquerque, 1986), 177–80, 196; Barbara Buhler Lynes, Lesley Poling-Kempes, and Frederick W. Turner, *Georgia O'Keeffe and New Mexico: A Sense of Place* (Princeton, 2004), 11–12, 78–79, 112; Jensen, *One Foot on the Rockies*, 74–76.

21. Eldredge, "The Faraway Nearby," 152–53; D. H. Lawrence to Mary Cannan, 27 September 1922, in *The Letters of D. H. Lawrence*, Vol. 4: June 1921–March 1924, eds. Warren Roberts, James T. Boulton, and Elizabeth Mansfield (Cambridge, 1987), 345; Rudnick, *Luhan*, 208–9, 210; Luhan to Collier, 21 November 1922, in Smith, *Reimagining*, 195; Luhan, *Lorenzo in Taos*, 35, 52; Luhan, *Edge of Taos Desert*, 101; Rushing, *Native American Art*, 27–29; Lasch, *New Radicalism*, 130. Lawrence, in turn, was a disappointment to Mabel, who complained that all his ideas about Indians—"evil," "witchlike," and "full of hate"—originated with James Fennimore Cooper. Luhan to Austin, 28 November [1922], Austin MSS, AU 3581. This item in reproduced by permission of The Huntington Library, San Marino, CA. For Lawrence's account of his experiences, see Keith Sagar, *D. H. Lawrence and New Mexico* (Salt Lake City, 1992), 5–6, 17, 21.

22. Rudnick, *Luhan*, 169, 175–76, 180, 182; Luhan, *Lorenzo in Taos*, 45, 276–77.

23. Smith, *Reimagining*, 200, 202, 205–7; Rudnick, *Luhan*, 155, 225, 238–40.

24. Luhan to Austin, 28 November [1922], Box 95, Austin MSS. This item in reproduced by permission of The Huntington Library, San Marino, CA.

25. Lasch, *New Radicalism*, 68, 128. Ashley Baker suggests that after the frustrations of Lawrence's disappointing sojourn in Taos in 1922, Mabel Dodge Luhan's relations with female visitors—especially Austin and Cather—deepened. Baker, "We Are Part of the Spectacle," 85.

26. Rudnick, *Luhan*, 316, 324; Burke, "Finding What They Came For," 363 (quoting Toomer), 370–71.

27. Carter Jones, "'Hope for the Race of Man': Indians, Intellectuals and the Regeneration of Modern America, 1917–1934" (PhD diss., Brown University, 1991), 3, 331; Rushing, *Native American Art*, 39.

28. Lawrence C. Kelly, *The Assault on Assimilation* (Albuquerque, 1983), xiii, 3, 16–17, 19, 23–24, 32–36; John Collier, *From Every Zenith* (Denver, 1963), 69, 71, 80. For the intellectual sources of Collier's mystical ideas, see Jenkins, *Dream Catchers*, 88–90.

29. Kelly, *Assault*, 48–49, 51, 59, 96, 103; Collier, *Zenith*, 79–80, 83–84.

30. Kelly, *Assault*, 107; Collier, *Zenith*, 93–94, 119, 123.

31. Collier, *Zenith*, 126; Kelly, *Assault*, xvi–xvii, 118–20; Kenneth R. Philp, *John Collier's Crusade for Indian Reform, 1920–1954* (Tucson, 1977), 4–5, 17, 24. For Collier's spiritual inspiration from Pueblo religious ritual, see Jenkins, *Dream Catchers*, 88–90.

32. John Collier, *The Indians of the Americas* (New York, 1947), 20, 25; Rudnick, *Luhan*, 165–66, 172–73; John Collier, "The Red Atlantis," *Survey* (October 1, 1922): 18; Jenkins, *Dream Catchers*, 110–12; Richard H. Frost, "The Romantic Inflation of Pueblo Culture," *American West* 17 (January–February 1980): 59.

33. Thompson, *American Character*, 308–10; Kelly, *Assault*, 133; Collier, *Zenith*, 131, 135, 203; Philp, *John Collier's Crusade*, 238–39.

34. Collier, *Indians of the Americas*, 18, 244–46.

35. Frost, "Romantic Inflation," 60; Collier, *Zenith*, 126.

36. Frost, "Romantic Inflation," 59–60; John Collier Jr., introduction to Kelly, *Assault*, xii–xiii.

37. John Collier, "Does the Government Welcome the Indian Arts," *American Magazine of Art* 27 (September 1934): 11; Lawrence to Mabel Dodge Sterne, 8 November 1923, in *The Letters of D. H. Lawrence*, Vol. 4: June 1921–March 1924, 527.

38. Jacobs, *Engendered Encounters*, 72, 180–81.

39. Rudnick, *Luhan*, 144–45, 192–93; Rudnick, introduction to Luhan, *Edge of Taos Desert*, vii–viii.

40. Deacon, *Parsons*, 1–30; Louis A. Hieb, "Elsie Clews Parsons in the Southwest," in Parezo, *Hidden Scholars*, 63–64; Rosalind Rosenberg, *Beyond Separate Spheres: Intellectual Roots of Modern Feminism* (New Haven, 1982), 152–54.

41. Deacon, *Parsons*, 46–47; Zumwalt, *Wealth and Rebellion*, chaps. 4–5.

42. Zumwalt, *Wealth and Rebellion*, 47–50.

43. Ibid. 171–76; Deacon, *Parsons*, 111–12, 130–31; Hieb, "Parsons," 66–67.

44. A. L. Kroeber, "Zuni Kin and Clan," *Anthropological Papers of the American Museum of Natural History*, Vol. 18, Pt. 2 (New York, 1917), 47–48, 78, 88, 90, 105.

45. Deacon, *Parsons*, 94, 97, 108–10; Louise Lamphere, "Feminist Anthropology: The Legacy of Elsie Clews Parsons," in *Women Writing Culture*, eds. Ruth Behar and Deborah A. Gordon (Berkeley, 1995), 88–89; Zumwalt, *Wealth and Rebellion*, 162–66. When Parsons went off on her field trips, her thirteen-year-old daughter Lissa assumed considerable responsibility for the care of her younger brothers (ibid., 156–57).

46. Lamphere, "Feminist Anthropology," 88; Rosenberg, *Beyond Separate Spheres*, 175–77; Peter H. Hare, *A Woman's Quest for Science: Portrait of Anthropologist Elsie Clews Parsons* (Buffalo, 1985), 136–37; Zumwalt, *Wealth and Rebellion*, 136–37.

47. Deacon, *Parsons*, xi–xii, 161, 187, 194; Zumwalt, *Wealth and Rebellion*, 257.

48. Deacon, *Parsons*, 222–23, 226.

49. Ibid. 309; Zumwalt, *Wealth and Rebellion*, 257, 273.

50. Hieb, "Parsons," 72–73; Deacon, *Parsons*, 230, 309, 312, 314.

51. Deacon, *Parsons*, 219–20, 356–58.

52. Ibid. 221–22.

53. Ibid. 259–60, 264; Lamphere, "Feminist Anthropology," 85–87.

54. Zumwalt, *Wealth and Rebellion*, photograph following p. 122; Rosenberg, *Beyond Separate Spheres*, 169–70; Ruth Behar, "Writing in My Father's Name," in Behar and Gordon, *Women Writing Culture*, 79.

55. Deacon, *Parsons*, xi.

56. Hare, *A Woman's Quest for Science*, 7, 21; Barbara Babcock, "Elsie Clews Parsons and the Pueblo Construction of Gender," introduction to *Pueblo Mothers and Children: Essays by Elsie Clews Parsons, 1915–1924*, ed. Barbara A. Babcock (Santa Fe, 1991), 4; Jacobs, *Engendered Encounters*, 57–58.

57. Deacon, *Parsons*, 259–60, 264.

58. Rosenberg, *Beyond Separate Spheres*, 175–77; Deacon, *Parsons*, xi.

59. Jacobs, *Engendered Encounters*, 57–58; Deacon, *Parsons*, 111, 130–31; Rosenberg, *Beyond Separate Spheres*, 177.

Chapter Five

1. Marshall Hyatt, *Franz Boas, Social Activist* (New York, 1990), 3–4; Franz Boas, "An Anthropologist's Credo," *The Nation* 147 (August 1938): 201.

2. Douglas Cole, *Franz Boas: The Early Years, 1858–1906* (Seattle, 1999), 79–81, 280, 285; Claudia Roth Pierpont, "The Measure of America," *The New Yorker* (March 8, 2004): 51–52.

3. Hyatt, *Boas*, 12, 49; Cole, *Boas*, 7, 59; Marvin Harris, *The Rise of Anthropological Theory* (New York, 1968), 298; George W. Stocking Jr., "Anthropology as *Kulturkampf*: Science and Politics in the Career of Franz Boas," in *The Ethnographer's Magic and Other Essays in the History of Anthropology*, ed. George W. Stocking Jr. (Madison, 1992), 95–96. Julia E. Liss suggests that Boas demonstrated "a destabilized sense of self—one formed out of experiences of perpetual marginality." Julia E. Liss, "Patterns of Strangeness: Franz Boas, Modernism, and the Origins of Anthropology," in *Prehistories of the Future*, eds. Elazar Barkan and Ronald Bush (Stanford, 1995), 114–15, 120.

4. Cole, *Boas*, 204–5, 271, 275.

5. Ibid. 132–33, 275.

6. Hyatt, *Boas*, 43, 50, 56, 61–62, 112–14; Liss, "Patterns of Strangeness," 397n9; Conn, *History's Shadow*, 155, 191–93, 195, 199.

7. Elazar Barkan, *The Retreat of Scientific Racism* (Cambridge, 1992), 77–78, 342–43.

8. Boas to Parsons, 9 July 1920, 20 June 1927, in Deacon, *Parsons*, 251, 254–55; Zumwalt, *Wealth and Rebellion*, 169, 171; Nancy J. Parezo, conclusion to *Hidden Scholars*, 348; Hilary Lapsley, *Margaret Mead and Ruth Benedict: The Kinship of Women* (Amherst, MA, 1999), 60.

9. Esther S. Goldfrank, *Notes on an Undirected Life*, Queens College Publications in Anthropology 3 (1978), 8.

10. Deacon, *Parsons*, 255–58, 264; Rosenberg, *Beyond Separate Spheres*, 166.

11. Hyatt, *Boas*, 85–86, 97–99; Stocking, "Anthropology as *Kulturkampf*," 35. Except for Parsons, who was born in 1874, Boas's closest "family" members (Benedict, Bunzel, Goldfrank, and Gladys Reichard) were born between 1887–98, all but Reichard in New York. Bunzel and Goldfrank were Jews; like Parsons, they graduated from Barnard College, while Benedict graduated from Vassar. Among Boas's "daughters," Benedict, Bunzel, and Goldfrank all had lost their fathers by the age of ten. Rachel Hart, Wellesley College (Class of 2002), gathered biographical information about these women and discerned some revealing patterns and parallels in their lives.

12. Judith Schachter Modell, *Ruth Benedict, Patterns of a Life* (Philadelphia, 1983), 22–24, 50; Ruth Benedict, "The Story of My Life," in *An Anthropologist at Work: Writings of Ruth Benedict*, ed. Margaret Mead (Boston, 1959), 108–9.

13. Modell, *Benedict*, 55, 65–66, 71, 73, 78; Benedict Journal 1912–14, in Mead, *Anthropologist at Work*, 120.

14. Modell, *Benedict*, 84–87, 90, 95–99, 102, 109; Mead, *Anthropologist at Work*, 132, 143, 491, 519.

15. Barbara A. Babcock, "'Not in the Absolute Singular': Rereading Ruth Benedict," in Behar and Gordon, *Women Writing Culture*, 106–8; Modell, *Benedict*, 110–13, 116–17, 121–22; Lois W. Banner, *Intertwined Lives: Margaret Mead, Ruth Benedict, and Their Circle* (New York, 2003), 147.

16. Modell, *Benedict*, 144–45, 150, 154; Lapsley, *Mead and Benedict*, 48, 50–51, 53. For a probing psychological inquiry into the Benedict-Mead relationship, see Banner, *Intertwined Lives*. Banner notes that after her father's death, Benedict's mother, who grew up within a tradition of educated women who worked outside the home, became "the family breadwinner" who "played the masculine role." Ruth, deprived of her father at an early age, "found her real self in relationships with women" (30, 63, 144). Banner acknowledges, however, that in important respects Boas and Benedict "were like a father and a daughter" (290).

17. Modell, *Benedict*, 180–81; Mead, *Anthropologist at Work*, 289, 344–46; Parezo, conclusion to *Hidden Scholars*, 348.

18. Mead, *Anthropologist at Work*, 67, 346, 356.

19. Deacon, *Parsons*, 275–77; Lapsley, *Mead and Benedict*, 61–63; Mead, *Anthropologist at Work*, 3, 66, 341–43.

20. Judith Schachter Modell, "Ruth Benedict," in *Women Anthropologists: A Biographical Dictionary*, eds. Ute Gacs, Aisha Khan, Jerrie McIntyre, and Ruth Weinberg (New York, 1988), 3; Modell, *Benedict*, 136, 147; Diamond, *In Search*, 223.

21. Barkan, *Retreat*, 127–28; Babcock, "Not in the Absolute Singular," in Behar and Gordon, *Women Writing Culture*, 108–9; Modell, *Benedict*, 163–64.

22. Margaret M. Caffrey, *Ruth Benedict: Stranger in This Land* (Austin, 1989), vii, viii–ix, 14, 92, 97–98, 110; Lapsley, *Mead and Benedict*, 64.

23. Benedict to Mead, 6 August and 29 August 1925, in Mead, *Anthropologist at Work*, 191, 295; Lapsley, *Mead and Benedict*, 2–4.

24. Modell, *Benedict*, 166–67; Lapsley, *Mead and Benedict*, 226, 290; Mead, *Anthropologist at Work*, 346–47. I am grateful to Professor Nan A. Rothschild of Barnard College who clarified the issue of Benedict's appointment for me.

25. Babcock, "Not in the Absolute Singular," in Behar and Gordon, *Women Writing Culture*, 116; Lapsley, *Mead and Benedict*, 177–78; Ruth Benedict, *Patterns of Culture* (Boston, 1934), 79, 87.

26. Benedict, *Patterns*, 2–3, 11, 14, 20, 57, 59, 93, 95–96, 99, 101–2.

27. Ibid. 74, 79, 101, 106–7, 120, 126, 263; Mead, *Anthropologist at Work*, 293.

28. Benedict, *Patterns*, 67, 73, 103, 106, 122, 231.

29. Ibid. 276–77, 278.

30. Ibid. 74–75, 126, 129; Caffrey, *Benedict*, 213.

31. Caffrey, *Benedict*, 1, 5; Modell, *Benedict*, 205–6.

32. Benedict to Mead, 5 September 1925; Benedict, "Psychological Types in the Culture of the Southwest" (published in *Proceedings of 23rd International Congress of Americanists, September 1928*), in Mead, *Anthropologist at Work*, 206, 212, 248–49, 260–61, 276; Benedict, *Patterns*, 80.

33. Babcock, "Not in the Absolute Singular," in Behar and Gordon, *Women Writing Culture*, 111, 123–24.

34. Ibid. 121–22, 128; Mead, preface to Ruth Benedict, *Patterns of Culture*. With a new preface by Margaret Mead (New York, 1959), ix.

35. Charles H. Lange, "The Contributions of Esther S. Goldfrank," in Parezo, *Hidden Scholars*, 222–27; Gloria Levitas, "Esther Schiff Goldfrank," in Gacs and others, *Women Anthropologists*, 120–21, 124; Goldfrank, *Notes on an Undirected Life*, 1–4, 26–27, 40–42, 92–93, 98–99, 110–11.

36. Margaret Ann Hardin, "Zuni Potters and the Pueblo Potter: The Contributions of Ruth Bunzel," in Gacs and others, *Women Anthropologists*, 260.

37. Ruth L. Bunzel, *Pueblo Potter* (New York, 1929), 1–2, 49, 54, 88; Dilworth, *Imagining Indians*, 171–72.

38. David M. Fawcett and Teri McLuhan, "Ruth Bunzel," in Gacs and others, *Women Anthropologists*, 30–32, 35; Hardin, "Bunzel," 261–63; Deacon, *Parsons*, 324; Bunzel quoted in *Margaret Mead: A Life*, by Jane Howard (New York, 1984), 69.

39. Parezo, conclusion to *Hidden Scholars*, 341, 346.

40. George W. Stocking Jr., ed., *Selected Papers from the American Anthropologist, 1921–1945* (Washington, DC, 1976), 7–8.

41. Jacobs, *Engendered Encounters*, 180–81; Parezo, conclusion to *Hidden Scholars*, 357–59. See Jacobs, *Engendered Encounters*, chap. 2, for an analysis of varieties of female missionary experience.

42. Parezo, conclusion to *Hidden Scholars*, 355–56; Rosenberg, *Beyond Separate Spheres*, 170, 226; Jacobs, *Engendered Encounters*, 77. The claim of close Anglo-Native friendships formed in the pueblos, at least in more recent times, has been challenged by Jill D. Sweet. According to Sweet, who researched the impact of tourism on Pueblo Indians during the 1970s and 1980s, "Anglo friends never became fully accepted or formally adopted members of a Pueblo community." "'Let 'em Loose': Pueblo Indian Management of Tourism," *American Indian Culture and Research Journal* 15, no. 4 (1991): 62 .

43. Behar, "Writing in My Father's Name," 79; Jacobs, *Engendered Encounters*, 77–79.

44. Deborah Gordon, "Among Women," 129–30, 132–33.

45. Ibid., 130, 132.

46. Ibid., 133.

47. Ibid., 133–34.

48. Jaime de Angulo to Ruth Benedict, 19 May 1925, in Mead, *Anthropologist at Work*, 296–97. Benedict, disregarding the advice, continued to gather information from (male) informants, while complaining, "they aren't telling me anything sacred"— confirmation that the locus of pueblo power was with men (302). She relied primarily upon older Zuni men, whose idealization of the past may have helped to shape her emphasis on harmony in Zuni, which in fact was torn by conflict that the intrusiveness of anthropologists seems to have exacerbated. See Triloki Noth Pandey, "Anthropologists at Zuni," *Proceedings of the American Philosophical Society* 116 (August 1972): 328–29, 332, 334.

49. Behar and Gordon, *Women Writing Culture*, xi–xii; Ruth Behar, introduction to Behar and Gordon, *Women Writing Culture*, 8, 11–12.

50. Jacobs, *Engendered Encounters*, 20–21, 180.

51. Ibid. 61.

52. Ibid., 22–23; Lapsley, *Mead and Benedict*, 2, 104.

53. Marianna Torgovnick, *Gone Primitive: Savage Intellects, Modern Lives* (Chicago, 1990), 17–18, 153, 187, 244–45, 247.

54. Roscoe, *The Zuni Man-Woman*, xi; Jacobs, *Engendered Encounters*, 87–95.

55. Jacobs, *Engendered Encounters*, 91, 94–95, 103–5, 154–55, 169–70.

56. Mead, *Anthropologist at Work*, 295; George W. Stocking Jr., "The Ethnographic Sensibility of the 1920s and the Dualism of the Anthropological Tradition," in Stocking, *Romantic Motives*, 217–20, 235, 249.

57. Barbara A. Babcock and Nancy J. Parezo, *Daughters of the Desert* (Albuquerque, 1988), 2; Nancy J. Parezo, "Anthropology: The Welcoming Science," in Parezo, *Hidden Scholars*, 3–4; Mullin, "Consuming the American Southwest," 57–58, 60–61, 74, 87–88.

Chapter Six

1. Jennifer Fox, "The Women Who Opened Doors: Interviewing Southwestern Anthropologists," in Parezo, *Hidden Scholars*, 294; Parezo, conclusion to *Hidden Scholars*, 336–37; Babcock and Parezo, *Daughters of the Desert*, 1; Bryant, *Culture*, 127.

2. Lamphere, "Feminist Anthropology," 96, 98, 100; Babcock and Parezo, *Daughters of the Desert*, 1; Weigle and Babcock, *The Great Southwest*, 4, 157.

3. Tedlock, *The Beautiful and the Dangerous*, xi, xiv; Barbara Tedlock, "Works and Wives: On the Sexual Division of Textual Labor," in Behar and Gordon, *Women Writing Culture*, 272, 279–80.

4. Parezo, *Hidden Scholars*, xi–xiii, 4, 6, 29, 31. The volume, an excellent collection of biographical essays, is the scholarly product of her inquiry.

5. Babcock, *Pueblo Mothers and Children*, x, 6, 19, 20.

6. Weigle and Babcock, *The Great Southwest*, 67–68; Barbara A. Babcock, "Mudwomen and Whitemen: A Meditation on Pueblo Potteries and the Politics of Representation," in Norris, *Discovered Country*, 182; Barbara A. Babcock, "First Families: Gender Reproduction and the Mythic Southwest," in Weigle and Babcock, *The Great Southwest*, 207, 210.

7. Babcock, "First Families," 207, 211, 214; Barbara A. Babcock, "'A New Mexican Rebecca: Imagining Pueblo Women," *Journal of the Southwest* 32 (1990): 400, 403–4, 430.

8. Babcock, "A New Mexican Rebecca," 400, 402–3, 404, 406, 428–30; Helen Carr, "In Other Words: Native American Women's Autobiography," in *Life/Lines*, eds. Bella Brodzki and Celeste Schenck (Ithaca, 1988), 150, quoted in Babcock, "A New Mexican Rebecca," 432–33; Judith Williamson, "Woman is an Island: Femininity and Colonization," in *Studies in Entertainment*, ed. Tania Modleski (Bloomington, 1986), 110–12; Luce Irigaray, *This Sex Which Is Not One* (Ithaca, 1985), 177.

9. Barbara A. Babcock, "Bearers of Value, Vessels of Desire: The Reproduction of Pueblo Culture," *Museum Anthropology* 17 (October, 1993): 43–44, 52–53.

10. Weigle and Babcock, *The Great Southwest*, 69, 157–58.

11. Ibid. 208–12; Phoebe S. Kropp, "'There is a little sermon in that': Constructing the Native Southwest at the San Diego Panama-California Exposition of 1915," in Weigle and Babcock, *The Great Southwest*, 41, 43–44; Dilworth, *Imagining Indians*, 3–6, 78–79, 104–6, 137–38.

12. Wade, "Ethnic Art Market," 167, 169, 171, 174; Babcock, "A New Mexican Rebecca," 400, 402–3, 428–30, 432–33. Martin Padget suggests that not until the end of the twentieth century were Pueblo Indians "affirming their right to contest the terms of incorporation imposed upon them" (*Indian Country*, 8–9, 127, 216).

13. Babcock, *Pueblo Mothers and Children*, x, 6–7, 17, 19–20; Babcock, "Mudwomen," 180, 182, 187–88; Babcock, "First Families," 217.

14. Edward Said, *Orientalism* (New York, 1978), 1, 3, 5, 204, 206, 283; Patrick Williams and Laura Chrisman, "Colonial Discourse and Post-Colonial Theory: An Introduction," in *Colonial Discourse and Post-Colonial Theory*, eds. Patrick Williams and Laura Chrisman (New York, 1994), 4–5, 8.

15. Said, *Orientalism*, 283, 300–301, 328, 333. For a critique of Said's approach, see David Cannadine, *Ornamentalism: How the British Saw Their Empire* (New York, 2001), xv, xix.

16. Lummis, *Land of Poco Tiempo*, 70; Dorsey, *Indians of the Southwest*, 87–88; Weigle and Babcock, *The Great Southwest*, 4–5, 102–4, 158, 207–9; D. H. Thomas, *The Southwestern Indian Detours* (Phoenix, 1978), 196.

17. Bourke, *Snake Dance of the Moquis*, 363; Dorsey, *Indians of the Southwest*, 23–24.

18. Said, *Orientalism*, 5–6; Weigle and Babcock, *The Great Southwest*, 6–7, 157, 209; Dilworth, *Imagining Indians*, 5–6, 58; Babcock, "Mudwomen," 187–88; Jacobs, *Engendered Encounters*, 96. The same analytical categories have not been applied by contemporary feminist scholars to women who went to the Southwest to write and sell their books about Pueblo Indians.

19. Mary Louise Pratt, *Imperial Eyes: Travel Writing and Transculturation* (London, 1992), xi, 2, 4, 62, 65, 95, 97, 152.

20. Ibid. 166–68.

21. Thierry Hentsch, *Imagining the Middle East* (Montreal, 1992), ix–x, 5–8, 23–24, 41, 45, 49–50, 75, 112, 119, 130, 159; Said, *Orientalism*, 290.

22. Holly Edwards, "A Million and One Nights: Orientalism in America," in *Noble Dreams, Wicked Pleasures: Orientalism in America, 1870–1930*, ed. Holly Edwards (Princeton, 2000), 22–23, 34–35; Gerald Ackerman, *American Orientalists* (Paris, 1994), 162–77, 186.

23. Dilworth, *Imagining Indians*, 162; Howard and Pardue, *Inventing the Southwest*, 126, 128, 131; Wade, "Ethnic Art Market," 167.

24. Rita Simmons, "Ila McAfee," *Southwest Art* (September 1990): 100, quoted in D'Emilio and Campbell, *Visions and Visionaries*, 100; Babcock, "Bearers of Value," 49–50; Babcock, "A New Mexican Rebecca," 400, 402–3, 428–30, 432–33; Moore, "Ellie Meets the President," 22–24, 28.

25. Mary Austin, *Land of Journeys' Ending* (New York, 1924), 4–5; Smith, *Reimagining*, 165.

26. Parezo, conclusion to *Hidden Scholars*, 359, 361; Smith, *Reimagining*, 213–14; Rudnick, "Re-Naming," 243n28; Mary Austin to Henry Seidel Canby, 1 April 1930, AU 1076, Box 57, Austin MSS. This item is reproduced by permission of The Huntington Library, San Marino, CA; Babcock and Parezo, *Daughters of the Desert*, 4.

27. Curtis M. Hinsley, "Authoring Authenticity," *Journal of the Southwest* 32 (Winter, 1990): 462; "Cincinnati Arts Pottery," *Harper's Weekly* (January 10, 1880): 342; Carr, "In Other Words," 150; Sylvia Rodriguez, "Art, Tourism, and Race Relations in Taos: Toward a Sociology of the Arts Colony," *Journal of Anthropological Research* 45 (1989): 93; Williamson, "Woman is an Island," 110–12.

28. Parezo, conclusion to *Hidden Scholars*, 365; Smith, *Reimagining*, 217; Jacobs, *Engendered Encounters*, 58. Clifford Geertz has noted "the long, unbalanced, difficult, and ambiguous special relationship, at once intimate and arm's length, between the Native American population and the American anthropological profession." See Geertz, "Morality Tale," *New York Review of Books* 51 (October 7, 2004): 6.

Conclusion

1. Martha A. Sandweiss, *Laura Gilpin: An Enduring Grace* (Fort Worth, 1986), 12, 16, 44–45, 69.

2. Laura Gilpin, *The Pueblos: Camera Chronicle* (New York, 1941), photograph facing title page, Preface, 1, 29, 33, 81, 85–89, 114, 123–24. Her photographs suggest that the romanticized "male" gaze, excoriated in contemporary feminist scholarship, was not restricted to men.

3. *New Mexico: A Guide to the Colorful State* (New York, 1940), v, 43, 45, 47, 213, 218, 219, 373; Collier, *Zenith*, 223.

4. Edward Robinson, *Biblical Researches in Palestine, Mount Sinai, and Araba Petraea*, 3 vols. (London, 1841), 1:46.

5. F. H. Cushing, "The Need of Studying the Indian in Order to Teach Him," *28th Annual Report of the Board of Indian Commissioners* (Washington, DC, 1897), 12.

6. Oleg Grabar, "Roots and Others," in Edwards, *Noble Dreams, Wicked Pleasures*, 4, 8; Lester I. Vogel, *To See a Promised Land* (University Park, PA, 1993), xv, 31, 47, 72, 76–78, 216. Twain's observations, in *Innocents Abroad*, appear in Hilton Obenzinger, *American Palestine: Melville, Twain, and the Holy Land Mania* (Princeton, 1999), 191, 221. For an exploration of American attitudes toward Islam and Arabs, locating them in "a Christian quest for Zion," see Fuad Sha'ban, *Islam and Arabs in Early American Thought* (Durham, NC, 1991), i–iv, 125, 128, 182–86, 189. For Indians as remnants of the Lost Tribes, see Hillel Halkin, *Across the Sabbath River: In Search of a Lost Tribe of Israel* (Boston, 2002), 120–23.

7. Davis, *Landscape of Belief*, 41–51, 88, 94; Vogel, *Promised Land*, 213–15; Eric Gibson, "When it was Chic to Paint Sheiks," *Wall Street Journal*, August 11, 2000.

8. Hinsley, "Authoring Authenticity," 463, 476–77; Frost, "Romantic Inflation," 9, 56.

9. Parezo, conclusion to *Hidden Scholars*, 354, 356; Tedlock, "Works and Wives," 279; Babcock, "Mudwomen," 180, 182. "The essential quality of a frontier, of course, is the opportunity for self-invention. That's why the West attracted not only explorers, pioneers and entrepreneurs but also utopians, fantasists and zealots of all kinds." Jonathan Kirsch, "How the American West Was Discovered and Invented," *Los Angeles Times Book Review* (November 17, 2002), R8.

10. McFeely, *Zuni*, 167.

11. Ibid., xi, 164–67. Pueblo Indians may be the most intensely studied tribal culture in history, but to historians (including, of course, the author) the Anglo-Americans who encountered the Pueblo Indians have become even more fascinating than the natives themselves.

Index

Eden: America as, 1–2, 164–66; California as, 54; Southwest as, 6–11, 13, 15, 42–43, 56–57, 72–73, 80, 82, 96, 116, 148, 153, 159, 162–63, 165–67; Southwest as, in contrast to Middle East, 153; Southwest as feminist, 96, 119, 142, 144, 147; Taos as, 100–101, 105, 187n14; Zuni as, 35, 42, 163

Edge of Taos Desert (Luhan), 99–100

Ellie of Ganado, 61, 154–55

"Elsie Clews Parsons and Lissa, 1902," 112

"Elsie Clews Parsons in the Southwest, 1915," 118

ethnography. *See* feminist ethnography

Evans, Karl, 97

Family, The (Parsons), 111

feminism, 12–13, 93–94, 96, 110–14, 116–17, 119, 123–24, 126, 134, 138, 141; the New Woman, 12, 89, 95, 138, 141, 143

feminist ethnography, 146, 166

"feministopia," 152–53

feminist scholars, 145–59, 194n18; connection with predecessors, 145–47, 158; and Orientalism, 150–55

feminist utopia, pueblos as. *See under* pueblo culture, idealization of

Fergusson, Erna, 94–96, 156, 158; Indian Detours, 151, 186n6; Koshare Tours, 94–95; *Our Southwest*, 96

"Frank Hamilton Cushing Before His Departure to Zuni," 19

"Frank Hamilton Cushing Returns to Washington, D.C.," 31

Franklin, Ben, 2

Fred Harvey Company, 11, 13, 55, 57–71, 83, 85–87, 94, 146, 148–51, 154–56, 162; and Anglo artists, 85–88; and native artists, 59–63, 69–70, 154–56; criticism of, 146, 148–151; *The Great Southwest*, 67; Harvey's Indian Tours, 94; Indian Building at Alvarado Hotel, 60, 67; Indian Department, 60–61, 64; promotional materials, 63, 67, 86–87, 156; providing opportunity, 58, 60–61, 156; and Santa Fe Railroad, 57–71, 86–87, 94, 145–46, 148–49, 151, 154–56,

158, 163 *See also* Nampeyo; Harvey Girls; Schweizer, Herman

Fred Harvey Postcards, postcards, 64, 67–68, 69–70, 74, 86–87, 148, 156; *65–66, 68, 76*

Fremont, John C., 3

Frost, Richard H., 109

Fulton, Ruth. *See* Benedict, Ruth

Ganson, Mabel. *See* Luhan, Mabel Dodge

gender roles, 10, 12, 44–45, 85, 89, 94, 95–96, 110–11, 124, 127, 129, 134, 137–38, 142–44, 147, 156, 158, 166–67; Benedict and, 125, 129; domesticity, 36, 40, 45–46, 51, 52, 62–67, 104, 129, 134–35, 138, 146, 148, 154, 166; Fred Harvey Company and, 61, 156; Luhan and, 97–98, 99, 104–5; Parsons and, 111, 113–14, 119, 124; Stevenson and, 45, 46–51. *See also* imperialism: and gender; masculinity; We'Wha

gender roles, pueblo, 10, 62, 64, 68, 93, 94, 96, 110, 115, 117, 119, 131–33, 135–36, 138, 141, 157–58; domesticity, 65–67, 93, 115, 133, 135, 141, 147–48, 158, 162; labor, 10, 63, 141; "matriarchate," 114–15

Gilpin, Laura, 13, 160–62, 164; *The Pueblos*, 162

Goddard, Pliny Earle, 113–14, 119

Goldfrank, Esther S., 12, 123, 127–29, 134–38, 166; at Cochiti, 134–35; Jewish identity, 127–28, 134, 138; *Notes on an Undirected Life*, 135

Goldfrank, Walter S., 134

Gordon, Deborah, 51, 139–40

Grand Canyon, 17, 57, 59, 60, 113

Great Depression and southwest tourism, 13, 160, 162

Great Southwest, The (Fred Harvey Company), 67

Green, Jesse, 20, 37–39, 179n31

Grieve, Lucia, 33–34

Hale, Edward Everett, 32

Harriman, E. H., 78

Harvey, Fred, 11, 44. *See also* Fred Harvey Company

George Wharton James, 77; Lummis, 53–54, 73–74; Frederick Monsen, 83–84; "A New Mexican Rebecca," 80, 147; pueblo responses to, 83, 184n20; Matilda Stevenson, 47, 140; and the railroad, 59. *See also* Curtis, Edward S.; Gilpin, Laura; Kodak; Vroman, A. C.

Photostint. *See* postcards

Pino, Patricio, 21, 22, 30

Pomeroy, Earl, 56

Pool of Zuni and Water Carriers, 5

postcards. *See* Fred Harvey Postcards

pots and pueblo women, representations of, 161, 162; feminist scholars on, 147–48, 158

potters, 62, 154–55; as anthropological subject, 135–36; *See also* Nampeyo; native arts and crafts

Powell, John Wesley, 17, 37, 45–46

Pratt, Mary Louise: on "feministopia," 152–53

primitivism, 8, 9–10, 39, 70–71, 110, 142–43, 155; and masculinity, 40; and pueblo art, 62

Promised Land: America as, 1–4, 159, 163–64; the frontier as, 9; the Southwest as, 43

pueblo acceptance of visitors, 83, 192n42; Bunzel, 136; Cushing, 24, 27–28; Goldfrank, 134

pueblo civilization, in contrast to other tribes, 10, 43, 93, 130–32

pueblo culture: as Apollonian, 130–34, 157, 160, 167; as blend (Parsons), 116; misperception of distinctiveness of, 7, 22, 25, 54, 55, 59, 63, 64, 79, 82, 156

pueblo government, 77

Pueblo Indian Religion (Parsons), 117

"Pueblo Indians Selling Pottery," 68

"Pueblo Women Making Bread," 65

pueblos, idealization of, 13, 53, 64, 70, 77, 84, 87, 96, 109, 130, 132, 138, 141, 160; as feminist utopia, 94, 110, 119 144, 157, 166–67; as primitive ideal, 7, 8, 57, 86; as imperialist, 148–49

pueblos, modernity's effect on, 29–30, 96, 155–56, 163

pueblos, "orientalized." *See* Orientalism

Pueblos, The (Gilpin), 162

pueblos as potential salvation of modern America, 10, 13, 53, 77, 88, 103. *See also* social reform

pueblos as refuge: from modern America, 6, 8, 9, 13, 38–39, 54; personal, 116

pueblos as utopian alternative to modern America, 8, 35, 42, 62, 69, 87, 89, 115, 128, 143, 165, 185n29

Puritans, 1–2, 43, 132, 159, 164

railroad. *See* Santa Fe Railroad

Rebecca imagery, 4, 6, 8, 10, 20, 29, 43, 57, 64, 80, 136, 147–48, 151, 162, 164, 165, 169. *See* "New Mexican Rebecca, A"

Reception at Wellesley College, The, 34

Reed, John, 98–99

Reichard, Gladys, 119

religious ceremonies, 6, 46, 77, 99, 100, 180n7; and Cushing, 24, 27–28; as spectacle, 75, 77–78, 82–83. *See also* Hopi snake dance

Remington, Frederic, 40, 85

Riis, Jacob A., 70, 76

Rinehart, Frank A., 11

Roberts, David, 6

Robinson, Edward, 164

Roosevelt, Franklin D., 109

Roosevelt, Theodore, 40, 51, 78, 155

Roscoe, Will, 50, 167

Rosenberg, Rosalind, 119

Rudnick, Lois Palken, 97, 104

Russell, Charles M., 85, 153

Said, Edward, 150, 153. *See also* Orientalism

San Francisco State Teachers College, 108

San Ildefonso Pueblo, 52, 68, 80, 113

Sandweiss, Martha A., 73

Santa Clara Pueblo, 87, 155

Santa Fe, 20, 52, 53, 59, 89, 98, 99, 117, 156

About the Author

Jerold S. Auerbach is the author of *Labor and Liberty* (1966); *Unequal Justice* (1976), a *New York Times* Noteworthy Book; *Justice Without Law?* (1983); *Rabbis and Lawyers* (1990); *Jacob's Voices* (1996); and *Are We One? Jewish Identity in the United States and Israel* (2001). He has been a Guggenheim Fellow, Fulbright Lecturer at Tel Aviv University, and Visiting Scholar at the Harvard Law School, and he is the recipient of two College Teachers Fellowships from the National Endowment for the Humanities. He is a professor of history at Wellesley College.